New Orleans

RIVER REGION RENAISSANCE

by Diana Pinckley

Corporate Profiles by Garry Boulard and Elizabeth Donze

Featuring the Photography of Jackson Hill/Southern Lights Studio

Produced in cooperation with The Chamber/New Orleans and the River Region

New Orleans
RIVER REGION RENAISSANCE

MARDI GRAS

New Orleans

River Region Renaissance

Produced in cooperation with
The Chamber/New Orleans and the River Region
David Crumrine, Communications Director
601 Poydras Street, Suite 1700
New Orleans, LA 70130
(504) 527-6900

By Diana Pinckley
Featuring the photography of Jackson Hill/Southern Lights Studio
Corporate profiles by Garry Boulard and Elizabeth Donze

Community Communications, Inc.
Publishers: Ronald P. Beers and James E. Turner

Staff for New Orleans: River Region Renaissance
Publisher's Sales Associate: John Hecker and Bill Koons
Executive Editor: James E. Turner
Managing Editor: Candy Strickland
Design Director: Camille Leonard
Designers: Katie Bradshaw and Russell Hailey
Photo Editors: Katie Bradshaw and Candy Strickland
Production Manager: Corinne Cau
Editorial Assistants: Katrina Williams and Emlyn Saunders
Sales Assistant: Annette Lozier
Proofreader: Connie Sessions
Accounting Services: Sara Ann Turner
Printing Production: Frank Rosenberg/GSAmerica

Community Communications, Inc.
Montgomery, Alabama

James E. Turner, Chairman of the Board
Ronald P. Beers, President
Daniel S. Chambliss, Vice President

*F*oreword

The rich history of the New Orleans area is inextricably intertwined with the history of the business community and its people. This book is dedicated to the people and businesses of the New Orleans Region, who for over 200 years have worked to build the New Orleans area into one of the world's unique places—a distinctive location to visit, to work, to live. The Chamber/New Orleans and the River Region is proud to tell these stories of renaissance—of change and the success that has extended across three centuries.

New Orleans' history has perhaps made it best-equipped to deal with the changes and challenges accompanying the dawn of the 21st century. We've had a long and varied experience, from our foundations on the deep and sometimes shifting silt washed down the Mississippi, at taking the circumstances we're given and making them work for the good of all. In New Orleans, we have managed to take each successive wave of change and divert it, making it fit our view of the world. While not always the author of the change, we have made it our change, and made the change fit our needs, our people, our culture, and our style. We have taken revolution and turned it into evolution.

This book is about that change, from our birth on the banks of the Mississippi, to our status as one of the top 10 international business Meccas. Our region is on the emerging edge of a renaissance—literally a rebirth. It is not the rebirth of the Phoenix, rising from the ashes. It is the metamorphosis of the butterfly, first being one thing, and then transforming itself into another. We have held onto our history. From the houses we live in, to the clothes we wear, to the food we eat, the celebrations we have, and the language we speak, our history is all about us. It is the foundation of our future.

This book tells the story of the *new* New Orleans, an international center of business, and a destination unlike any other in the world. When you read our story you will know why we have become one of the very top sites for conventions and travel.

You may see a visitors walking down a street, marveling at the architecture, paying close attention to the ironwork on a front gate—while New Orleanians around them seem oblivious to charms they see everyday. Notice the glint in their eye, the smile on their face. You can be sure they will return—maybe even to become a New Orleanian. It's a renaissance on a personal scale and it happens here every day.

Preface

When my husband and I checked into a hotel in downtown Vancouver one summer, the clerk took note of our address—and her eyes widened. "Ooooh, New Orleans," she said. "That's where the magic happens."

Even from more than 2,000 miles away, she knew. New Orleans is where magic happens. It can be as simple as the smell of confederate jasmine on a humid summer night, the scent of coffee, or even the raunchy odor of shrimp shells left out for the garbage. (You always know that someone has enjoyed a good meal earlier when you hit that aroma!) It's the wrought-iron and live-oak-tree sense of place that permeates the area. You can't confuse New Orleans with any other American city, no matter how hard you might try. We're distinctive—from our European/African/Caribbean-infused history to our world-class food, from our bustling ports to our thriving downtown.

Perhaps the most special part of New Orleans is the people— the folks who are willing to work hard to get their own jobs done and then put the same energy toward addressing the challenges of an urban area. After all that, it's time to kick back and hear a little music together, or maybe go get some iced coffee. Those are the kind of people who can change things, who'll make a difference—and who'll have a great time doing it.

I've spent almost half my life in New Orleans (the other half has been in the Tennessee mountains and the North Carolina piedmont); and working on New Orleans: River Region Renaissance lets me remember why I like the city so much. I've learned a lot, too, and I've tried to pass it on in a fairly amusing fashion. But I've also had to leave some things out, for reasons of space or forgetfulness. You'll just have to explore the city and find them for yourself.

My own favorite part of the book is the photography by Jackson Hill, who has been showing off the places and people of New Orleans for years now. If you like what you see, check out Jackson's Southern Lights site on the World Wide Web. It's also been nice to get the team back together—Jackson, profile writers Elizabeth Donze and Garry Boulard, and I have worked on many Tulane University communications projects together over the years.

I've had a lot of help with the book. Chamber Communications Director David Crumrine has supplied everything from historic dates to favorite Zydeco artists, as well as a lot of moral support. Susan Larson, one of my best editors, listened to me talk about the book, read the whole thing, and made her usual cogent comments in her consistently supportive and cheering fashion. My husband John Pope, my other best editor, knows that the key is in the details—many of which he either supplied or checked. (Don't ever play him at Trivial Pursuit!)

I've enjoyed writing about New Orleans. I hope it gives residents a new spin on their city and out-of-towners the impetus to come join us.

— Diana Pinckley

The New Orleans Story

Distinctive swamps and marshes just outside New Orleans add an element of natural beauty to the urban environment. Photo by Jackson Hill/ Southern Lights Studio.

"'Unique' is a word that cannot

be qualified. It does not mean rare or

uncommon; it means alone in the

universe. By the standards of grammar

and by the grace of God, New Orleans

is the unique American place."

Charles Kuralt
from Charles Kuralt's America

For almost three centuries, New Orleans has mixed amazing persistence, ingenuity, optimism, tolerance, and just plain old high spirits to create the uniqueness that Kuralt—among many others spread across generations—found so mesmerizing. There was no other way for the city to survive and flourish.

"The Mississippi River demands a city at its mouth, but fails to provide any place for one," writes geographer Peirce F. Lewis, in *New Orleans, the Making of an Urban Landscape*. In that one sentence, Lewis summarizes the basis of much of New Orleans' history, challenges, achievements, greatness, and destiny. Because there was the Mississippi, there was New Orleans.

Swampy ground. No rock anywhere nearby. Elevations from 15 feet above sea level to a dozen feet below. Water on three sides, with the only strip of livable land running right along the river. Floods and disease a fact of everyday life. The New Orleans of 300 years ago wasn't exactly an urban planner's dream.

But there, a hundred miles upstream from where the Mississippi meets the Gulf of Mexico, was the sole eighteenth- and nineteenth-century gateway to the heartland. There were no roads, no trucks, no railroads. The richness of the farms and natural resources all across a great continent must be made available to Europeans and other trading partners. And the mighty Mississippi was the only outlet to the rest of the world. So was New Orleans destined to become and remain a queen city of trade, with more than 1.5 million people in the greater metropolitan area in 1996.

New Orleans has a history unlike any other in America. Founded by the French, the city was given to the Spanish in 1762, went back to the French briefly in 1800, and was sold to the United States in 1803 as part of the Louisiana Purchase—600 million acres ranging from New Orleans to Canada to the Rockies— for $15 million, or about 2.5 cents an acre. That means the nine parishes in the greater New Orleans region cost a total of about $75,000. Three centuries of multicultural heritage continue to be clearly expressed in the region's music, art, food, business, architecture, and, most of all, distinctive personality.

In April, 1682, more than 140 years after DeSoto became the first European to record a sighting of the Mississippi, French explorer Robert Cavalier, Sieur de LaSalle, floated an expedition down the big river to its mouth, raised a cross, unfurled the flag of Bourbon France, and claimed the valley for Louis XIV, the king of the most influential nation in Europe. But the king didn't care about Louisiana. He gave LaSalle four ships to go to Mexico and find gold. Like

millions of people since, LaSalle had already succumbed to the charms of South Louisiana. He came back to put a settlement at the mouth of the river, whatever his king said. But he couldn't find it. LaSalle spent two years searching, until finally his men had had enough and murdered him.

France ignored Louisiana for another 15 years, until, in the waning days of the seventeenth century, Spain tried to lay claim to the territory. That set off a race among Spain, England, and France to place a settlement at the mouth of the Mississippi and so control the vast interior wealth of the continent. France's entry was a fleet commanded by the French Canadian Pierre Le Moyne, Sieur de Iberville, and including his younger brother Jean Baptiste, Sieur de Bienville. Iberville sailed to the Gulf Coast in 1699, moved quietly past Pensacola where the Spaniards were busy building a settlement, and floated into the mouth of the Mississippi the day before Mardi Gras. They were 200 miles upriver before they were sure they had landed their prize.

Some Choctaw guides took Bienville and Iberville to a strip of relatively high ground close to the river, near where the Native Americans carried their canoes from the river to Lake Okwata (now Pontchartrain). Bienville noted it as a good place for a settlement, though it would require his

In 1727, the Ursuline nuns came to teach children and care for the sick. They began the first school in Louisiana—and the first all-girl school in the country—and ran a military hospital. Photo courtesy of The Historic New Orleans Collection, accession no. 1981.329.2.

repeated efforts for 19 years—until 1718—to establish Nouvelle Orleans, named for the regent Phillip, Duke of Orleans.

The struggling settlement (population 68) strung out along the river bank in what is now the French Quarter had to cope with constant flooding in the first four years of its existence, and in 1722 a hurricane practically wiped it out. But the city continued to grow. In 1727, the Ursuline nuns came to teach children and care for the sick. They began the first school in Louisiana—and the first all-girl school in the country—and ran a military hospital. The next year, to the great enthusiasm of the male population, the "casket girls," young marriageable French women of good character, came to Louisiana, taking their name from their government-supplied clothes and linens carried in casquettes, or chests.

During colonial times, slightly less than half the population of the city was of European ancestry, primarily French and Spanish, and slightly more than half was of African-Caribbean ancestry. About half the blacks were slaves, about half were "gens de couleur libres"— free people of color. Free people of color were successful tradesmen, skilled craftsmen, and landowners. Some were wealthy, and some even held slaves themselves.

(following page) The Presbytere, facing Jackson Square adjoining St. Louis Cathedral, was completed in 1813 as the bishop's palace and administrative building for church functions. Featuring historic art and relics, including Civil War armaments, the Presbytere is now a part of the Louisiana State Museum. Photo by Jackson Hill/Southern Lights Studio.

According to most historians, the color line in New Orleans was never as firmly drawn as it was in other parts of the South. Creole French and Spanish heritage, and the presence of a large number of free people of color, meant more tolerance for the races mixing in day-to-day commerce, housing, or romance. The Code Noir, a 1724 document which regulated slavery, handed down brutal sentences for slaves who ran away, stole, or hit a white person. But it also mandated that slaves be properly fed and clothed, instructed in Catholicism, and not required to work on Sundays or Holy Days.

In 1731, with a population of 7,000, New Orleans was exporting lumber, bricks, tar, meat, sugar, and rum; and importing silk, leather, spices, cocoa, silver, and porcelain. But France wasn't making any money, so in 1762, it gave the entire Louisiana Territory to Spain by secret treaty. When New Orleanians found this out, 600 of them rioted. One reason: they couldn't get the good French Bordeauxs they were used to, but had to drink inferior Catalonian wines instead.

For the most part, New Orleans was uninvolved in the American Revolution, although the Spanish governor Bernard de Galvez did capture 11 English cargo ships on the Mississippi in 1777 to show his support for the revolutionaries.

Fire has always shaped the city's history, dating to the time in 1699 when the French, hoping to make friends with the Indians, built a hut and a fire for a friendly Choctaw only to see him perish in an out-of-control blaze and his colleagues disappear into the woods. On Good Friday in 1788, some drapery blew across a candle on an altar of a private chapel in a home on the corner of Chartres and Toulouse streets, starting a fire that burned down between 800 and 900 structures in the French Quarter—more than four-fifths of the total. Six years later, a fire, which began when some children playing in a house on Royal Street accidentally ignited some hay, burned 212 buildings. The only building in the area to survive both fires was the Ursuline Convent. Thus most of the architecture of the French Quarter actually dates from Spanish times.

The threat of fire still looms over the oldest part of the city. In 1988, the Cabildo in Jackson Square, the old Spanish seat of government, caught fire from a welder's torch, but the damage was confined to that building.

In the last years of the eighteenth century, more and more flatboats and keelboats came down the Mississippi from Ohio, Tennessee, and Kentucky; some loaded with grain or tobacco or lumber, some just logs lashed together to sell. Driving them were the "Kaintocks," a rowdy, rugged bunch who did their business in New Orleans, made their money, partied, and, often, walked home. The Creoles in residence were offended by the Kaintocks' behavior and annoyed by their boats, so the Spanish began levying heavy

General Andrew Jackson at the famous Battle of New Orleans, on January 8, 1815. Photo courtesy of The Historic New Orleans Collection, accession no. 1964.06.

New Orleanians display their sense of living history every year by recreating their most famous battle. Photo by Jackson Hill/Southern Lights Studio.

Opera has a long tradition in the city, which staged the first performance in North America 200 years ago. The French Opera House, built in 1835, was the most opulent on the continent and a city landmark until it burned in 1919. Photo courtesy of The Historic New Orleans Collection, accession no. 1974.25.36.22.

The architecture of downtown New Orleans combines the best of traditional and modern styles. Photo by Jackson Hill/Southern Lights Studio.

tariffs. Kentucky and Tennessee, in turn, threatened to leave the Union they had just joined unless President Thomas Jefferson did something to control the situation.

At about the same time, Spain gave the Louisiana Territory back to the United States's arch-rival Napoleonic France, which worried Jefferson a great deal. With two good reasons, he arranged to buy the entire 600-million-acre territories for $15 million. It took only two weeks of negotiation to lead to what has been called "the greatest real estate deal of all time." The Louisiana Purchase of 1803 set the stage for the American phase of New Orleans history.

The Americans flocked to town, but they were not precisely welcomed by the Creoles. So they established their own part of the city in Faubourg St. Mary, what is now the Central Business District, across Canal Street from the Creole-dominated French Quarter. Business blossomed, with banks, shipping firms, and exchanges where cotton, sugar, tobacco, and other commodities were auctioned. Beginning in 1812, steamboats also plied the river, bringing commerce to an even more fevered pitch. Some people from each side did meet to shop on Canal Street—at 171 feet reputedly the world's widest, with an aptly-named "neutral ground" as its median—but the two worlds were quite separate, and often hostile.

Shortly after Louisiana joined the Union in 1812, war broke out between Britain and the United States. The final engagement was the famous Battle of New Orleans, on January 8, 1815. General Andrew Jackson and his troops, including Creoles, Americans, free men of color, and pirates who sailed with the renowned Jean Lafitte, pounded home a decisive victory in about half an hour. There were almost 3,500 British killed or wounded, compared to 71 American casualties. General Jackson's statue rules Jackson Square, at the heart of the French Quarter, and every January 8, the battle is re-enacted. As it happened, however, the whole enterprise was unnecessary. A treaty ending the war had been signed about two weeks previously, but the message didn't reached the warring parties in time to abort the battle.

The middle part of the century was the golden age for New Orleans, still propelled by the engine of the river and the port. The city had grown from just over 8,000 in 1803 to 41,000 in 1820 and more than double that by 1840, becoming the fourth-largest in the nation. Some of the earliest growth was traced to the Acadian French (or Cajuns) who had begun to come to the region in 1764 after their expulsion from Canada. In 1809, nearly 6,000 people who had fled a slave insurrection in Santo Domingo arrived in the city. From 1820 to 1860, about a million immigrants came through New Orleans—the nation's primary destination after New York. In 1844, a ticket from Ireland to New Orleans could be had for as little as $12, and many Irish came fleeing the famines of their homeland. There were succeeding waves of Germans and Sicilians, who established one of the earliest Italian colonies in the U.S. in the 1840s.

New Orleans was becoming a shining beacon for civilization in the Americas. After all, the first opera in North America had been staged in here in 1796. The city had a theatre, built in 1835 by James H. Caldwell, whose lavishness was surpassed by only three others, all of which were in Italy. Caldwell also built the St. Charles Hotel, the first of the great American hotels that, according to historian John Chase, "rose from the pigsties and butterbean sections of Pierre Percy's truck garden to dominate the New Orleans skyline. Departing guests passed through its Corinthian portico to spread its fame to the world." Caldwell brought light to New Orleans, quite literally, when he arranged for the city to become one of the first four in the nation lit by gas. And there was much to see. The first Mardi Gras parade rolled in 1838, the harbinger of an event with an economic impact of almost a billion dollars more than a century-and-a-half later. In 1847, New Orleans was the leading horse racing center in the country, and it still has the nation's third-oldest racetrack.

The seeds of the city's decline during and after the Civil War, however, were already being sown. The Erie Canal and the emergence of railroads meant that the Mississippi River

637 COMMON ST.
THE
KINGS
JESTERS

was no longer the only way to market for the center of the country. But the merchants of the city didn't realize the import of such changes.

According to many historians, New Orleans came through the Civil War better than most of its Southern counterparts. The city was blockaded in 1861 and occupied by federal troops about a year later. The occupation lasted for 15 years, giving New Orleans the dubious distinction of having a Reconstruction government longer than any other Southern city.

By the 1870s and 1880s, commerce was beginning to pick up again—and the formation of the Association of Business and Commerce, the forerunner of The Chamber/ New Orleans and the River Region, was just one sign of economic health. A system for dredging the mouth of the Mississippi River, Captain Eads' jetties, reopened the Port of New Orleans to international trade, though the port didn't recover its pre-war levels until World War I. Railroads linked New Orleans with the rest of the world for the first time, banks were founded, and there was a steady growth in the cotton and sugar industries, in which New Orleans led the nation. The city was also host to the 1884 World's Exposition, held to celebrate the 100th anniversary of the first shipment of cotton from the United States. It didn't do much for economic development, as it had promised, but it did plant the seeds for the tourism industry that has become so important to the region.

The turn of the century saw the birth of jazz in the famous red-light Storyville district, the distinctive voice of New Orleans that was to make its way up the river to

Mardi Gras is New Orleans' most famous celebration. From Twelfth Night (January 6) to Mardi Gras itself (the day before Lent), people celebrate with formal balls and massive parades, with elaborate colorful floats bearing riders who toss tons of trinkets to the cheering throngs. Photo by Jackson Hill/Southern Lights Studio.

For a different view of New Orleans, take a ride on the historic streetcar down St. Charles Avenue through the Garden District and university neighborhoods. Photo by Jackson Hill/Southern Lights Studio.

The Crescent City Connection, with its twin bridges spanning the Mississippi River, joins two parts of Greater New Orleans—the west bank and downtown.
Photo by Jackson Hill/Southern Lights Studio.

St. Louis and Chicago and from there to the world. An important engineering advance made it possible for the first time to pump water up and out of the below-sea-level parts of the city, opening them to development and making the entire area much less vulnerable to floods. Fifty automobiles were driven around the city in 1904, and electric streetcars were introduced. Oil was discovered in Louisiana in 1901 and a gas strike was hit 15 years later, developments that would define the economy of the New Orleans region in the latter half of the century.

The Depression hit New Orleans as it did the rest of the country, with five banks failing and the controversial populist politics of Huey Long—first as governor, then senator, then martyr—filling the atmosphere. Works Progress Administration projects in the mid-'30s restored the Pontalba buildings and the French Market, as well as building much of City Park, one of the largest urban green spaces in the nation. And in 1933, the first bridge was built across the Mississippi.

During World War II, local shipyards worked around the clock, building PT boats, landing craft for the Navy, and the Higgins boat, which made possible the D-Day landing on the beaches at Normandy. German submarines operated in the Gulf, sinking 12 boats, and Mardi Gras was cancelled for only the third time in history. Air raid drills and rationing were the norm.

The first offshore oil well was hit in the Gulf of Mexico in 1947, launching an industry that was to shape the economic destiny of the region for many years and make Louisianians the world's experts in offshore drilling skills. Skyscrapers, many of them occupied by oil companies, soared in the city during the 1960s; the architecturally distinctive Rivergate was built to serve the growing convention industry, and the 76,000-seat Louisiana Superdome—one of the first and largest of its kind in the world—became a distinctive addition to the horizon in 1975.

The New Orleans region is fortunate because history here is not something that's preserved in a museum or a collection of books. It's all around us. We live it every day. In fact, *New Orleans Magazine*, looking back over the past 30 years in the city, tags "an appreciation of preservation" as one of the 10 ways New Orleans has improved, adding "New Orleans survives partially because it is better-preserved than many cities."

According to many preservationists, the 12-block long, 6-block-wide French Quarter is the most important historic district in the country. The Vieux Carre Commission, created in 1936 and used as a model worldwide, is in large part responsible for the intact fabric of this living neighborhood. The French Quarter was designated as a National Historic Landmark District in 1966 and is also included on the National Register of Historic Places. And our living history isn't restricted to the oldest part of town. Most neighborhoods are listed in the National Register of Historic Districts, including Uptown, the largest district in the country with 10,000 buildings on 2,250 acres. Historic plantations are but a short

drive away, and historic houses dot the French Quarter, offering their view of life in a wide range of bygone times. Archival resources and museum collections—including the Historic New Orleans Collection, the Louisiana State Museum, and the planned D-Day Museum—preserve life in New Orleans as it was in order to inspire life and work in the city as it is and will be. ◆

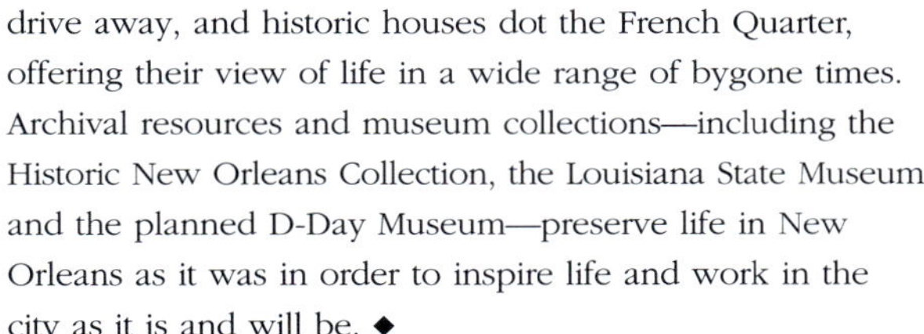

The French Quarter was designated as a National Historic Landmark District in 1966 and is also included on the National Register of Historic Places. Photo by Jackson Hill/Southern Lights Studio.

Getting Down to Business

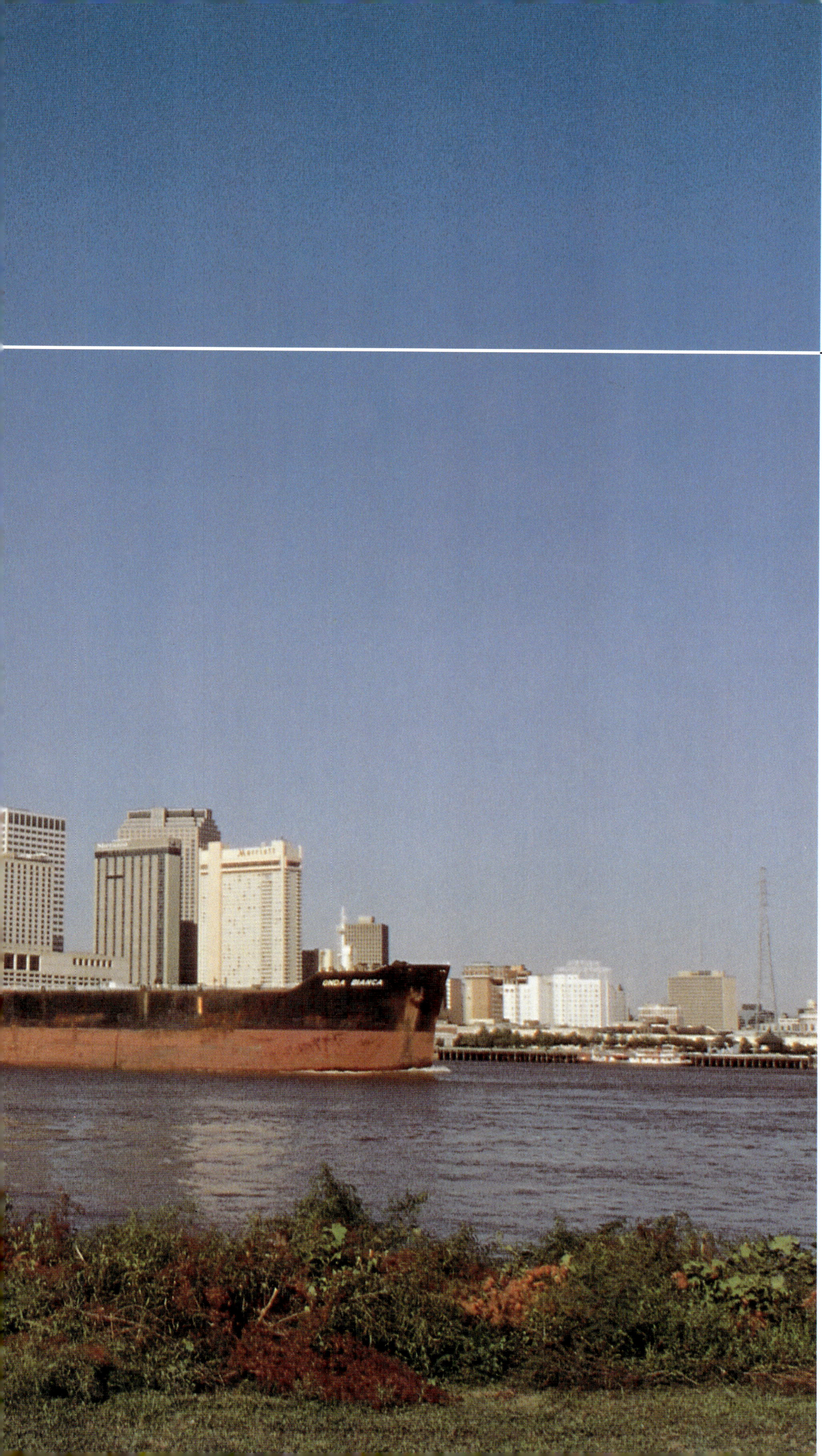

CHAPTER 2

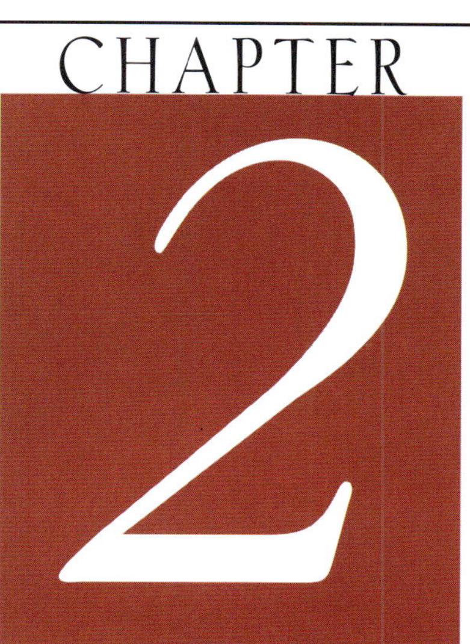

Because there was the Mississippi River, there was New Orleans. Photo by Jackson Hill/Southern Lights Studio.

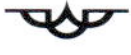

"New Orleans has long been

world–famous for its unique, rich

cultural tradition. For many, the quality

of its business infrastructure—and its

low cost of living—may be surprising."

Trade and Culture *magazine*

As a misty dawn breaks over New Orleans, the booms are swinging, loading up a container ship that will sail to Tokyo with its cargo of grain. Upriver, the refineries are running, producing the oil that fuels the nation and the chemical byproducts that are used in everything from pharmaceuticals to swimming pools.

A computer programmer, here for a major convention, strolls from her French Quarter hotel to Decatur Street to pick up a beignet and a cup of café au lait. Skilled craftsmen swarm over the steel frame of a new tanker destined for Russia, welding here and there; while on the other side of town, other workers are engineering the fuel tanks for the newest generation of space shuttles.

A surgeon snaps on his gloves to begin his latest transplant with procedures that he developed—and the world follows. Traffic is heavy as students go to class, professionals head for the offices in the Central Business District and the suburban towers, and shops and restaurants open their doors for a new day.

New Orleans works—every day presents a new example of just how well. In 1996, some 600,000 people were employed in the New Orleans area, the highest number ever recorded and an increase of more than 80,000 jobs since 1987. The New Orleans region ranks in the top third of all metropolitan areas for economic growth, with a growth rate of four times the national average from 1990-1995. We've created more jobs than Birmingham, Memphis, Phoenix, or Miami.

The vignettes above illustrate the major segments of the local economy. The maritime industry and oil and gas each provide 19 percent of New Orleans jobs, with tourism following close behind at 16 percent. Shipbuilding and the aerospace industry together employ 11 percent of New Orleanians, 9 percent are involved in business and professional services, 7 percent provide educational services, and the remaining 15 percent have jobs in a variety of areas, including the military. According to statistics from MetroVision, the economic development partnership for New Orleans and the River Region, the area has an above-average number of workers in professional specialties, technical areas, administrative support, and service occupations.

Some of the major employers have been destined by history. For example, New Orleans' site as the gateway to the Mississippi River has meant more than 200 years as one of the most important ports in the world. The ports of the New Orleans region lead the world in cargo tonnage, handling about 15 percent of the U.S. total waterborne cargo each year. Over 4,000 ships annually call at the four area

entities that together comprise the largest inland port in the U.S. (the Gulf of Mexico is more than 90 miles down the Mississippi). Common cargos include steel, coffee, agricultural commodities, and bulk liquid commodities such as petroleum and chemicals. Japan is a principal trading partner, accounting for 13 percent of the port's activities, followed by Mexico, Canada, the United Kingdom, and Argentina. The port also handles about 18 percent of total U.S. trade with Africa.

A year after the beginning of the twentieth century, when oil was struck in Jennings and Whitecastle in the southwest part of Louisiana, an economic powerhouse was born. The engine of oil and gas, including offshore exploration, would drive the New Orleans economy for the last half of the century and beyond.

Louisiana ranks third after Texas and Alaska in crude oil production, with about 17 percent of total U.S. output

in 1994, and second only to Texas in natural gas, with 27 percent of total U.S. production. There are more than 27,000 producing wells in the state. About half the refining capacity in Louisiana is located in the New Orleans region. In fact, if New Orleans were a state, it would be fourth in the nation (after Texas, Louisiana, and California) in refining capacity. Local refineries can process more than 1.1 million barrels of crude oil a day, or about one in every 12 barrels in the U.S.

While the flow of oil and gas revenues into salaries and the local tax base has ebbed from its height in the mid-80s, the industry is still arguably the most significant economic sector of the region. Although one in every four jobs in oil and gas was lost between 1990 and 1995, it still accounted for more than $600 million in earnings in 1994, or almost a quarter of the economy of the New Orleans metropolitan area. And, according to local evidence and a 1996 national Arthur Andersen survey, the oil and gas industry is stronger than it's been since the boom days more than a decade ago as it enters a period of significant growth.

About three-fourths of the nation's offshore oil activity is within Louisiana, much of it in the New Orleans region. And the industry is growing each year. In the last two years, 10 companies operating in deep water have found the equivalent of 3.5 billion barrels of oil in the 25 fields discovered so far. In 1996, the rig count stands at 170, the highest since 1985, and one of the most active offshore federal lease sales ever brought in $511 million. The offshore industry leads the world in wells drilled, number of producing wells, and future production. Both the U.S. Geological Survey and the

oil industry rate the Central Gulf region south and southwest of New Orleans as having the highest resource potential of all outer continental shelf regions. Some have even projected that the oil and gas reserves of the once-thought-to-be-played-out Gulf of Mexico will exceed the riches of Alaska's Prudhoe Bay.

Effective use of new technology is one reason for the turnaround, and the offshore industry in Louisiana is full of examples. Shell Offshore's 31-story, $1.2 billion Mars oil and gas platform—the world's tallest—was installed in the Gulf 130 miles southeast of New Orleans in the spring of 1996, where it floats in almost 3,000 feet of water over a field estimated to contain 700 million barrels of oil and gas. Mars, its big brother Ursa Major—scheduled for installation in 1998 as the Gulf's largest platform, working in 4,000 feet of water—and other similar ventures are made possible by a technological breakthrough called a tension leg platform. Instead of rigid steel supports anchored to the ocean floor, these platforms float on the surface, held in place by low-cost steel tendons.

The people play a part in offshore oil's success, too. New Orleans area rig workers are famous from to the North Sea to Australia, and points in between, for their willingness to share their knowledge about offshore oil and gas—not to mention cooking lessons and party pointers.

More than 11 million visitors come to the New Orleans region every year, spending an estimated $3.5 billion. Some come for renowned events such as Mardi Gras or the New Orleans Jazz & Heritage Festival. Others prefer cultural attractions such as writers' festivals or blockbuster art

If New Orleans were a state,
it would be fourth in the nation in
refining capacity. Local refineries
process about one out of every 12
barrels of oil in the United States.
Photo by Jackson Hill/Southern
Lights Studio.

The New Orleans region ranks
in the top third of all metropolitan
areas for economic growth, with a
growth rate of four times the
national average from 1990–1995.
Photo by Jackson Hill/Southern
Lights Studio.

ESSO AFRICA
NASSAU
ESSO

Shipping by water has meant prosperity for the city and its surrounding region. Photo by Jackson Hill/Southern Lights Studio.

exhibits. Some choose quieter times for the architectural, musical, and epicurean joys of the city that's been called the most European in America. And some are in town for conventions. The region is second only to Washington D.C. as a top convention site, and the number of convention delegates has almost doubled over 10 years, to reach more than 1.1 million in 1995. The third phase of the Ernest N. Morial Convention Center, which broke ground in 1996, will give the convention industry a facility with more than a million square feet under one roof, able to serve the largest conventions in the country—sometimes two at a time!

The fourth-largest New Orleans sector is ship and boat-building and aerospace manufacturing. Although ships have been built in New Orleans virtually since the city's founding, the industry's modern development dates to World War II, when many Navy PT boats and the landing vessels that made the D-Day beach invasion possible were built at Higgins Shipyard, Avondale, and other companies. New Orleans industries are responsible for about 10 percent of the nation's shipbuilding and repair activities. With some reduction in defense expenditures, many firms are exploring new markets, including land-based defense vehicles, surface-effect patrol craft, pleasure/excursion vessels, ferries, and work boats for clients that range from the individual pleasure-boat buyer to the government of Russia. Adept with craft for water or air, workers at Lockheed Martin assemble external fuel tanks for the NASA space shuttle program.

Business and professional services in the city range widely, but many have a distinct New Orleans flavor. To cite only one example: Because European-rooted civil law is in force in Louisiana—as opposed to the British-inspired common law that reigns the other 49 states—New Orleans attorneys often find their services sought by clients across the globe. Thirty-four banks with well over 225 branch offices serve the region, with combined deposits of $11.4 billion. Some of the larger local banks have earned national recognition for their leadership in small business programs and lending to under-served parts of the community, among other accomplishments.

The eight universities, two medical centers, two law schools, three seminaries, and two community colleges within the region bring a continuing flow of students, faculty, research money, and cultural events to bear on the economy and the flavor of the city.

Military operations play a major part in the New Orleans region, providing 8,000 jobs and adding about $2.2 billion to the economy each year. More than 30 commands of the Navy, Navy Reserve, and U.S. Marine Corps are stationed in the region, including the Naval Support Activity, the Naval Air Station, and the Naval Reserve Force Command Headquarters. The Louisiana National Guard and the U.S. Coast Guard Eighth District—the largest in the country, covering 26 states—are also headquartered here. With 1,300 full-time employees and a payroll of $60 million, the U.S. Army Corps of Engineers maintains navigation routes, carries out flood control, and conducts environmental projects.

The list of major corporations who have selected New Orleans for their headquarters is an impressive one. It would include, among many others, Avondale Industries (shipbuilding), Entergy Services (utilities), Freeport-McMoRan (natural resources), McDermott International (construction engineering), Pan American (life insurance), Petroleum Helicopters, Inc., (oil services), Stewart Enterprises (death services),

The Freeport–McMoRan building on Poydras Street is home to one of the leading oil, gas, and mineral firms in the world. Photo by Jackson Hill/Southern Lights Studio.

and Tidewater (marine services). Small businesses—those with annual revenues of $10 million or less—account for 98 percent of all businesses in the region, and they are growing in every sector of the economy.

The New Orleans region has also seen an unprecedented surge of $13.1 billion in capital investment and infrastructure improvements in the last four years, focusing on traditional industries (shipbuilding, maritime, oil and gas services), new growth industries (tourism, health care, communication, food processing, apparel manufacturing), infrastructure (air, water, and land-based transportation) and projects that will enhance the environment. It's the highest rate in the history of the city, and among the leaders in the nation.

New Orleans' economic health can be attributed to several factors. Our workers are productive: according to statistics from the U.S. Department of Commerce, the value added per manufacturing employee in Louisiana is the highest in the South and second-highest among all states. Our cost of living is the fourth-lowest among metro areas with more than a million people, and that translates to a lower cost of doing

Military operations play a major part in the New Orleans region, providing 8,000 jobs and adding about $2.2 billion to the economy each year. Photo by Jackson Hill/Southern Lights Studio.

business. Top-flight office space is readily available, at one of the most competitive rates in the entire country. "This is a relatively cheap city to live in, with low taxes, low (cost) housing and low levels on other costs," University of New Orleans College of Business Dean Tim Ryan told *Trade and Culture* magazine. "It offers a climate where international business is understood and valued. But what makes New Orleans especially attractive is that it's an exciting city. There are things for people to do here."

Traditionally, New Orleans has been the gateway to Latin America. It's a gateway that's becoming steadily busier. MetroVision, the private-public economic development partnership that covers the nine-parish New Orleans region, launched a marketing program in 1995 called InterCambio 2000 to increase trade with Latin America by developing trade leads and positioning the region as a major international trade center. Its goal—to add $2 billion in economic impact and 10,000 jobs to the region by the turn of the century. Early indicators are good. Trade between the New Orleans region and Latin America for the first three quarters of 1995 totaled more than $10 billion—up about 15 percent from the comparable period in 1994 and growing at a rate about eight times the national average. Guatemala has also opened a trade office in the city, the first new trade office for New Orleans in 20 years. Hibernia National Bank has led a trade finance revival in the city, according to *U.S./Latin Trade* magazine, and is working to match small and medium-sized companies with Latin American markets. A federal import/export center came to New Orleans in 1994, adding to the critical mass for trade.

An economic development partnership of 200 investor organizations from business, education, labor, government, and media, growing from The Chamber/New Orleans and the River Region, MetroVision works with the state and parish offices of economic development, the World Trade Center, and other organizations to market the New Orleans region. These organizations have identified the region's competitive strengths and targeted the industries to whom those strengths appeal most—information services, textiles and garments, chemicals and plastics, and medical devices. In 1995, 2,400 permanent jobs with an economic impact of $58 million were created by five companies—in the information service, manufacturing, and medical sectors—that had expanded in or relocated to the region. Corporations who are seriously considering moving to New Orleans have increased almost seven-fold in the last three years, to reach 163 at the end of 1995. These benchmarks are evidence of progress toward a goal of creating 20,000 new jobs.

Both MetroVision and The Chamber encourage regional cooperation among governments on issues ranging from waste disposal to the criminal justice system to funding for transportation initiatives. MetroVision's 25-member Council of Governments, composed of parish presidents, mayors, and parish council representatives from the nine parishes, is a national model for cities working effectively with surrounding regions. Results have included more than $65 million annually in state and federal funds for transportation projects, a proposal for a regional partnership for a solid waste disposal system that can save up to $155 million over 20 years, and an unprecedented spirit of cooperation. The New Orleans Police Foundation, supported by The Chamber, is a leader in the effort to revamp the New Orleans Police Department, building grassroots and corporate support for the department's needs.

New Orleans mayor Marc Morial has received national kudos for his successful efforts to control crime. In 1995, the number of murders dropped 14 percent citywide—and by as much as half in some high-risk neighborhoods where community policing was introduced—while overall crime rates placed the city 31st among major metropolitan areas.

It's all adding up to success, and people across the nation are taking notice. "I have never seen as dramatic a turnaround in a business climate as I have in the New Orleans region between 1989 and 1996," said consultant Ross Boyle, president of the Growth Strategies Organization. As evidence, he cited a 45 percent reduction in workers' compensation costs, a 30 percent cut in unemployment insurance costs, the elimination of the inventory tax, the focus on funding for and quality in public education, a major upgrade of area roads and water systems, a political climate more responsive to business concerns, and more than a 50 percent increase in per capita income in seven years.

Combine fabled charm with high productivity rates, the world's best food and lodging with low cost of living, distinctive European/African/Caribbean roots with a global view of job development through trade, and the inimitable New Orleans spirit with a careful plan for creating tens of thousands of jobs and billions of dollars in economic impact. The result is true renaissance. ◆

In large businesses and small, the seafood industry provides the fuel for human energy, from oyster po–boys and catfish dinners to boiled crabs and gumbo. Photo by Jackson Hill/Southern Lights Studio.

The Destination City

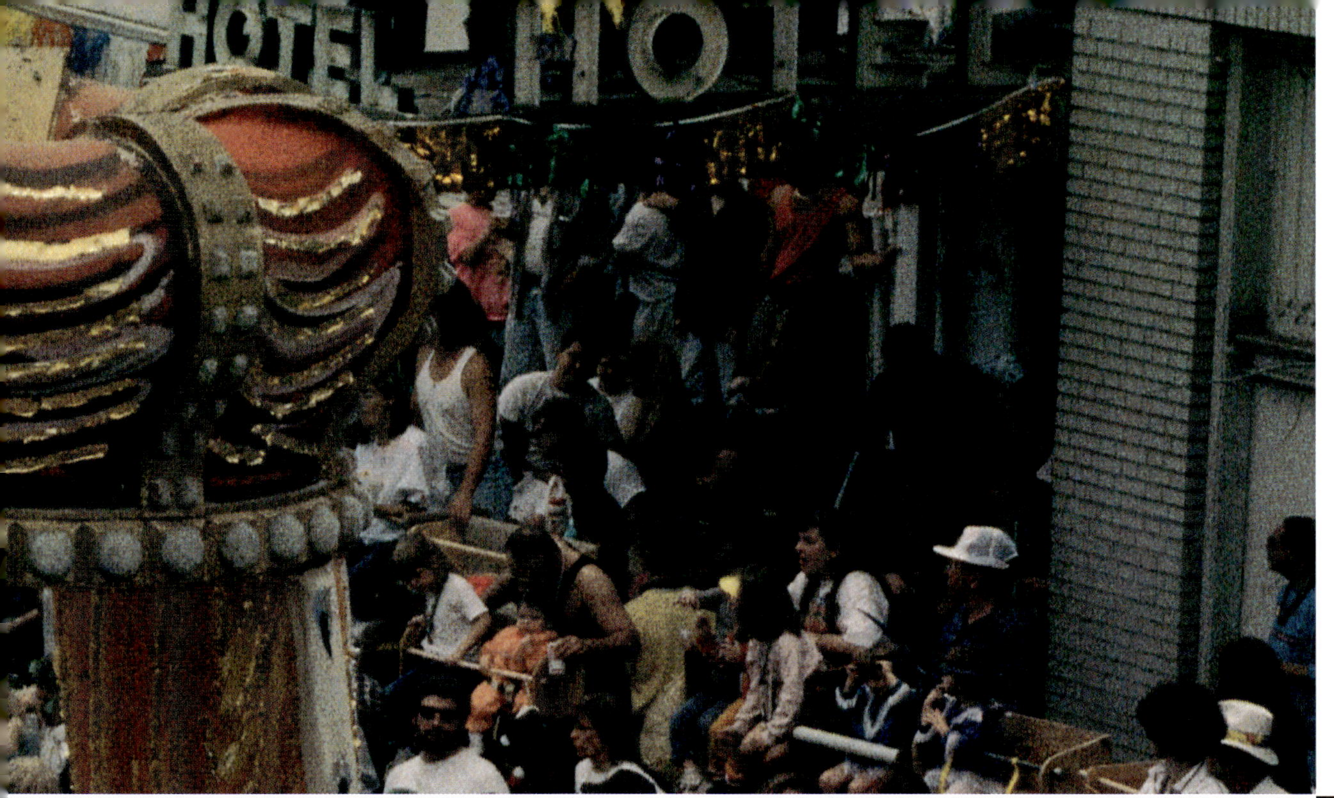

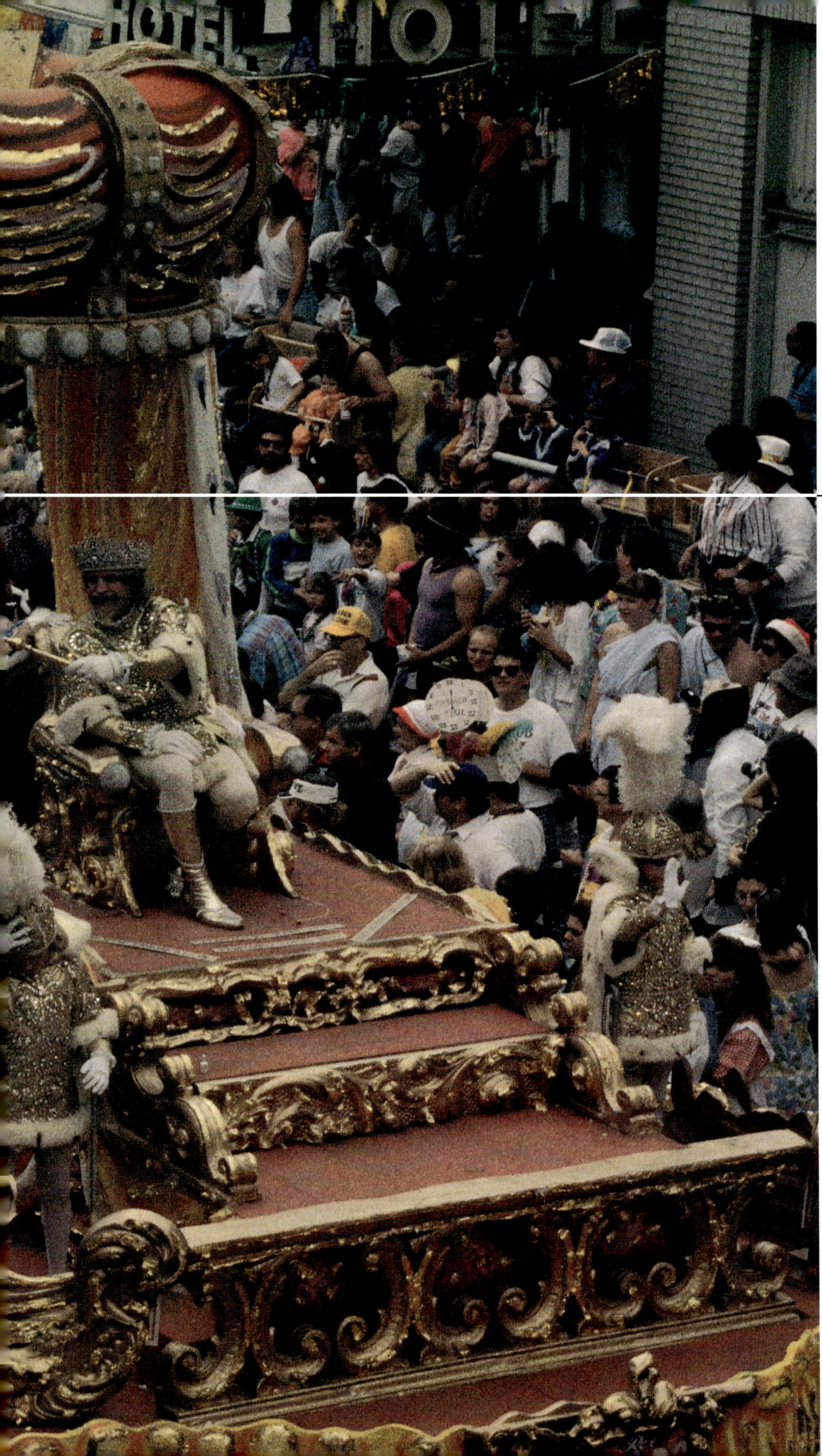

CHAPTER 3

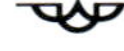

Rex reigns over Mardi Gras each year. Photo by Jackson Hill/ Southern Lights Studio.

"To the tourist, the city is first of

all a place to eat, drink and be merry....

many of them, Thackeray and Mark

Twain included, have communicated their

appreciation for the 'American Paris'

to the world."

WPA Guide to New Orleans, *1938.*

Given the way people love to come see her—throughout nearly 300 years—you'd think New Orleans would change her nickname from the Crescent City to Destination City.

Almost 11 million people visit the New Orleans area every year, for a variety of reasons. Over 1.1 million come to attend conventions, making New Orleans second only to Washington, D.C. as a top U.S. meeting venue. Millions fill the streets during the two weeks of Mardi Gras parades, while millions of others prefer to visit the city during JazzFest, the NOKIA Sugar Bowl, the Crescent City Classic Road Race, Halloween, Creole Christmas celebrations, or simply whenever they get a chance to enjoy her charms.

More than 3 million visitors a year—30 percent of the region's total—come to visit family and friends. That fact won't surprise anyone who has moved to New Orleans and almost immediately finds the spare room (and the floor space) booked with excited acquaintances. Some 27 percent of travelers to New Orleans come for business, 17 percent for pleasure, 13 percent for a special event, and 10 percent as part of general touring.

The region, with its strong mix of international flavors, is also a popular destination for people from outside the United States, with more than half a million visiting each year. Some are attracted by our unique-to-the-U.S., tax-free shopping program for international visitors. More than 46,000 people took advantage of the sales-tax rebate program in 1994.

Tourism is a sizable, and growing, economic sector in the River Region. The industry has doubled in the last 20 years and now accounts for 16 percent of the employment in the region—more than 61,000 jobs. Its impact is second only to the oil and gas and maritime industries, each of which holds a 19 percent employment share. Visitors spend approximately $3.5 billion in the city annually, including almost $1 billion on accommodations, $800 million on food, and $500 million on retail purchases. The average visitor spends $65 a day, stays for three nights, and is traveling with two other adults.

And what do they do while they're here? According to a recent survey by the New Orleans Metropolitan Convention and Visitors Bureau, Inc., 87 percent visit the French Quarter, with 90 percent also saying they want to see the Mississippi River and to visit Jackson Square. Just over 40 percent express an interest in taking a riverboat tour. More than a third plan to see the Aquarium of the Americas, a fifth intend to visit Audubon Zoo, and about a quarter want to see the Lakefront, with about the same number planning to visit City Park. About 14 percent intend to go to the New Orleans Museum of Art in City Park, while about one in four expresses some interest in visiting a riverboat casino.

But the statistics can't tell you why people love to discover New Orleans—and then to come back again and again and again. Native daughter Anne Rice, the best-selling author of *Interview with the Vampire* and other novels, creator of Louis, Lestat, Claudia, and a universe of vampires and witches, has the words. Of her move to New Orleans after 25 years in California, she told *Lear*'s magazine, "For the first time I'm

DIXI
TIPITIN
e's

CUSTOM MADE HATS
TO ORDER

The Louisiana Swamp Exhibit at the Audubon Zoo—with its rare white alligators—was recently named one of the top five zoo exhibits in the nation by The Zoo Book. *Photo courtesy of the Audubon Zoo.*

The newly expanded Louisiana Children's Museum offers many hands-on learning opportunities for children and adults. Photo by Jackson Hill/Southern Lights Studio.

a residential neighborhood, too, with New Orleanians who've lived there for decades rubbing shoulders with artists, musicians, writers, and Hollywood stars who've discovered its gentle European charms. For example, journalist and mystery writer Kevin Allman, who recently moved to the city from Los Angeles, says his favorite thing about New Orleans is the respite from what he terms architecture fatigue. "In Los Angeles, anything built before 1960 is historic, and if a building is remotely attractive, people race to tear it down. In the French Quarter, all I have to do is walk outside my gate and look around. The architecture here is a tonic. It clears my head."

The Audubon Zoo and the Aquarium of the Americas—with its new Entergy IMAX theater—together draw more than 2.5 million visitors each year, most of them from outside the New Orleans area. Both are managed by the Audubon Institute, a not-for-profit corporation which oversees Audubon Park, Aubudon Zoo, Woldenberg Riverfront Park, the Aquarium of the Americas, the Entergy IMAX Theatre, the Louisiana Nature Center, Wilderness Park, the Freeport-McMoRan Audubon Species Survival Center, the Audubon Center for Research of Endangered Species, and a planned Insectarium—the largest collection of natural science facilities in the country. The popularity of the zoo and the aquarium has made Audubon Institute facilities the top year-round tourist attraction in the city. They're also highly rated nationally. Both the zoo and the aquarium place first on *Good Housekeeping*'s list of similar facilities, and the LL&E-sponsored Louisiana Swamp Exhibit—with its rare white alligators—was recently named one of the top five zoo exhibits in the nation by *The Zoo Book*.

The zoo, extending from the river to Magazine Street in Audubon Park uptown, has earned acclaim for its turn-around in the last two decades from one of the country's worst zoos to one of its best. In addition to the distinctive swamp exhibit, with its focus on Cajun life and culture, zoo features include a reptile encounter, a tropical bird house, an Asian domain starring Suri, the white tiger; the world of primates, an African savanna, North American grasslands,

actually able to write with the sound of the rain falling on the banana trees, the smell of the river breeze coming in the window; and every night the twilight, the golden moment when the sky is shot with red and purple and gold, is just incredible . . . [New Orleans] is a place in the United States where you're not really in this country any more."

The French Quarter, which adds Spanish heritage to the French, then seasons with bits of Caribbean, African, and Anglo-Saxon culture, has earned its distinctive flavor throughout history. In the 12-block-by-6-block neighborhood, strollers pass renowned restaurants, lush tropical flowers and trees, the wrought-iron balconies that represent New Orleans in so many photos, the townhouses with hidden patios, and shops that offer items ranging from top-of-the-line antiques to the most modern crafts to exotic masks to Louisiana foods. There's the raunchy fun of Bourbon Street, with burlesque mixing with bars, fine restaurants, and souvenir shops, and the attractions of the farmer's market and flea market in the historic French Market buildings.

General Jackson presides over his square, with the Cathedral in the background and the MoonWalk leading to a spectacular view of the river just across the street. The square is flanked by the Pontalba buildings, the red-brick structures that are among the first apartments in the United States, developed in 1850 by Baroness Micaela de Pontalba. Their terrific living space is still in demand. The Quarter is

From antiques to high fashion, the French Quarter is full of shops that cater to the whims and pocketbooks of every shopper. Photo by Michael Varisco/Southern Lights Studio.

The Aquarium of the Americas, located where Canal Street meets the Mississippi, attracts more than a million visitors a year to explore the watery worlds of the Caribbean Reef, the Gulf of Mexico, the Mississippi River, and the Amazon Rainforest. Photo by Jackson Hill/ Southern Lights Studio.

Aquarium
of the Americas

Commander's Palace was named the number one restaurant in America by the readers of Food & Wine Magazine. *"With three times as many mentions as any other establishment, Commander's Palace . . . is clearly a culinary mecca for many of you, whether you live in New Orleans or not," wrote the editors. Photo by Jackson Hill/Southern Lights Studio.*

and South American pampas, with their native animals; and frequently changing exhibits. Its annual benefit, the Zoo-to-Do, is the largest nonmedical fundraiser in the country and serves as a model for similar events from coast to coast.

The Aquarium of the Americas rose in 1990 at the site where Canal Street meets the Mississippi, as the anchor for the riverfront Woldenberg Park. Since then, it's become the busiest aquarium-related building in the country, attracting some two million visitors in 1996 to explore the watery worlds of the Caribbean Reef, the Gulf of Mexico, the Mississippi River, and the Amazon Rainforest. Special donut-shaped tanks, huge cylinders, and other innovative habitat designs let visitors see creatures from all angles.

As part of a $25-million, 66,000-square-foot aquarium expansion, the Entergy IMAX Theatre opened in 1995, bringing dramatic state-of-the-art images of living seas, tropical rain forests, mountain gorillas, great sharks, and planets to a screen that's a five and a half stories tall. One of only five IMAX 3-D theaters in the nation and the first to be housed within an aquarium, it's a popular place. Projections were for 500,000 visitors in the first year; more than 750,000 actually turned up to see giant IMAX wonders.

Visitors who come to New Orleans for family fun will also enjoy walking tours of literary, ghostly, and/or historic sites in the city. The newly expanded Louisiana Children's Museum, tripling its space in a $2.8 million Warehouse District renovation, attracted more than 200,000 visitors in 1995. They enjoy a wide range of exhibits, including a gigantic microscope for a closer look at bugs or human cells; a child-scale grocery store, restaurant, television studio, and tugboat; a toddler labyrinth; a waterworks display; an interactive exploration of music; and let's-pretend play-spaces with Cajun cabins, pirogues, dress-up clothes, and other imagination-sparkers inspired by Louisiana's diverse heritage. The museum is rated as one of the top 10 children's museums in the country by *Your Family* and *Parenting*.

Tourism by African-Americans is on the increase in New Orleans, with the Essence Festival and conferences of the Links, the Full Gospel Mission, and the Urban League bringing thousands of visitors to the region just in the summer of 1996. Special tours focus on the region's African and Caribbean heritage, and a growing niche within the industry also targets big African-American family reunions.

More than a million visitors to the New Orleans region each year come for conventions, which increased from 893 in 1980 to 2,434 in 1994. Some events bring only a few dozen or a few hundred people; others, like the Pittsburgh Conference, the American Heart Association, the National Association of Television Production Executives, or the Republican Convention, bring tens of thousands.

The city's larger conventions are held at the Ernest N. Morial Convention Center, a riverfront complex downtown which was part of the 1984 World's Fair before being developed into a convention center in 1985 and named in memory of the first African-American mayor of New Orleans. Delegates to conferences at the convention center alone— about half the annual conventioneer total—added almost $2.75 billion to the area economy in 1995, money that created some 35,000 jobs in the region. Currently, the facility offers 733,360 square feet of exhibition space and ranks among the top convention centers in the country. A third phase of its construction, to be completed in 1998, will add over 400,000 square feet of exhibition space in four halls, giving the Morial Convention Center the largest contiguous exhibition space in the United States. The new construction will add 73 meeting rooms to the existing 83, making it possible to accommodate 300,000 more conventioneers annually and host two major trade shows at once. More than 600 future meetings are already booked using the expanded facility, with a value of at least $8 billion.

Undoubtedly the most famous New Orleans tourist magnet is Mardi Gras. It's billed as the biggest free show on earth, but in point of fact, Mardi Gras is nearly a $1 billion business, attracting over 2 million visitors every year with more than 50 parades and close to 100 balls in the four- to six-week period between January 6 (Twelfth Night) and Ash Wednesday.

Mardi Gras—which is often called simply Carnival—is an intrinsic part of New Orleans culture. Perhaps it was fated by the mere fact that the French explorers d'Iberville and de Bienville who would go on to found New Orleans camped near the mouth of the Mississippi on Mardi Gras, 1699. New Orleanians celebrated with costumed balls as early as 1740,

The Great Hall at the 1984 World's Fair was transformed into the core of the Ernest N. Morial Convention Center. Photo by Jackson Hill/Southern Lights Studio.

All over the New Orleans area during Mardi Gras, costumes abound, many of them simultaneously witty and racy. Photos by Jackson Hill/Southern Lights Studio.

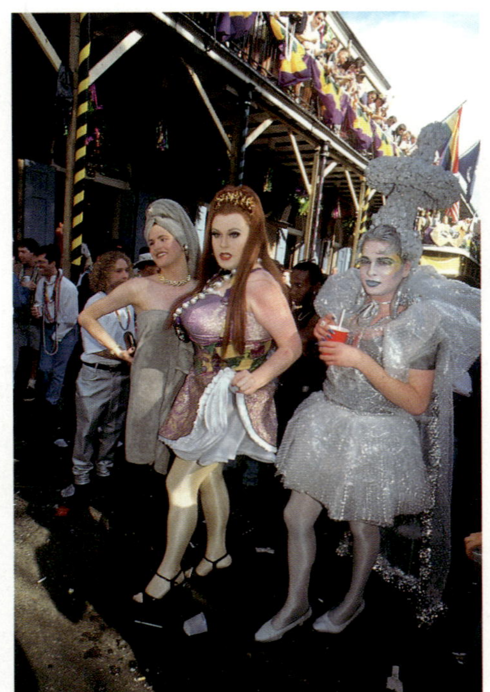

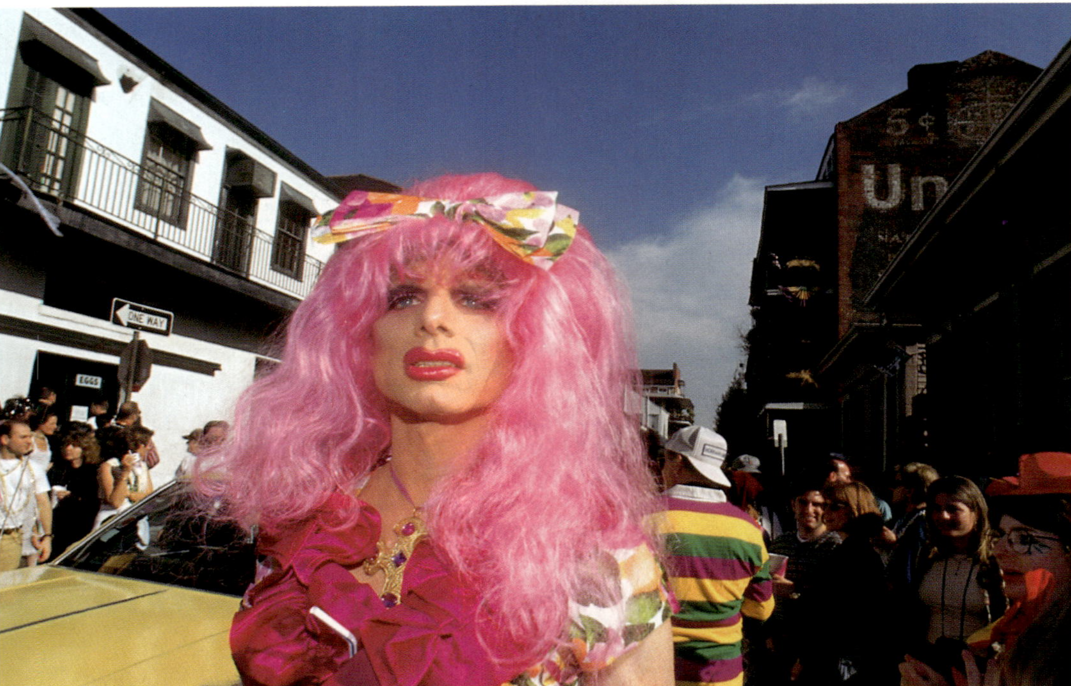

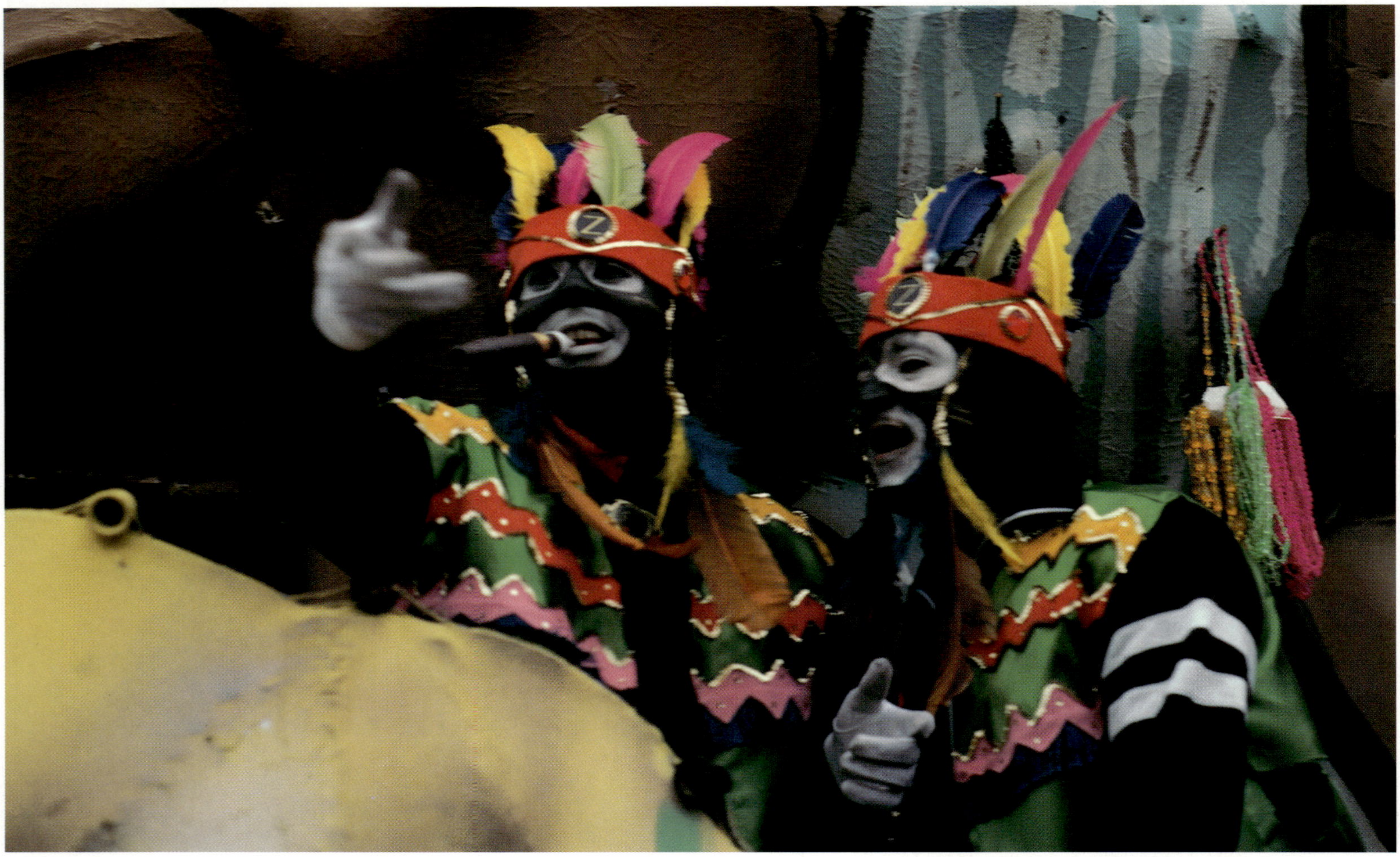

The African-American based Zulu Social and Pleasure Club sponsors a parade each year, with float riders tossing highly coveted beads and spears, and occasionally handing down a painted coconut to a favored spectator. Photos by Jackson Hill/Southern Lights Studio.

The Superdome is one of the top sightseeing attractions in the South, with an annual attendance of more than 75,000 for its daily tours. Photo by Jackson Hill/Southern Lights Studio.

and Mardi Gras was the occasion for public masking during the colonial period, but the first parade float did not appear until 1837. The first organized parade was the Mystick Krewe of Comus, formed by nine men in 1857.

Balls begin on January 6. Most of them are quite formal but others are more along the lines of a party for 10,000 close friends, with famous rock'n'roll musicians performing in the Superdome. The balls and parades are sponsored by krewes, or organizations of people who band together for such Mardi Gras purposes. Some krewes are all-male, some are all-female, and some consist of both genders. Some are small; Endymion and Bacchus each have more than 1,000 members. Some of the krewes are based on family and society lineage, others invite out-of-town guests to be parade riders, for a price.

Prime parade season begins about 10 days before Mardi Gras, with at least one parade a day, and works to a fever pitch of non-stop, region-wide parading on the weekend preceding Fat Tuesday. A parade is usually put together by one krewe (though some have done joint ventures for the sake of economy recently). It consists of 20 or more floats, each with at least 10 riders, with bands and other marching groups inserted between the floats. In perhaps the main distinction between a Mardi Gras parade and those quieter events in other cities, each rider is throwing things—plastic beads, metal coin-like objects called doubloons, go-cups emblazoned with the logo of the krewe, toys, spears, and other innovative, tossable items. And the spectators are catching— sometimes at the expense of each other. If a parade-goer doesn't come back to the hotel room with a neck laden with beads and a foot-tall stack of go-cups, he or she hasn't been trying. For example, in the super parades of Bacchus and Endymion, held the weekend before Mardi Gras, 2,300-plus members toss more than 1.5 million cups, 2.5 million doubloons, and almost 29 million strings of plastic beads.

On Fat Tuesday itself, Zulu and Rex are the highlights. The positions of Rex, King of Carnival, and King Zulu are considered top civic honors in the city. The two traditional parades are followed by truck parades, where any family, PTA, organization, or group of friends with enough energy can decorate a flatbed truck, don a costume, hop aboard, and throw things to crowds that number in the millions. In the French Quarter, costumes abound, many of them simultaneously witty and racy. In other city neighborhoods, the Mardi Gras Indians make an appearance, African-American "tribes" whose colorful and intricate feathered costumes and call-and-response rhythm patterns serve as reminders of an incident in the 1790s when local Chickasaw tribes sheltered runaway slaves.

One of the most popular icons of Mardi Gras is the king cake—essentially a large Danish with purple, green, and gold sugar on top and a plastic baby about as long as your fingernail somewhere inside. According to tradition, whoever is served the slice containing the baby must buy the next king cake. More than 500,000 king cakes are sold in New Orleans each year between Twelfth Night and Fat Tuesday, with another 50,000 shipped across the country.

Promptly at midnight on Fat Tuesday, the Mardi Gras season ends and the city enters into the Lenten season. No one ever really celebrates overtime, either, at least not in the

French Quarter. At the stroke of 12, the garbage trucks begin to roll through Quarter streets, preceded by police announcing over bullhorns to the partying masses, "Mardi Gras is over. Go home."

Sometimes they do. And sometimes they come back for the New Orleans Jazz and Heritage Festival just a couple of months later. A tradition of the last weekend of April and the first weekend of May, JazzFest is a celebration of music, food, and crafts that brings more than 400,000 people to the New Orleans Fair Grounds, and another 50,000 to evening concerts. At the Fair Grounds, stages showcase more than 75 musical acts every day—traditional and contemporary jazz, rhythm and blues, ragtime, gospel, Cajun, zydeco, bluegrass, rock, African-Caribbean, Latin, fusion, rap, reggae, and everything in between and beyond. Visitors can sample local and regional food from dozens of vendors, or wander through a juried craft show, a Louisiana folk art exhibition, an African marketplace, and tents with books and music rooted in local heritage. According to a recent study, JazzFest generated about $200 million in economic activity in 1995, more than the NCAA Final Four and the SEC basketball tournament, and possibly exceeding the Super Bowl.

Sports special events bring many visitors to the Crescent City. In early 1997, the city and its Superdome Stadium host championships for national collegiate football in the NOKIA Sugar Bowl and for the pros in Super Bowl XXXI, which is expected to draw 150,000 visitors. That will mark the eighth time the Super Bowl has been played in New Orleans, a record for any city. The annual Thanksgiving weekend Bayou Classic, one of the largest African-American sporting events in the country, matches the Grambling State University Tigers and the Southern University Jaguars in a head-to-head battle for bragging rights—for the football team and for the marching bands.

The Dome is also a popular site for basketball championships—the NCAA Men's Final Four has been held here three times and the NCAA Women's Final Four was here once, and the Southeastern Conference Championships came to town in 1996. The Freeport-McDermott Golf Classic, with a purse of $1.2 million, is a popular stop on the PGA. Each spring brings the Crescent City Classic 10K Road Race, with over 30,000 participants from every state and 23 nations—the fifth-largest run in the United States. The fall sees a different kind of road race in the Acxiom Grand Prix du Mardi Gras, the series finale for the International Motor Sports Association's Exxon World Sports Car Championship.

Whether in town for a convention, an event, or just plain fun, New Orleans visitors have plenty of places to stay. When the 2,000 new rooms under construction or committed to be built are completed, the metropolitan area will boast nearly 30,000 hotel rooms. Among those coming on line in 1996 downtown are the Wyndham Riverfront, the Omni Royal Crescent, and the Holiday Inn Select. New hotels are also going up near the airport in Kenner, in Metairie, on the Westbank of New Orleans, and in Covington. The new hotels have a high standard to meet—The Windsor Court,

famed for afternoon tea, luxurious suites, and the finest restaurant cuisine, is ranked as the top hotel in the United States by *Condé Nast Traveler* magazine.

The same *Condé Nast* survey, published in November, 1995, tagged New Orleans as the third among U.S. cities for fine dining, behind San Francisco and Santa Fe, calling it "the little city that outscored both Paris and New York." The city ranked seventeenth in the world overall, a tally based on cuisine, cultural enrichment, people, and ambiance.

The city's cuisine receives constant kudos for food in the smallest of our 2,000 restaurants or some of the most famous. One example—Commander's Palace was named the number one restaurant in America by the readers of *Food & Wine* magazine. "With three times as many mentions as any other establishment, Commander's Palace . . . is clearly a culinary mecca for many of you, whether you live in New Orleans or not," wrote the editors. In 1996, Commander's also was chosen as America's outstanding restaurant by the prestigious James Beard Foundation.

To provide staff for the finest restaurants and hotels in New Orleans, the University of New Orleans has developed a program in hotel, restaurant, and tourism administration that ranks in the top handful of such programs nationwide.

Those New Orleanophiles who don't live in the city—or even those who do—now have various ways to get information about it from dozens of sites on the World Wide Web. This book is even posted on one of them—The Chamber Business Network, introduced in 1995 by The Chamber/New Orleans and the River Region as a national pioneer in web sites for chambers of commerce. The Chamber Business Network, in co-operation with the Greater New Orleans Freenet, also contains information on events, businesses, and organizations in the seven-parish New Orleans region. ◆

Bourbon Street—still a popular place for people to tap their feet! Photo by Jackson Hill/Southern Lights Studio.

The Living Arts

CHAPTER

4

The arts—in their every aspect—
reflect the beauty, energy,
and grace of the city.
*Photo by Jackson Hill/
Southern Lights Studio.*

"In other places, culture comes

down from on high. In New Orleans,

it bubbles up from the street."

Jazz musician and teacher Ellis Marsalis

Listen to the music—all kinds of sounds in all kinds of places. Gaze at the art—in galleries, on the sides of buildings, in museums, in tiny stores on Magazine Street. Watch the movies, and see the best location of them all. Read the words and get a thousand stories of New Orleans, each of them evocative. Hear the ring of famous lines from a stage, or discover a tiny new theater troupe. In New Orleans, there's no avoiding it. Art is all around.

"There is an indigenous, creative energy in the arts here, and it expresses itself in many ways, from architecture to music," says Shirley Trusty Corey, executive director of the Arts Council of New Orleans, in *New Orleans Magazine*. "We do have more of it than most places in the United States, even places with more money."

Corey and her staff point with pride to the richness and diversity of the visual arts scene; the neighborhood orientation of much of the performing arts universe ("Little bitty grassroots organizations are out there doing wonderful stuff at a low-key level," says one Arts Council staffer); the synergism among different branches of the arts (theater and music presentations often have exciting visual components, for example); and the fact that many performances are free.

As the official arts agency and grant allocator for the city, the Arts Council provides cultural planning, advocacy, public art, economic development, arts education, and grant and service initiatives for the community. Its purview is broad—its 1995-96 directory lists 133 galleries, 31 arts media outlets, 25 cultural festivals, 31 dance troupes, 27 multicultural arts organizations, 22 museums and historic homes, 22 music concert series, and 36 theater groups. And that's just in Orleans Parish. The Arts Council also has much to be proud of—over a period of just three years in the mid-1990s, it managed to raise the ranking of arts funding in Louisiana from 56th, behind every U.S. state and territory, into the top 20.

Jazz is the art form most associated with New Orleans in the mind of the world. In fact, the city has a long history of virtually every kind of musical innovation. "I'm not sure, but I'm almost positive, that all music came from New Orleans," says New Orleans R&B artist Ernie K-Doe, famous for "Mother-in-Law." The first opera in North America was staged in New Orleans in 1796, and native composer and concert pianist Louis Moreau Gottschalk toured Europe in the mid-nineteenth century, to the acclaim of Chopin and Berlioz, among others. In the first half of the nineteenth century, New Orleans was the only city that permitted its slaves to sing in African languages, do African dances,

and play African instruments. The performances that took place at Congo Square on the edge of the French Quarter, were the ancestors of both jazz and other popular American music.

At the turn of the century, jazz was born from the marriage of brass band music and African rhythms. It was originally music for outdoor processions and celebrations, not simply played inside the brothels of Storyville. "Man, I sure had a ball growing up in New Orleans," jazz legend Louis Armstrong said in *Life* magazine in 1966. "We were poor and everything like that, but music was all around you. Music kept you rolling." By the 1920s, the "jazz age" in American culture, most of the major jazz musicians—Jelly Roll Morton, Buddy Bolden, Nick LaRocca, Sidney Bechet, and Armstrong—were performing and recording in New York and Chicago. But jazz hung on in New Orleans, too. Its latest renaissance was in the 1980s, starring performers like Wynton Marsalis (perhaps the foremost of the thirty-something jazz generation, who is now director of jazz programming at Lincoln Center), Branford Marsalis, Terence

Blanchard, and Harry Connick, Jr., all of whom began in New Orleans and moved to global musical success.

"Jazz is one of the nation's great treasures, one worthy of preservation and celebration," says Louisiana Senator J. Bennett Johnston. "In fact, music is one of this country's few commodities for which we enjoy a large trade surplus with the rest of the world." The point of origin for this popular export is tagged in the typically whimsical fashion of the city. At the Holiday Inn on Loyola Avenue, an 18-story, 150-foot clarinet painted on the side of the building marks a spot that is right across the street from the "birthplace of jazz"—Louis Armstrong grew up at the current site of City Hall, and the Supreme Court Building is located at the former site of Funky Butt Hall, where the father of jazz, Buddy Bolden, played.

The New Orleans Jazz and Heritage Festival, continuing to hold in its 27th year the record as the largest paid music event in the world, transforms the city into a musical mecca for two weeks in April and May. Nearly 10,000 musicians, cooks, and craftspeople welcome more than 400,000 people, almost half of them from outside the city, to the New Orleans Fair Grounds for music, food, crafts, sun, and sightings of friends who long ago moved away. But they all come back from wherever they are and bring their new friends. No wonder. There aren't many places where you can pay a daily admission of $15 and sample all you want of more than 75 musical acts every day—traditional and contemporary jazz, rhythm and blues, ragtime, gospel, Cajun, zydeco, bluegrass, rock, African-Caribbean, Latin, fusion, rap, reggae, and more. Then there are dozens of food booths serving all kinds of local and regional delicacies, and a juried craft show with contemporary work, traditional Louisiana folk art, and an African marketplace. Evening concerts, with attractions like Joan Baez, Joan Osborne, B.B. King, Cassandra Wilson, Van Morrison, Aretha Franklin, and Ladysmith Black Mambazo, attract another 50,000 audience members each year. The *Boston Globe* calls JazzFest "America's Best Festival." Most locals would agree.

While JazzFest is the New Orleans musical frenzy, with clubs all over town hosting national headline acts, music indeed bubbles up from the streets all year. Driving through

New Orleans neighborhoods, you're likely to hear the sound of a trombone and a trumpet, then a drum will join in. It may be members of the St. Augustine High School Band practicing for the next parade or football game, or it may be people that you'll see soon in your favorite small club. On an average weekend, newspaper listings carry news of two dozen concerts and perhaps 150 more clubs, restaurants, and other places to hear live music.

Traditionalists wouldn't miss Preservation Hall, the French Quarter home of traditional Dixieland. There's no air conditioning, few seats, and no cocktail service—just the sounds that are most associated with New Orleans across the globe, played by some of the people who have spent decades moving the rhythms of traditional jazz from the city to the world.

If Cajun music and its cousin, zydeco, are more your taste, you might enjoy dancing to the fiddles at Michaul's or Mulate's, or a hot zydeco accordion at the Rock'n' Bowl, perhaps America's only combination bowling alley/top music spot. The legendary Tipitina's hosts almost every kind of music, particularly New Orleans rhythm and blues; and the newcomer House of Blues combines headline national acts and local artists with one of the best collections of folk art you'll find. For bluegrass, go across Lake Pontchartrain to the tiny town of Abita Springs, where the nationally-acclaimed Piney Woods Opry holds forth once a month in the town hall, recreating an old "opry" radio show with the best fiddlers, banjo players, and guitar pickers—steel and otherwise—the region has to offer.

New Orleans music has received more and more international attention, both in the sounds going out from New Orleans to the world and big names traveling from the world to New Orleans. City-based artists including Dr. John, Aaron Neville, the Neville Brothers, the Iguanas, and Better than Ezra, have all hit the pop charts. In the summer, the Essence Music Festival brings some of the biggest names in music to the city, including Luther Vandross, Patti LaBelle, Gladys Knight, B.B. King, Queen Latifah, Boyz II Men, Mary J. Blige, Anita Baker, and Earth, Wind, and Fire. It also features scores of local entertainers and national personalities such as Jesse Jackson and Bill Cosby. In 1995, 142,000 people turned out for the weekend event, which had an impact of $75 million on the city. The Reggae Riddums International Arts Festival, billed as the premier Caribbean food & entertainment festival in the country, showcases traditional Caribbean music—reggae, zouk, steel drum, soca, and Latin-Caribbean— and features curry goat and jerk chicken. Its 30,000 attendees in 1995 had an economic impact of $5 million.

The Louisiana Philharmonic Orchestra, the only musician-governed and operated orchestra in the country, presents more than 50 classical concerts every year, in addition to special programs for young people and concerts with its affiliate, the Symphony Chorus. In keeping with the city's history, opera still flourishes as the New Orleans Opera Association offers crowd-pleasers like *Carmen, Madame Butterfly,* and *Don Giovanni,* each season. The New Orleans Ballet Association, the Delta Festival Ballet, and the Jefferson Performing Arts Society add to the full spectrum of the arts in the region.

To hear a wide range of New Orleans music in the comfort of your home or car, simply turn on your radio and tune it to a not-for-profit station. WWOZ, the community station supported in part by Jazz and Heritage Foundation,

Louisiana
HERITAGE
FAIR
STAGE
1

offers a sensational sampling of local and regional music year-round. WTUL, the student radio station at Tulane University, was named the top such outlet in the country in 1996; and WWNO, at the University of New Orleans, is the city's public radio affiliate. Or if words without music are more your style, tune in to WRBH, the pioneering radio station with volunteers who read everything from novels to the want ads over the air.

To keep the music flowing, New Orleans is keeping the learning going. Ellis Marsalis, father of Wynton and Branford, heads the jazz programs at both the New Orleans Center for Creative Arts, for high school students, and at the University of New Orleans. Each program adds new talent from the city and region to the musical mix of the world. The William Ransom Hogan Jazz Archive at Tulane, one of the foremost sources for the history of jazz in the country, contains thousands of records, taped interviews with jazz greats and peripheral players, sheet music, and photographs. A New Orleans Jazz National Historic Park is planned to preserve the origins and early history of jazz, provide visitors with opportunities to experience the sights, sounds, and places where jazz evolved, and implement innovative ways of establishing jazz educational partnerships.

The biggest player in the New Orleans visual arts world is the 85-year-old New Orleans Museum of Art, in City Park. A 1993 renovation almost doubled the museum's size to more than 130,000 square feet, making room for more extensive display of its almost-40,000-piece, $200-million collection. NOMA has particular strength in African art, Asian Edo period Japanese paintings, decorative glass arts, American art pottery, and nineteenth century French porcelain; the finest

photography collection in the Southeast, and an impressive array of pre-Columbian Mexican and Central American art, as well as European and American art. In 1995, the museum hosted the blockbuster exhibit of 22 of Claude Monet's later paintings, drawing more than 234,000 people during its two-month tenure. The major cultural tourism event inspired spin-offs all over the city, including performance art on Julia Street, special Monet meals in three restaurants, art contests, murals, and streetcar decorations crafted by Orleans Parish Prison inmates. The crowd, whose economic impact was more than $25.5 million, was the largest for any exhibit at the museum since the Treasures of Tutankhamen, which drew 870,000 people from September, 1977 through January, 1978.

The gallery scene is lively all over the city. "New Orleans art is available everywhere and to everyone," says an Arts Council staffer. "You don't just go to a museum to see a painting. You can go all over town and buy all kinds of things. It's all so interwoven." There's particular excitement on gallery opening nights along Magazine Street, in the Warehouse District, and in the French Quarter. Usually, there are coordinated openings on the first Saturday of each month. Art for Art's Sake in October and White Linen Night in August feature celebrations that spill from the galleries to the streets and on to the Contemporary Arts Center, which is the cornerstone of alternative and experimental art, music, dance, performance art, and theater in the city.

Glass arts are flourishing, based on Tulane's influential program led by Gene Koss; the New Orleans School of Glass Works; Studio Inferno; and Lighthouse Glass. And the color-fully dramatic painted furniture, Swatch watches, and fabric designed to cover chairs at the United Nations have earned

Glass arts are flourishing in New Orleans. Photo courtesy of the New Orleans School of Glass Works.

The Louisiana Children's Museum is rated as one of the top 10 children's museums in the country by Your Family and Parenting magazines. Photo by Jackson Hill/Southern Lights Studio.

Native daughter Anne Rice is the best-selling author of Interview with the Vampire and other popular novels. Photo by Jackson Hill/Southern Lights Studio.

The biggest player in the New Orleans visual arts world is the 85-year-old New Orleans Museum of Art, in City Park. Photo by Jackson Hill/Southern Lights Studio.

international acclaim for Young Artists/Young Aspirations (better known as YA/YA), a group of young New Orleans artists, many of whom are still in high school, led and inspired by Jana Napoli. Sculptor John Scott, a faculty member at Xavier University, was recently honored with a MacArthur "genius grant" for his work—one of his current commissions is the Monument to Children in the 14-acre Woldenberg Park on the Mississippi River in the French Quarter. The public art collection there is one of the most impressive in the city, featuring sculptors including Scott and Ida Kohlmeyer. Other public art has been funded through The Arts Council's Percent for Art program. Beginning in 1987, the program has used one percent of major building budgets to add art to public places—police stations, fire stations, streetcar stops, schools, parks, the zoo, and even neutral grounds (medians) of major thoroughfares.

New arts developments are on the drawing board for Lee Circle, near the Contemporary Arts Center and the Warehouse District. The Roger H. Ogden Museum of Southern Art is planned by the University of New Orleans in conjunction with art collector Ogden, and the Arts Council is developing the Louisiana Artists' Guild. The Guild, an $11-million project, will provide state-of-the-art studio and retail space for visual artists and craftspeople, bringing visitors into the creative process and becoming a major tourist destination.

From the Oscar-winning *Panic in the Streets* (1950) to the Oscar-winning *Dead Man Walking* (1996), New Orleans has had a fascination for filmmakers and audiences internationally. Who can forget *A Streetcar Named Desire*? Or *Pretty Baby*? Or *Cat People*? Or *The Big Easy*? Or *The Pelican Brief*? Or Oliver Stone's epic revisionist history, *JFK*? Then there was that vampire flick with Tom Cruise. It's all in keeping with history—the first theatre showing regularly scheduled movies was established in New Orleans in 1896. The local film industry is also a growing business. For example, the economic impact of shooting *Interview with a Vampire* in New Orleans is estimated at $12 to $15 million. In 1995 alone, projects shot on location in the city had an impact of more than $435 million, according to statistics from the New Orleans Film and Video Commission, and film activity in the first quarter of 1996 indicated the arrival of a blockbuster year.

For more than a century, New Orleans has been so closely associated with so many different writers that a listing of them sounds like an American literature major's bookshelf. Consider: Mark Twain, Walt Whitman, Kate Chopin, Sherwood Anderson, William Faulkner, F. Scott Fitzgerald, Tennessee Williams, Truman Capote, William Burroughs, Jack Kerouac, Lillian Hellman, Walker Percy, and John Kennedy Toole. And those are just the ones whose writing careers are over. Local novelist Richard Ford won the 1996 Pulitzer for his novel *Independence Day.* Anne Rice and her vampire and witch chronicles rise to the top of the best-seller lists as soon as the books hit bookstores nationwide. Pulitzer Prize winners Shirley Ann Grau and Robert Olen Butler, and National Book Award-winner Ellen Gilchrist are fiction writers with close ties to the city. The literary scene

The Chosen Few Brass Band, and others like it, give a distinctive beat to the rhythm of the city. Photo by Jackson Hill/Southern Lights Studio.

has a good stock of children's book writers and illustrators, led by Berthe Amoss; an active romance writers' community including Rexanne Becnel, Meghan McKinney, and Deborah Martin; and a cunningly good array of mystery writers, like Kevin Allman, Tony Dunbar, Skye Moody, Laura Joh Roland, Julie Smith, and Chris Wiltz.

The city's literary lights shine nationwide in the nonfiction arena as well. In one week in 1996, *Dead Man Walking*, by New Orleans native Sister Helen Prejean, was number one on the *New York Times* nonfiction paperback best-seller list; *We're Right, They're Wrong*, by area native and political consultant James Carville was number two. Number three on the hardback nonfiction list was *Undaunted Courage*— New Orleanian Stephen Ambrose's look at the Lewis & Clark exploration. Ambrose is also the author of biographical works on Eisenhower and Nixon, a Presidential adviser, and a renowned chronicler of World War II. Douglas Brinkley, Jimmy Carter's biographer, directs the Eisenhower Center at the University of New Orleans; and Andrei Codrescu's distinctive voice—on National Public Radio, in the film, *Road Scholar*, or in books like *The Muse is Always Half-Dressed in New Orleans*—comes to the world from the Crescent City. Many renowned writers, including Valerie Martin, Andre Dubus, Nicholas Lemann, and Michael Lewis, began their careers in New Orleans and return often to visit even as they write from elsewhere.

When they do, they find an active bookselling scene, with particular strength in neighborhood stores and antiquarian booksellers. New Orleans is home to the New Orleans/Gulf South Booksellers' Association, which is involved in community projects ranging from the book tent at the JazzFest to an annual distribution of children's books to social service agencies in the region. It is a stop on national book tours, with frequent readings at bookstores. The Maple Leaf Bar's Sunday afternoons dedicated to poetry and fiction, which began in 1979, make up the longest continually running reading series in the South. Faulkner House Books, on Pirate's Alley just off Jackson Square, is a landmark for Southern literature fans. They visit for its history—Faulkner wrote his first novel, *A Soldier's Pay*, when he lived there in the 1930s; its extensive stock of first editions; and its annual fall literary festival.

The Tennessee Williams/New Orleans Literary Festival celebrates the city, its best-known playwright, its current writers, and its famous imaginations each year. The weekend-long spring festival, which celebrated its 10th anniversary in 1996, attracts more than 6,000 people to events including seminars and master classes featuring renowned writers, walking tours, theater, musical performances, and even a Stanley and Stella Shouting Contest.

The theater scene is active year-round, with perennial and new stars including the Black Theatre Festival, DramaRama, NORD Theatre, Southern Rep, Rivertown Rep, Northstar Rep in Mandeville, True Brew, the Saenger for road companies of Broadway shows, the Contemporary Arts Center's theatrical presentations, Le Petit Theatre, and various college organizations.

The New Orleans region has a full complement of print and electronic media. WWL-TV, the CBS affiliate, began with the Gulf South's first AM radio broadcast in 1922 and has

become a national broadcast legend since
by reflecting the flavor of New Orleans. The
New Orleans market leader for more than
two decades—and winner of an unprecedented five George Foster Peabody awards
for its news excellence—WWL-TV is consistently ranked among the nation's top five
stations, year after year. WDSU-TV has just
moved to state-of-the-art studios near the
Warehouse District, marking rising ratings
and a commitment to "making a difference
in New Orleans." Viewers also enjoy programming on WGNO (ABC), WVUE (Fox),
and WNOL (Warner) as well as dozens of
cable channels and radio stations. Among a
wide range of major print media are the
memorably-named *Times-Picayune*, the daily newspaper
(a picayune, a coin worth 6 1/2 cents, was once its cost),
Gambit Entertainment Weekly, *Citybusiness*, *The Louisiana
Weekly, New Orleans Magazine*, and *Offbeat*, devoted to
the local music scene.

When you put all the strengths of New Orleans culture
together with its architecture, historic houses, other museums,
and general ambiance, you have a wonderful opportunity
for attracting visitors. That's just what the new Arts Tourism
Partnership is designed to do. The partnership, which includes
New Orleans' umbrella arts and tourism organizations, is only
the second in any city in the country. Its programs include a
blanket admission to museums and historic houses, an arts
hotline, and a "New Orleans Host" initiative to supply
coupons, invitations, backstage passes, discounts, and other
offers to New Orleanians to encourage them to bring out-
of-town guests to arts events.

New Orleans is a national leader in
coming up with ways to have healthy arts
organizations. Founded in 1992 under the
auspices of the Arts Council, The Entergy
Arts Business Center is an arts incubator,
helping artists and arts organizations
acquire the skills they need to ensure their
growth as a business and to support the
artistic product. Success stories from the
incubator, only the second one in the country, include the symphony and ballet, both
of which are now on stable financial foot-
ings for the first time in many years, and a
small early music group, Musica da Camera,
which has begun to sell its own CDs and
build an endowment. The Entergy Arts
Business Center's success was recognized on a national basis
in 1994, when it won the Forbes Business in the Arts Award.
The arts are also economic drivers for blocks, whole streets,
or shopping centers. According to one Arts Council staffer, the
tone of Canal Place, a popular upscale mall, has been influ-
enced by the quality of the art by several nonprofits who have
space there—New Orleans Film & Video Festival, Southern
Repertory Theatre, RHINO Gallery, and Fyberspace. "Quality
art products are finding homes, while artists are being
entrepreneurial and charting their own courses." she says.

In all the arts, the common thread is New Orleans.
"Musicians come and go," says Harold Battiste, a saxophonist
who himself left the city for Los Angeles in the 1960s to
return in the late 1980s to teach in UNO's jazz program.
"Their creations always seem directed at the city. Because
after all is said and done, New Orleans is the star." ◆

*The innovative use of color and motion
characterizing the works of New Orleans
sculptor Ida Kohlmeyer brings a touch of
culture to a busy corner. Photo by
Jackson Hill/Southern Lights Studio.*

Water=Prosperity

CHAPTER

5

The mighty Mississippi and its endlessly fascinating traffic are a focal point for urban attention. Photo by Jackson Hill/Southern Lights Studio.

"I love the Mississippi River. The

beauty of it and the history of it. I'm

always blown away by the great deal of

commerce that moves by when I sit and

watch it for 10 minutes. There are so

many people's lives tied up with it,

present and past—riverboat gamblers,

people on houseboats, people who

made their living off it."

Paul Prudhomme in the Times–Picayune's
Insider's Guide to New Orleans

Despite the challenges posed by swamps and alligators, New Orleans was situated three centuries ago to take advantage of the positions of the Mississippi River and Lake Pontchartrain and the trade access promised by their confluence. Photo by Jackson Hill/Southern Lights Studio.

Water is undoubtedly the key element in the life of New Orleans. It always has been. Almost half of the city's total 363.5-square-mile area is water. Average annual rainfall is 60 inches, making New Orleans the wettest major city in the United States. It is bisected by the world's third-longest river, the Mississippi. After a journey of almost 2,300 miles, the river delivers its magnificence to New Orleans, where it climaxes at its widest point—2,200 feet—and its deepest—212 feet. Lake Pontchartrain, covering 621 square miles but only 15 feet at its greatest depth, boasts the world's longest bridge in the 24-mile Causeway. Even directions in the city are done by watery landmarks. North, south, east, and west are useless—but tell someone you live on the uptown river-side corner of a street that runs one-way toward the lake, and they'll understand exactly where you are.

New Orleans was situated—despite swamps and alligators—to take advantage of the juxtaposition of the Mississippi River and Lake Pontchartrain. Sharp economic minds realized that cargo could come down the Mississippi, be unloaded, go by wagon the short distance to Lake Pontchartrain, be loaded on another ship, go through Chef Pass, and have consistent, easy access to the Gulf of Mexico. Shippers didn't have to worry when the mouth of the Mississippi was blocked by sandbars, as was frequently the case until the advent of good dredging technology in the late nineteenth century.

From that time to this, water has meant prosperity for the city and its surrounding region. Today, about 22 percent of the area's economic activity stems directly or indirectly from port operations. That adds up to over 51,000 jobs for the metro area.

There are four deep-water ports in the area—the Port of New Orleans; the Port of South Louisiana; the Port, Harbor, and Terminal District of St. Bernard; and the Plaquemines Port, Harbor, and Terminal District. Each adds its own impact to the overall water equals prosperity economic equation for the region.

The region's ports are the largest inland ports in the United States and among the nation's leading ports for steel, coffee, agricultural commodities, and bulk commodities

including petroleum and chemicals. Together, the deep-water ports of the River Region lead the world in cargo tonnage, ranking number one every year since 1985. In 1993, the total was almost 314,000 tons, up by about 30 percent over the 1985 number. About 15 percent of the country's total water-borne commerce goes through a port in the region, with trade worth almost $44 billion in 1994.

Area ports host more than 4,000 ship-calls annually, by vessels flying the colorful flags of virtually every nation. Japan is the principal trading partner for the region, accounting for 13 percent of the total import and export cargo tonnage and dollar value. Next is Mexico, followed by Canada, the United Kingdom, and Argentina.

Trade with Latin America is an area of particular growth. In 1995, Latin American trade numbers for the New Orleans customs district (which stretches from Little Rock to Knoxville, but tracks about 75 percent of its total business to New Orleans area ports) totalled about $13 billion, up by around 15 percent from the same period in 1994. As one of the top three Latin American trade regions in the U.S., the

New Orleans is bisected by the world's third–longest river, the Mississippi. After a journey of almost 2,300 miles, the river climaxes here at its widest point—2,200 feet—and its deepest more than 200 feet. Photo by Jackson Hill/Southern Lights Studio.

NATCO 3

New Orleans region also compares well with its competitors. In the first three quarters of 1995, total U.S.-Latin trade was down by 2 percent and Miami, the leading U.S.-Latin trade district in the South, increased by only 7 percent—half the rate of the New Orleans rise.

Just south of New Orleans, in the Gulf of Mexico, is the Louisiana Offshore Oil Port, or LOOP, which allows large crude-oil tankers to unload offshore. Up to 1.4 million barrels of oil a day can be offloaded and shipped to the mainland. The Port of South Louisiana, just upriver from New Orleans, has 104 miles of deep water port, making it among the world's largest harbors. It's the largest port in the United States in cargo tonnage handled, with more than 73 million tons of imports and exports in 1994. The most common cargoes are grains, petroleum, and chemical products.

The Mississippi River is dredged to accommodate deepwater ships all the way to Baton Rouge. When the Port of Baton Rouge is included in the statistics, combined tonnage of all ports along the Mississippi River from the Gulf of Mexico to Baton Rouge increases to about 400 million tons, or almost 20 percent of total water-borne commerce in the U.S.

Although it is almost 100 miles from the Gulf of Mexico, the Port of New Orleans is the second largest in the nation, with most of the grain from the heartland passing through as it travels to world markets. Some 2,500 ships call at port facilities annually. In 1995, the port handled a record 10.4 million tons of bulk cargo—such as grain and oil—and a total of more than 37 million tons of bulk cargo and general cargo—containers, steel, rubber, plywood, and other goods.

Statistics comparing 1995 with the previous year yield some fascinating, telling details. Frozen chicken exports were up by 50.5 percent to 107.6 tons, baled cotton exports rose by 37.2 percent to 162.7 tons, coffee imports increased by 6.8 percent to 241.3 tons, and natural rubber imports climbed by 3.2 percent to 340 tons. Imported plywood held steady with 1994 statistics, at 314 tons, while exported forest products fell by 2.8 percent to 633 tons.

Steel represented the largest volume of a single commodity to move through the port in 1995. Exports of steel coils and pipes increased from just over 87,000 tons in 1994 to 756,000 tons in 1995. The growth promises to continue, thanks to a two-year contract awarded to the port early in 1996.

The ships loading and unloading at the port's 13.5 miles of wharves on the Mississippi literally crisscross the globe with their cargoes. Europe accounted for just over 35 percent of the port's trading volume in 1995, with Asia close behind at almost 32 percent. Central and South America represent 25 percent, Africa 4 percent, the Caribbean 2.4 percent, and Australia/New Zealand 2 percent.

1995 was quite a 100th birthday celebration for the Board of Commissioners of the Port of New Orleans! The port's indisputable success is anchored in a variety of recent developments. With 6 class-one rail lines, 70 steamship lines, 16 barge lines, and 75 truck lines, New Orleans sells itself as

Sailboats stand ready for launch in their Lake Ponchartrain harbor. Photo by Jackson Hill/Southern Lights Studio.

The ships loading and unloading at the Port of New Orleans' 13.5 miles of wharves on the Mississippi literally crisscross the globe with their cargoes. Photo by Jackson Hill/Southern Lights Studio.

The three remaining overnight paddlewheel steamboats in the United States, including the Mississippi Queen, make New Orleans their base of operation for cruises up the river. Photo by Jackson Hill/Southern Lights Studio.

"America's Most Intermodal Port," giving traders an unusually flexible, economical choice of methods with which to reach their final markets.

Then there are all those new facilities springing up. President Clinton was in town early in 1996 to dedicate the Nashville Avenue B Terminal and Wharf, the centerpiece of a $215 million capital improvement program begun by the port five years ago. The $22-million facility will be part of the longest contiguous berth in the world—a 2.1-mile linear wharf. Two giant gantry cranes to be installed later in the year can each hoist 70 tons.

In 1989, the 73-year-old New Orleans Public Grain Elevator gave way to Silocaf, a $12-million green coffee bean processing facility that is the world's largest. In an innovation that single-handedly modernized the coffee industry, the beans are sorted and held in the renovated and modernized grain elevator space until they are distributed to be ground and roasted—a sort of just-in-time coffee processing. Silocaf can handle more than 275,000 tons of coffee a year.

The Julia Street Wharf, on the edge of the historic Warehouse District downtown, is being modernized to handle cruise ships. The port also plans to develop its Perry Street Wharf in Gretna and upgrade its Esplanade and Mandeville wharves to better handle plywood, coffee, and rubber cargoes. A new dedicated port roadway—The Tchoupitoulas Corridor—is under construction to streamline traffic through uptown port facilities and remove it from neighborhood

streets. In mid-1996, port offices moved into a new $9-million facility just upriver from the Crescent City Connection. In the planning stages is a $40-million refrigerated cargo facility to help expand the port's share of the growing frozen meat, fruit, and vegetable cargo markets.

As the port creates state-of-the-art facilities, many of its older wharves in the downtown area are renovated for public recreation. Among the new uses for former wharf areas are the nationally renowned Aquarium of the Americas and its adjacent Woldenberg Park, giving strollers up-close vistas of the Mississippi and its unceasingly fascinating rhythms just upriver from the French Quarter.

Water is big business in New Orleans, but it's also a place to play. Sunny days bring out clusters of sailboats to wing their way around Lake Pontchartrain. Riverboat gaming has become popular in the city since the first boats were introduced in 1993. The Natchez' calliope fills the air in the French Quarter before the paddlewheeler leaves for one of several daily tourism cruises. The Delta Queen, the American Queen, and the Mississippi Queen—the last three overnight paddlewheel steamboats in the United States—make New Orleans their base of operation for cruises up the river. Their parent company, Delta Queen Steamboat, which relocated its headquarters here from Cincinnati 10 years ago, will move more than 40,000 passengers through the Port of New Orleans in 1996.

With the renovations of the Julia Street Terminal, cruise

ships are also starting to make New Orleans an important port of call. Since 1992, the city has more than doubled its passenger service, and projections for 1996 indicate a 65 percent gain over 1995. Royal Cruise Line and Holland America increased their number of calls in 1995, when three new ships called at the city for the first time. Commodore Lines has offered weekly cruises from New Orleans since 1992, and the city is the winter home port for Carnival Cruise Lines' Tropicale liner, which can accommodate almost 1,500 passengers and a crew of 670 in its New Orleans-themed space.

Rolling on the river may be the New Orleans tradition, but riding the rails and flying though the air are also important ways to connect with trade and people. Six major trunk-line railroads serve the New Orleans region, providing access to virtually all U.S. major markets. More than 400 trains and 8,800 railcars arrive and depart in the region every week, delivering and receiving cargo from the port community for distribution throughout the country. New Orleans is the only major seaport where main eastern rail trunks intersect with

their western counterparts. If it's people who are on the move, Amtrak service runs north, east, and west, with service from such classic trains as the Sunset Limited and the Southern Crescent.

At the New Orleans International Airport, 8.2 million passengers annually board flights of the 15 airlines that provide direct service to 74 domestic cities, and connections to destinations worldwide through the newly renovated international concourse. The renovation is only one element in an ambitious $650-million capital improvement program. A 3,000-car enclosed parking lot, a state-of-the-art baggage system, an air-conditioned transportation center, and a new 200-foot control tower with terminal Doppler weather radar have already been completed. Major projects in process include rebuilding two concourses, reflooring two others, extending runways, building new multi-modal cargo facilities, constructing new general aviation facilities, and establishing a new Federal Inspection Services Center. A new perimeter road will encircle the airport, and a canal that parallels a runway will be enclosed. The airport adds more than $1.8 billion in economic impact to the region every year. It directly provides 6,000 jobs and contributes to the creation of almost 25,000 more.

The juxtaposition of shipping, air facilities, railways, and interstate highways means that New Orleans is indeed the Big Easy for travelers—whether they be cargo containers or human visitors. ◆

Almost half of the city's total 363.5–square–mile area is water. Photo by Jackson Hill/Southern Lights Studio.

Education for Life

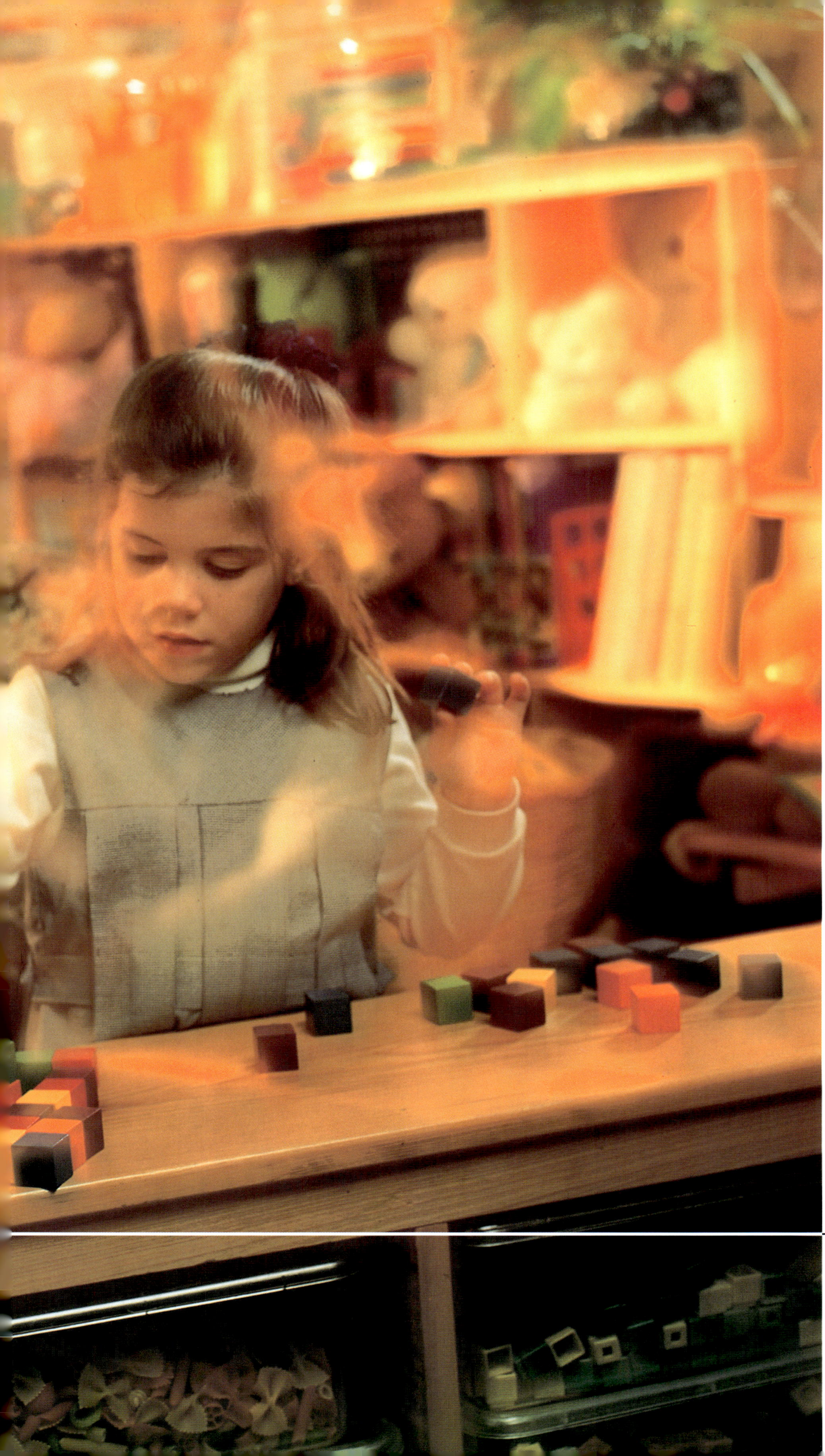

CHAPTER 6

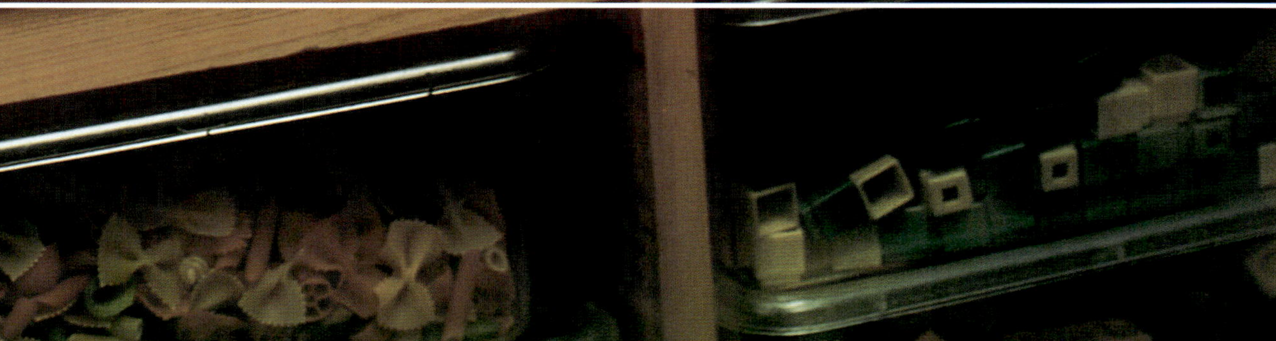

New Orleans has an educational network that includes innovative award-winning public, private, and parochial elementary and secondary schools that educate hundreds of thousands of students each year. Photo by Jackson Hill/Southern Lights Studio.

"This city is known for food and fun,

but it's also got the biggest heart,

because it cares for people."

Willard Scott
NBC–TV Today Show, *September, 1995*

Since the very beginning, New Orleans has focused on the importance of educating its citizens, helping those in need, and developing the spiritual side of life. Just nine years after the city's founding and three years after the completion of the French Quarter's St. Louis Cathedral as the first in the United States, six Ursuline nuns and two Jesuit missionaries arrived in 1727 to begin a school for girls, a hospital, an orphanage, and a general ministry to the spiritual needs of New Orleans. The nuns also taught slave and Native American children.

From that heritage has grown an educational network that includes innovative award-winning public, private, and parochial elementary and secondary schools that educate hundreds of thousands of students each year. Eight four-year colleges and universities (with professional schools in medicine, law, business, engineering, and architecture), two community colleges, two Catholic seminaries, a Baptist seminary, and nine vocational-technical schools provide a vast economic, cultural, training, and research resource. And broad-based public-private initiatives, including a new school-to-work program, school/business partnerships, and governance reforms, significantly strengthen the educational effort.

There are 327 public schools and 164 private schools in the New Orleans region. Catholic parochial schools comprise most of the private school sector, though there is a good representation of other church-affiliated and nondenominational schools as well. About one in every four students is enrolled in a private school.

Private or public, New Orleans schools win kudos for excellence from national sources. For example, the St. Tammany Parish school system, in suburban New Orleans, was recently cited by *Money* magazine as one of the 100 metropolitan districts "where your housing dollar buys super public schools." Five percent of the region's elementary and secondary schools have been honored for their excellence in leadership, teaching environment, curriculum, and parental support with the Blue Ribbon School Award from the U.S. Department of Education. Since 1982, the program has recognized 36 private and public schools in the region, including five schools in 1995. Three Catholic girls' high schools were cited—Archbishop Blenk; Archbishop Chapelle, which won its third award; and St. Mary's Dominican, which won its second award. Also honored were De La Salle High School, a parochial school for boys and girls, and the public Warren Easton Fundamental Senior High School. Easton, a magnet school where students and their parents sign a contract pledging to abide by discipline rules and other campus codes, drew 1,200 applicants for 300 slots in the fall of 1995. Graduates of New Orleans area schools go on to high honors as well. An example: In 1995, Rebecca Marier, an alumna of Metairie Park Country Day School, was the first woman to graduate at the top of her class at West Point.

The New Orleans public school system offers several other popular magnet programs at the elementary and secondary level. Among the latter are the New Orleans High School for Math and Science, founded in 1994, thanks in part to the efforts of two Tulane University Medical School faculty members, to train students in the high-tech fields that are expected to dominate the economy in the twenty-first century; McMain and Franklin High Schools, for academically talented students; and the New Orleans Center for Creative Arts, which has provided intensive instruction and professional apprenticeships in dance, music, theater, visual arts, and creative writing since 1973. Other magnet schools focus on vocational-technical careers. The school systems also feature

innovative programs to address many of the problems that
plague urban schools nationwide, including violence prevention, student health care needs, and low achievement.

An employee base that's well-prepared to work is an
important consideration in economic development initiatives.
Thus many programs have grown from the public and private
sectors to strengthen public education in the region.

The MetroVision economic development organization
leads a School-to-Work initiative, a partnership of education,
business, labor, and government representatives in the region
that works to make sure students are better prepared to
enter the workplace or continue their education after high
school. In 1995, the program received two federal grants to
develop occupation-based academies within 16 area high
schools, to prepare students more effectively for jobs in
banking, health care, and tourism. Ninety teachers interned

The New Orleans region offers many alternatives for single-sex and coed education, particularly in parochial schools.. Photo by Jackson Hill/Southern Lights Studio.

at more than 30 companies for firsthand experience with workplace needs. Then, at a special teaching skills symposium, they learned ways to make the classroom more relevant to the work their students will perform. In 1996, students from the 16 target schools are slated for internships at those organizations, working with specially trained business mentors.

A Partnerships in Education program, coordinated by the Metropolitan Area Committee (MAC) civic group, matches businesses with public schools in Orleans Parish to provide extra resources for those schools. Sometimes those resources are financial. Sometimes they are measured in time and bodies, with attorneys volunteering for a Saturday paint job, for example, or an oil company presenting a career day. MAC, supported by two national grants to its Educational Governance Task Force, is also working with grassroots school constituencies to arrive at new management systems based within individual schools.

The Chamber/New Orleans and the River Region has taken a leading role in addressing educational issues, with a Career Directions 2000 program introducing more than 5,000 high school students every year to the wide range of career possibilities available to them; a Dollars for Scholars initiative raising over $1 million a year for scholarships for needy students in Orleans and Jefferson parishes; and a total quality management training program providing principals with a business perspective to apply to the operation of their schools.

Delgado Community College and Elaine P. Nunez Community College offer two-year programs that prepare New Orleanians for work or for continuing their education at a local university. In 1996, Delgado celebrates, as its slogan puts it, "75 years of education that works." The college, which enrolls more than 14,000 students annually on three campuses, offers more than 50 associate degree programs and 28 one-year certificates in a variety of academic areas,

Fourteen institutions of higher education— private and public—enroll more than 78,000 students each year, many of whom remain in New Orleans to live and work after graduation. Photo by Jackson Hill/ Southern Lights Studio.

(following page) At the 327 public schools and 164 private schools in New Orleans— including the Academy of the Sacred Heart on St. Charles Avenue—emphasis is on learning to care for others as well as excelling academically. Photo by Jackson Hill/Southern Lights Studio.

including allied health, liberal arts, business, nursing, sciences, and technology. The school's pioneering Tech Prep program allows students who are still in high school to get a head start on their careers, by taking approved high school vo-tech courses and receiving credit toward a Delgado degree or certificate.

About 2,000 students attend Nunez College, which opened in 1968 and offers a variety of certificate and associate programs. In addition, the nine vo-tech schools in the New Orleans region enroll about 6,000 students, providing training in specific occupations.

Colleges and universities in the New Orleans region attract about 78,000 students annually—62,000 in four-year programs or professional/graduate schools.

The largest institution, with more than 15,000 students, is the public University of New Orleans. A member of the Urban 13, a prestigious association of the country's top urban universities, UNO prides itself on distinctive programs that reflect its location in New Orleans—jazz studies, naval

architecture, hotel, restaurant, and tourism; energy resources management, international business, and urban waste management and research, among others.

Running a close second in size, with more than 14,000 students, is Southeastern Louisiana University in Hammond, about 40 miles from the city. A public university, Southeastern is known for its programs in education, business, nursing, industrial technology, and liberal arts.

Tulane University, consistently rated among the top 2 percent of higher education institutions nationwide, enrolls about 11,000 students every year in 11 schools and colleges, including professional schools of medicine, law, architecture, business, engineering, social work, and public health and tropical medicine. Founded in 1834 as the Medical College of Louisiana, the private university has grown to be one of the largest private-sector employers in New Orleans. It shows particular strength in the environmental and international arenas, and its medical, law, and business schools rate high in national surveys.

Five percent of the region's elementary and secondary schools have been honored by the U.S. Department of Education for excellence in leadership, teaching environment, curriculum, and parental support. Photo by Jackson Hill/Southern Lights Studio.

Loyola University, a Jesuit institution, has been ranked in national publications as one of the top five regional colleges and universities in the South and as a "best buy" in higher education. It enrolls some 6,000 students in programs in the liberal arts and sciences, business, law, and music, and has earned particular renown for its communications offerings.

Southern University at New Orleans boasts over 4,400 students, a popular master's in social work program, and a curriculum in African Studies. The fall of 1996 marks the introduction of SUNO's master's degree program in criminal justice, which will be followed in the next two years by new masters' programs in urban teaching, computer information systems, addictive disorders, and transportation.

Xavier University, the only historically black, Catholic university in the United States, is known for its programs in science education. About 1,600 of Xavier's 2,650 undergraduate students are science, math, and engineering majors, and the university sent more black graduates to medical school in 1993, 1994, and 1995—a total of more than 180—than any other U.S. college or university. In 1995, Xavier received a $12.3-million federal grant to beef up its science, math, and engineering departments; recruit more students for those disciplines; and send more of them into post-graduate research. It has one of two pharmacy schools in the state.

Dillard University, established in 1869, has the first Japanese Studies program to be set up in any historically black college in the country. The campus also features the only national center for black-Jewish relations in the world. Dillard, a private university with an enrollment of just over 1,500 students, was elected to the 1995 Templeton Honor Roll for Character-Building Colleges, a poll which recognizes institutions that promote the development of character.

Our Lady of Holy Cross College, founded by the Maronite nuns in 1916, offers a bachelor's degree in nursing and a master's in marriage and family therapy among its programs. It enrolls over 1,300 students.

LSU's medical center, with 2,939 students, contains schools of medicine, nursing, dentistry, allied health professions, and graduate studies.

Three seminaries offer pastoral and spiritual education in the region. Notre Dame Seminary Graduate School of Theology and St. Joseph Seminary College are designed for Catholic seminarians and lay people; the New Orleans Baptist Theological Seminary, owned by the Southern Baptist Convention and educating 4,000 students, is one of the largest accredited seminaries in the world.

The presence of such extensive educational resources in the area makes a big difference to the cultural and economic life of the city. The schools attract students to the area, and many remain to live and work here. Partly because of their influence, for example, the New Orleans region was recently named one of the top areas for office operations in the country by the Wadley-Donovan Group (WDG). The consultants cited in their study the availability of diversified labor skills, high employee productivity and quality, "a significant under-tapped college-educated workforce," and an abundance of workers with multilingual skills. The area's colleges and

universities "guarantee a ready supply of entry-level profes-sionals in all fields," said the Wadley-Donovan report. "Over 13,000 students graduate from area colleges and universities each year with bachelor and graduate degrees, and WDG investigations show that many of these graduates prefer to remain in the metro area after graduation."

Libraries and archives in the region have played an important part in the formal education process, as well as the informal keeping up to date, satisfying curiosity on a particular point, or simply wanting a good book to read. There are 65 public libraries and three institutional libraries to serve the population. Consistent community support for the public library system strengthens the collections and brings opportunities for guest lecturers, book signings, and special events like the popular New Orleans Public Library Friends Fest. Institutional libraries including the Historic New Orleans Collection, the Orleans Parish Law Library, and the Orleans Parish School Board Library enrich area resources.

Lending essential support to those resources, as well as to writers, artists, filmmakers, and others in the region, is the Louisiana Endowment for the Humanities, which provides grants and seed money to wide-ranging projects statewide.

Education in New Orleans also concerns teaching people to care for others and for their own spiritual development.

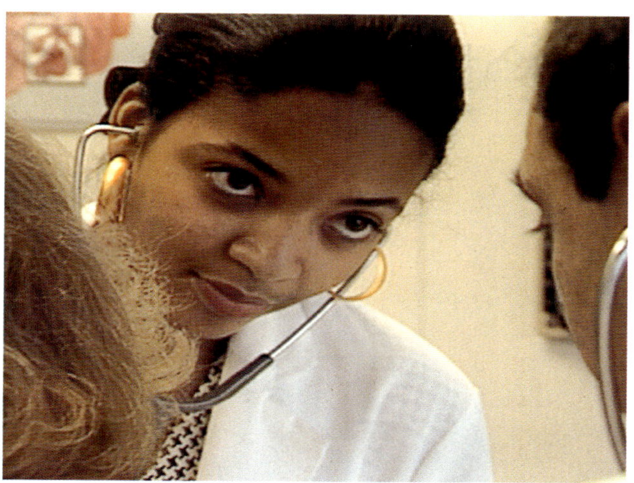

The not-for-profit sector in the city is thriving, and is led by United Way, which includes 66 agencies, and Associated Catholic Charities, whose work ranges from AIDS hospices to daycare centers. The history of caring in the city is strong as well. In the 1890s, one of the first settlement houses in the nation, Kingsley House, was founded here, and the Family Service Society was established. Both continue to flourish. Family Service of Greater New Orleans served more than 10,000 people in 1995, for example, and attracted NBC weatherman Willard Scott to the city to help celebrate its 100th birthday that year.

New Orleans is a culture rooted in Catholicism. In 1700, the year after Iberville's trek to the future site of New Orleans, the first Catholic church in the Louisiana territory was established at a Houma Indian settlement north of the region, and there was "a half a miserable warehouse, where Our Lord is worshipped," mentioned in a 1721 letter. A century later, Protestantism began to influence the city; and Judaism grew as well, with the first synagogue erected in 1828. In the late nineteenth century, the African-American Spiritual churches were established, combining elements of Catholicism, Pentacostalism, and voodoo. Even Mardi Gras, that most famous New Orleans holiday, has a religious aspect. It is celebrated on the day before Ash Wednesday, the beginning of the Lenten season.

Because much education and social service grows from religious roots, the New Orleans region's thousands of churches and synagogues form an influential base for volunteerism and spiritual growth.

The educational, social service, and quality of life elements all came together with a national splash in June, 1996, when New Orleans was chosen as one of ten an All-America Cities and Communities, in recognition of building coalitions to address the region's problems successfully. The presentation that earned the prestigious award, given by the National Civic League, included information about School-to-Work; the New Orleans Jobs Initiative, which supports employment for inner-city residents ages 18-35; the Lower Garden District Civic Association, which is re-energizing an historic urban neighborhood; and grass-roots techniques that are working to improve the environment, race relations, the arts community, public safety, and civic morale.

At the awards competition in Fort Worth in June—and in the New Orleans area every day—it has become clear that the Spirit of New Orleans and her people will prevail over any challenge. ◆

Solving the Tough Problems

Health care in New Orleans is based on a long tradition that includes the establishment of the first medical college west of the Allegheny Mountains and one of the oldest hospitals in the country. It is also a growth sector of the economy, with a focus on medical service and manufacturing industries. Photo by Jackson Hill/Southern Lights Studio.

"In overcoming the problems arising from the soggy nature of the subsoil, the low elevation of the city, climatic condi-tions favorable to malignant diseases, and the danger of Mississippi flood waters, New Orleans has made many contributions in scientific advancement."

WPA Guide to New Orleans, 1938

The nine-parish region boasts 44 hospitals, with more than 8,300 staffed beds, and about 8,100 physicians. Photo by Jackson Hill/Southern Lights Studio.

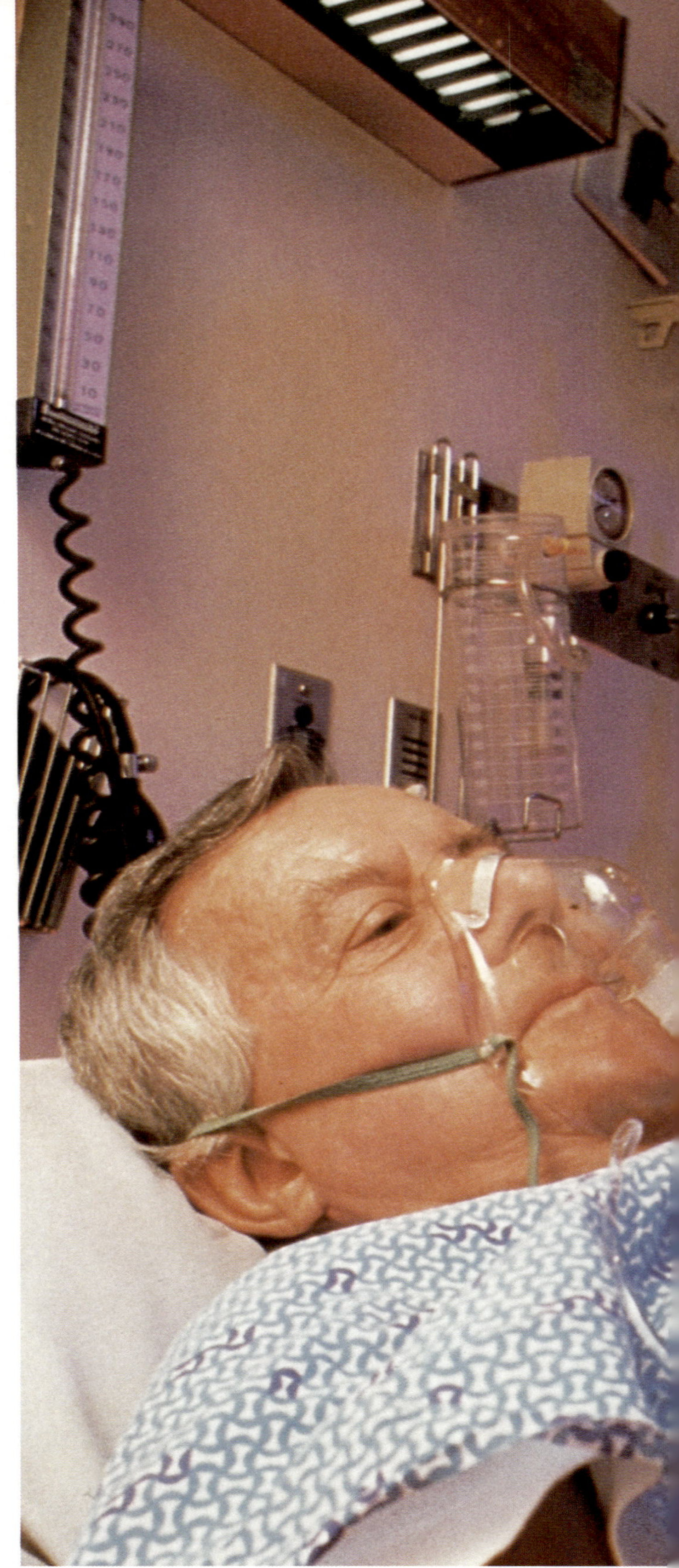

New Orleans has always been a marvel of technology, from the time the first levees were built to hold back the waters of the Mississippi River soon after the city's founding.

As you might expect from a city that is predominantly below sea (and river) level, flood control is a priority. The danger from Mississippi waters has been mitigated by an extensive levee system designed and maintained by the U.S. Army Corps of Engineers, and by the construction in 1937 of the Bonnet Carre Spillway, to divert water from the river to the lake when flooding threatens. The problem of rainwater with no natural place to drain was answered in the early twentieth century with the invention by Albert Baldwin Wood of the "screw pump," giant mechanisms that send the water into Lake Pontchartrain through a network of canals dwarfing their renowned counterparts in Venice. Then there's soupy soil, and a total lack of rock. "New Orleans is built on mush, literally," writes S. Frederick Starr in *New Orleans Unmasqued.* "The recipe calls for 200 feet of the best alluvial soil washed in from Minnesota, Nebraska, and Pennsylvania. Then soak the soil in water from the same sources to form a smooth, stratified pudding. No granite fundament lies beneath this, either. Instead, there is a layer of compacted sand just hard enough, with luck, to support a building." Those buildings—the skyscrapers that line Poydras Street in downtown New Orleans—are built on 190-foot, pre-stressed concrete pilings, hammered into the mush with a pile driver until they hit that layer of clay and sand more than 100 feet below the surface. Each piling is capable of bearing a 400-ton design load, and enough of them will support a structure like the 50-story One Shell Square, the city's tallest building.

Air conditioning has tamed the summers in New Orleans and the rest of the South, and public health measures in the late nineteenth and early twentieth centuries slowly but surely wiped out the yellow fever and cholera that plagued the city through so much of its life. In 1833, for example, a cholera epidemic caused 6,000 deaths in a city of 50,000; it was followed a few months later by a yellow fever epidemic. The next year, the Medical College of Louisiana was founded by seven physicians to study and treat "the peculiar diseases that prevail in this part of the Union." The first medical college west of the Allegheny Mountains, the institution was the forerunner of Tulane University and its world-renowned medical school. The state-run Medical Center of Louisiana at New Orleans/Charity Hospital campus was founded in 1736; the facility has 631 staffed beds and is one of the oldest continually operating hospitals in the country. It is particularly known for emergency medicine and for its outpatient services. Medical staff from Tulane and LSU medical centers see some 1,200 patients a day there and at its affiliated University Hospital a few blocks away.

Health care services in New Orleans rank with the best available in any metropolitan area. The nine-parish region boasts 44 hospitals, with more than 8,300 staffed beds, and about 8,100 physicians. The area has about six physicians per 1,000 people—twice the national average. The health

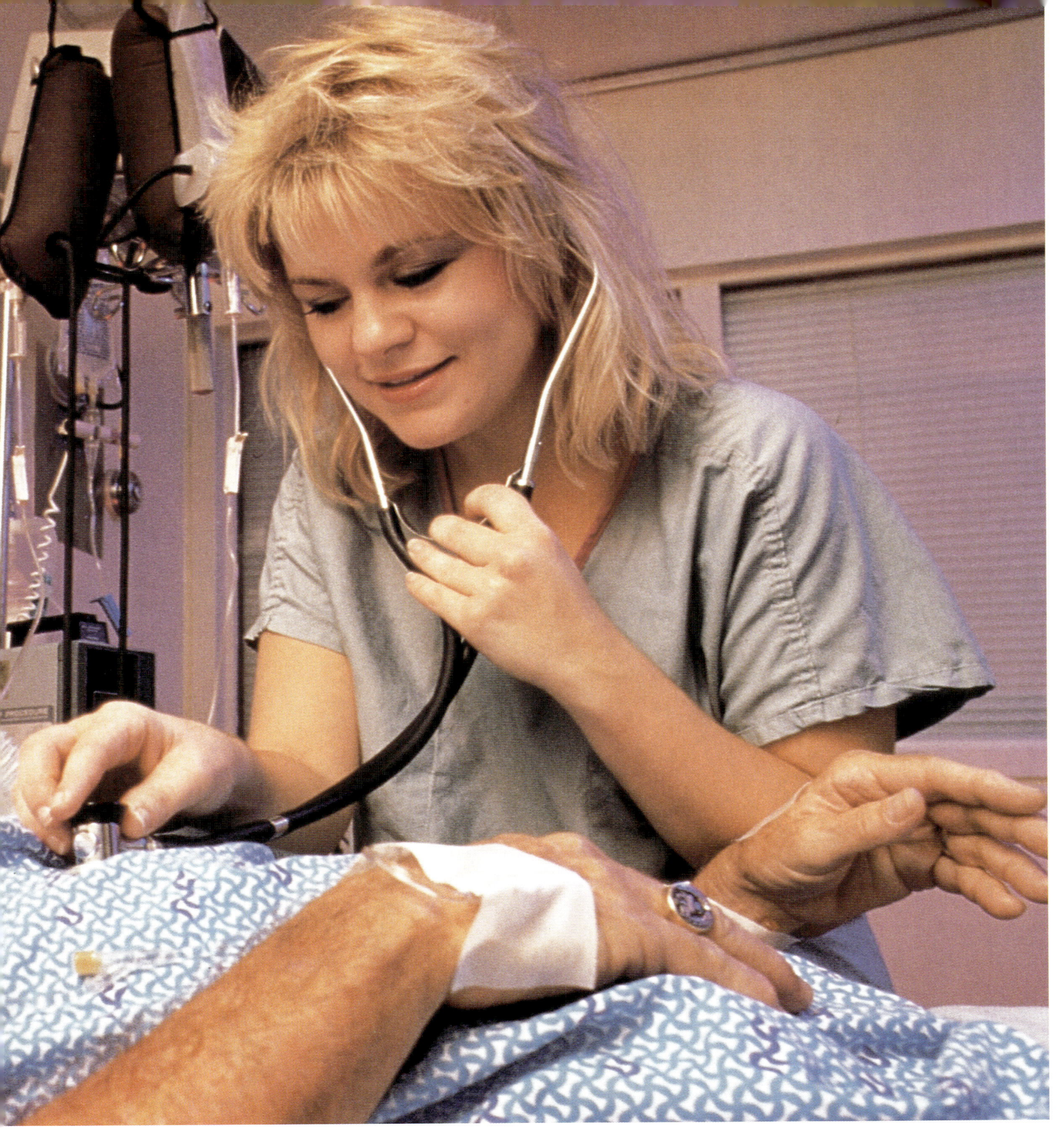

The Ochsner Medical Institutions attract more than 700,000 patients a year, a significant number of them from Latin America. The 532-bed hospital and clinic is among the top 1 percent of hospitals nationwide, as rated by U.S. News & World Report. Photo by Jackson Hill/Southern Lights Studio.

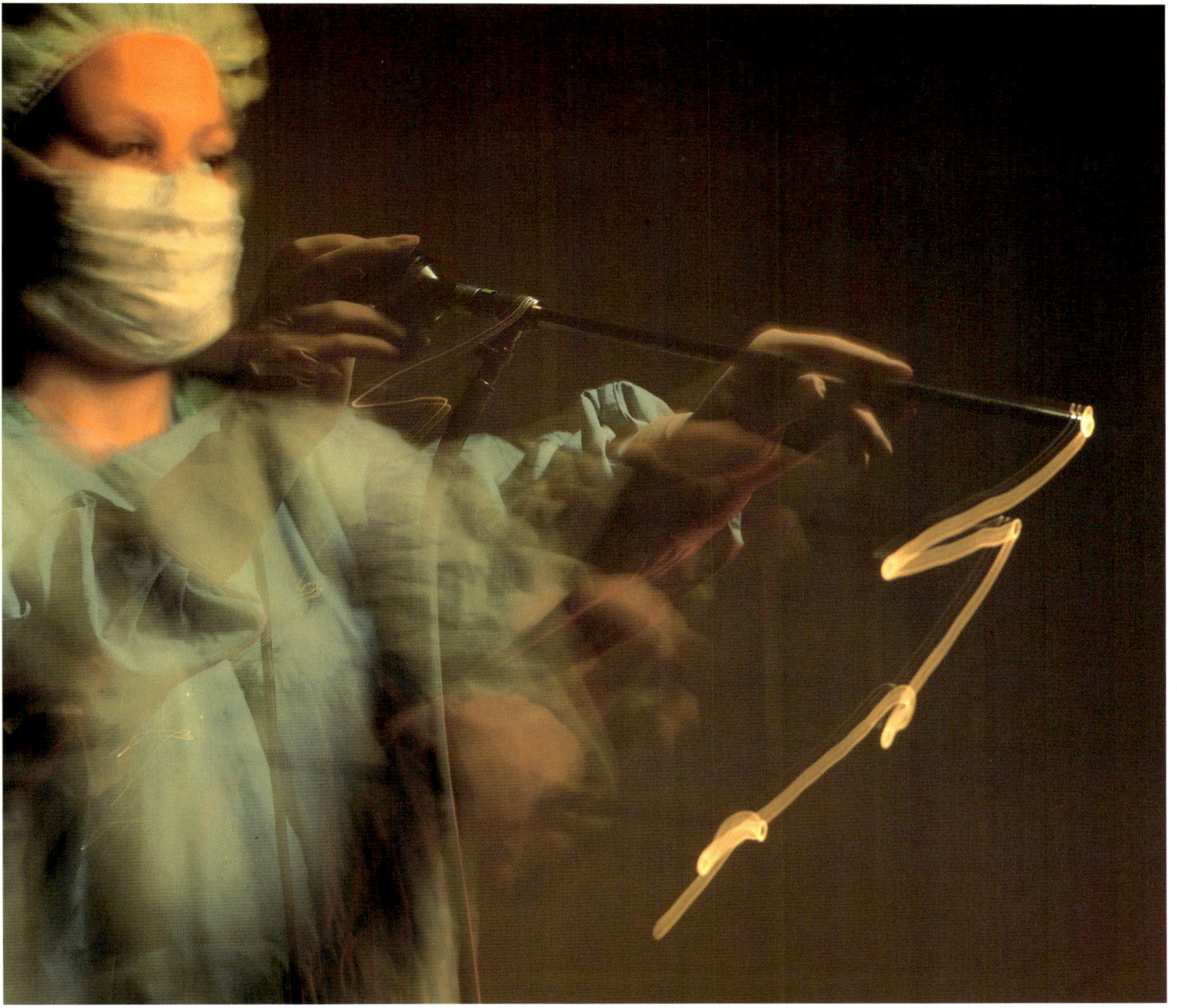

care industry has a total of about 48,000 employees, an increase of almost 18 percent since 1990. The sector accounts for one job in every 12 in the regional economy. Many people come from as far away as Latin America to take advantage of the health care resources of New Orleans. At Tulane University Hospital and Clinic, for example, more than one in every four of the 100,000-plus patients seen annually comes from outside Louisiana.

New Orleans has three academic medical centers—Louisiana State University Medical Center, Tulane University Medical Center, and Ochsner Medical Institutions. According to *New Orleans Magazine*, they're a big reason why Louisiana has long been out front in health care. "Over the past 30 years, the city has developed as a health center, not just because of the pioneering heart-transplant work done at Ochsner Medical Institutions, but also because of the research and training done in Tulane's and LSU's facilities."

LSU Medical Center boasts a school of medicine, a school of graduate studies, a school of nursing, and the state's only schools of dentistry and allied health professions. LSU Medical Center is also home to the world-renowned LSU Eye Center, the LSUMC-Stanley S. Scott Cancer Center, the LSUMC Cardiovascular Center, the Louisiana Area Health Education Center, and the LSU Neuroscience Center of Excellence, now under construction and scheduled for completion in 1997. The largest single holder of federal grant money in the region, LSU Medical Center has conducted path-breaking research leading to many medical advances including:

- the genetics of aging.
- a drug that helps regenerate damaged brain cells.
- pioneering work with the Excimer laser for myopia, cochlear implants, and dental implants.
- the region's premier bone-marrow transplant program.
- the discovery of a gene for lung cancer.
- the epidemiological study that led the Environmental Protection Agency to declare secondhand smoke a class A carcinogen.
- the discovery of the link between cigarette smoking and heart disease.
- the ability to grow mature heart cells in culture to help the heart repair itself after heart attacks.

Tulane University Medical Center features a school of medicine ranked among the top 20 in the country, the only school of public health and tropical medicine in the Gulf South, the Tulane University Hospital and Clinic; and the Delta Regional Primate Research Center, among other entities. Tulane is home to the Bogalusa Heart Study, the world's longest-running descriptive study of the early signs of cardiovascular disease, which extends its research to young children. Nobel laureate Andrew V. Schally was honored for his discovery and synthesis of the brain hormones that control production and release of other hormones from the pituitary gland, and he continues his work in neuroendocrine, neurobiological, and related neuroscience areas.

Tulane researchers developed the Tulane hip, a biologically attached total hip replacement system that has allowed thousands to walk again, and a soft plastic cornea that has restored sight to many patients who were totally blind. In 1995, four Tulane surgeons performed an intestinal transplant, in only the fifth such operation worldwide. Clinical

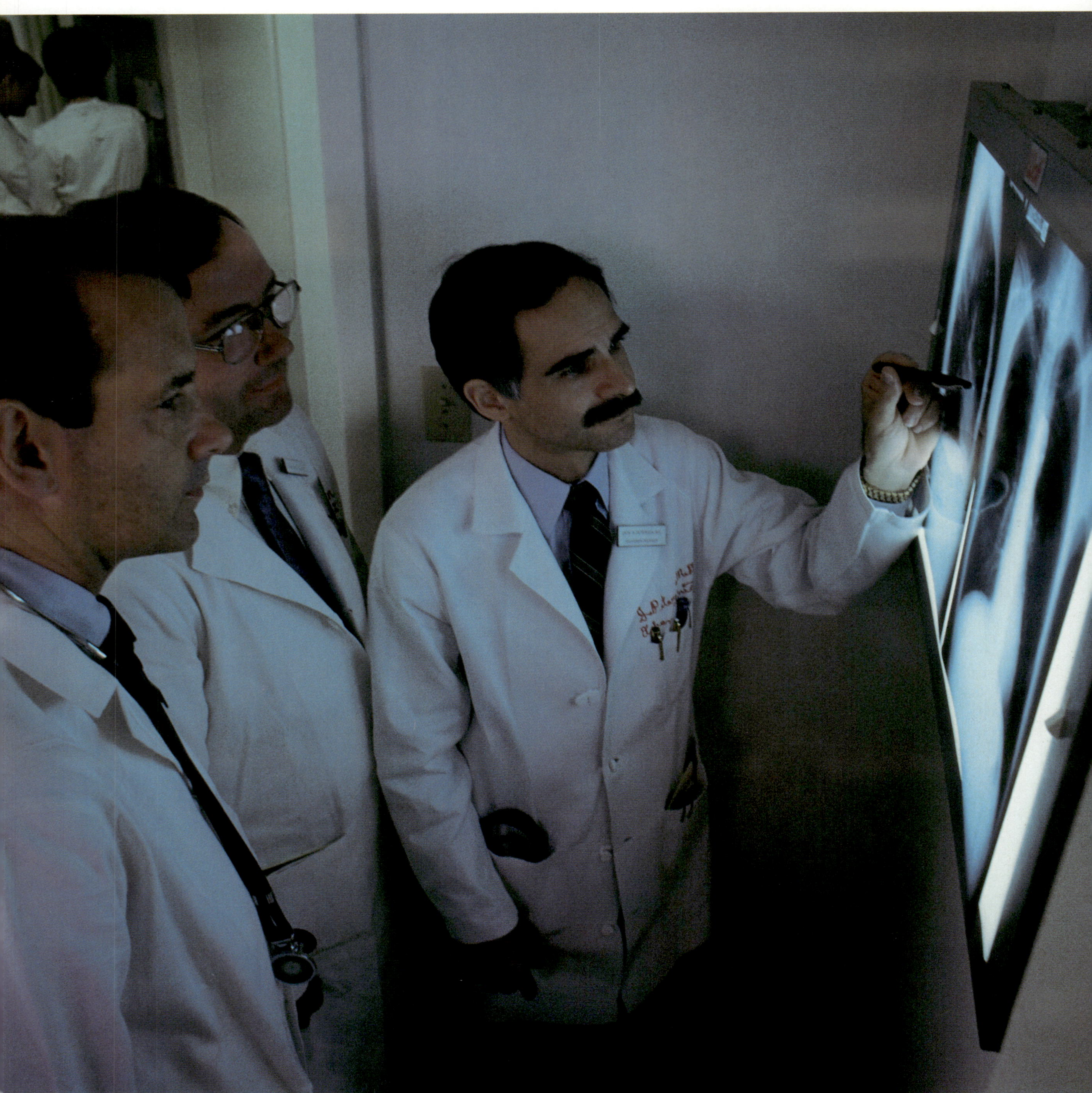

Discovering new ways to protect human health and ecosystems from the effects of air pollution and other environmental contaminants is an important area of emphasis in New Orleans at sites including the J. Bennett Johnston Center for Bioenvironmental Research, a joint venture of Tulane and Xavier universities. Photo by Jackson Hill/Southern Lights Studio.

immunologists conduct extensive studies on airborne
allergens—the molds, spores, and environmental pollutants
common to the state. The medical center recently began
development of a $2.45 million Tulane Cancer Center; and
in 1995, it established the Tulane University Hospital for
Children as a comprehensive pediatric health care resource
within existing hospital facilities. Tulane and LSU researchers
work together in the AIDS Clinical Trial Unit, testing a variety
of new diagnostic methods and treatment therapies while
providing nursing care, treatment, and support programs
for AIDS patients of all ages.

The Ochsner Medical Institutions is named in honor of
a founder, world-renowned surgeon Dr. Alton Ochsner, who
was the first physician to connect cigarette smoking with
cancer of the lung. It consists of a 532-bed hospital and clinic,
where more than 700,000 patients are seen annually by over
350 physicians and surgeons. Ochsner is noted particularly
for its leadership in organ transplantation. In 1985, the first
heart transplant with long-term success in the Gulf South
was performed by Dr. John Ochsner, son of the founder and
chief of thoracic surgery. Since then, more than 325 Ochsner
patients have received new hearts. Ochsner surgeons have
also performed many of the "firsts" in transplantation in
Louisiana—heart-lung, single-lung, double-lung, liver,
liver-kidney, and pancreas-kidney.

Ochsner consistently ranks high in virtually every survey
of physician and medical care quality. In August, 1996,
Ochsner was the only hospital in Louisiana or Mississippi
to be listed among America's best hospitals in *U.S. News &
World Report*. Out of 1,961 hospitals surveyed for the annual
listing, Ochsner was listed in the medical specialities of cardiology, endocrinology, gastroenterology, neurology, orthopedics,
and rheumatology, more than any other hospital in the five-
state region of Louisiana, Mississippi, Alabama, Georgia, and
Arkansas. *The Best Doctors in America—Southeast Region—
1996-97* also listed more individual Ochsner doctors, in more
specialties, than at any other hospital in Louisiana. Ochsner's
cancer center is recognized as one of the top 10 in the nation
by *Good Housekeeping* magazine.

Other medical institutions in the area have earned reputations for excellent, effective community health care, including
the Browne-McHardy Clinic, Children's Hospital, East Jefferson
General Hospital, Methodist Health System, Southeast Medical
Alliance, Touro Infirmary, and West Jefferson Medical Center.
Health care organizations Columbia/HCA and Tenet are
represented in the market, and the New Orleans Hospital
Alliance draws together a group of not-for-profit institutions
under one umbrella.

A coalition of eight organizations representing business,
public health, civic development, and education have joined
together to form the New Orleans Medical Complex, located
in a 40-block area of downtown New Orleans. The organizations include the Downtown Development District, created
as a special taxing district by the state legislature to help
revitalize and promote downtown New Orleans, Tulane
University Medical Center, LSU Medical Center, the Veterans

The health care sector accounts for 1 job in every 12 in the regional economy. Photo by Jackson Hill/Southern Lights Studio.

Affairs Medical Center, the Medical Center of Louisiana at New Orleans/Charity Hospital Campus, Louisiana Office of Public Health, Xavier University, and the City of New Orleans. Together, these entities boast annual research funding of $74 million. The umbrella New Orleans Medical Complex works to improve security and the physical environment of the medical complex area, develop shared services, and encourage additional medical research and development to locate in the area. It is also the moving force behind the Louisiana Biomedical Research and Development Park, which grants tax exemptions, rebates, and credits to biomedical companies who relocate to the park.

In a related project, the Downtown Development District has developed a New Orleans presence on an Internet database called Community of Science, cataloguing information on medical researchers and specialties at Tulane and LSU medical centers for wide exposure to the medical industry. This effective marketing tool allows pharmaceutical companies and other Internet users immediate access to information about the research strengths of the area.

Those strengths have attracted businesses to relocate or expand here, according to executives of MetroVision Economic Development Partnership, who have targeted pharmaceuticals, medical instruments, and medical products as one of four areas of competitive strength in the New Orleans area.

Fostering growth in the New Orleans-based technology industry is the mission of the New Orleans Technology Council, an initiative of the City of New Orleans' Economic Development Office. It emphasizes cooperative ventures and capital discovery for small business, among other things. Some of those involved in council include:

- Lockheed Martin Space Systems, which uses advanced lightweight construction, welding techniques, and rocket propulsion to manufacture the external tanks of the Space Shuttle.
- Information Technology Systems, Inc., a developer of pioneering software and information systems that allow complete integration of information across multiple platforms, solving one of the fundamental incompatibility problems of the computer industry. The company is winner of the 1994 Louisiana Innovative Company of the Year Award and the Southern Growth Policies Board 1995 Governor's Cup, the South's most prestigious award for technology innovation.
- ISI, which develops multi-media solutions to training challenges, using state-of-the-art equipment and technology.
- Cox Fibernet, builders of a fiber optic network throughout the greater New Orleans area. Cox Fibernet's parent company, Cox Communications, is part of the recently-announced Sprint Telecommunications Venture, offering wireless long distance and local services, cellular phone communications, and wireless cable TV.
- Textron Marine, a U.S. leader in the design and construction of advanced technology air-cushion vehicles, surface effect ships, combat vehicles, and advanced suspension systems.

Other companies on the technological cutting edge in the New Orleans region—and who are involved in the Technology Council— include Waldemar S. Nelson and Company, one of the nation's leading engineering consulting firms; PSC PrimeCo, a new wireless communications business; Network Teleports, specializing in satellite uplink and information distribution; Radiofone, BellSouth, and Entergy.

Resources at universities add to the technological richness of the area. For example, the University of New Orleans'

Because a healthy start is important to a healthy life, New Orleans health care professionals dedicate themselves to the city's youngest citizens as well as the oldest—and everyone in between. Photo by Jackson Hill/Southern Lights Studio.

Endoscopy being performed on a lioness at the Audubon Zoo Animal Health Care Center. Photo courtesy of the Audubon Institute.

Telecommunications Research Center, established in 1994 with a $1-million gift from South Central Bell, focuses on the application of new telecommunications technology in business and government. A new $9.3-million science annex features state-of-the-art lab equipment and facilities; and work has begun on a $53-million, 56-acre UNO Research and Technology Park adjacent to the Lakefront campus. The site will feature programs and facilities that support research and technology transfer in the neurosciences, pharmaceuticals, biotechnology, medical sciences, energy conversion and conservation, urban waste management, aquatic sciences, telecommunications, and robotics, to name a few. The park also includes the Center for Energy Resources Management and a Public Health Environmental Lab. UNO has the top naval architecture program in the United States. The Advanced Marine Technology Center, the only one of its kind in the country, helps U.S. shipbuilding become more competitive on an international scale by improving design and construction processes. And the UNO Technology Enterprise Center, an incubator in downtown New Orleans, helps smaller technology companies get the competitive edge in business.

Xavier University ranks first nationally in the number of black students receiving undergraduate degrees in physical sciences and second nationally in life sciences. It was selected for funding by the National Science Foundation as a Model Institution of Excellence in Science, Engineering, and Mathematics. The College of Pharmacy is number one in the nation in pharmacy degrees awarded to African Americans, having educated since 1927 nearly one in four black pharmacists practicing in the United States. Xavier is first in the nation in placing African-American students in medical schools, with an 80 percent acceptance rate. Some 95 percent of those who enter graduate.

In 1989, Tulane and Xavier received $33 million in federal money to begin the J. Bennett Johnston Center for Bioenvironmental Research, a scientific and policy research institute dedicated to finding new ways to protect human health and ecosystems from the harmful effects of environmental pollutants. Researchers at the center study pollution in the Mississippi River system and how to clean it up.

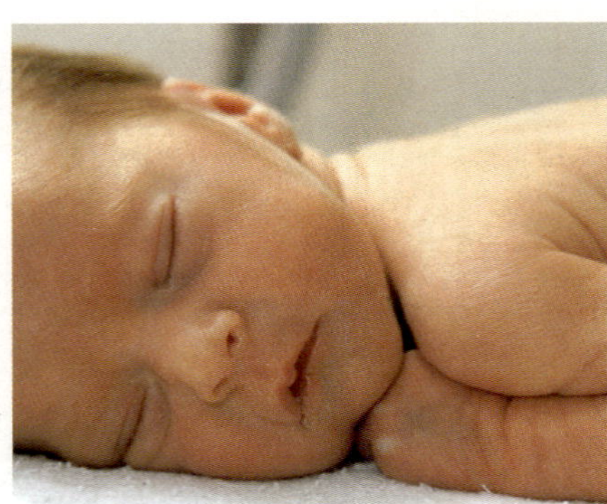

They look at how biohazards actually affect human health and how contaminated environments can be restored. They help the federal departments of Defense and Energy protect worker health, public health, and the environment; and they train employees in hazardous material management and emergency response. They are carrying out a comprehensive cancer study of Louisiana parishes bordering the Mississippi River between Baton Rouge and the Gulf. They have established a technology exchange with China, through the U.S./China Energy and Environmental Technology Center in Beijing. And they study climate patterns, oceanographics, and global warming through the National Institute for Global Environmental Change, one of six in the country. Between 1992 and 1994, the Center for Bioenvironmental Research received almost $70 million in funding for its projects.

Through Tulane's Environmental Law Clinic, the first of its kind in the South, law students represent otherwise under-represented citizens and organizations who are trying to protect Louisiana's natural environment.

Research at the Audubon Institute works to protect endangered species in Louisiana and throughout the world. The Freeport-McMoRan Audubon Species Survival Center, a 1,200-acre site on the West Bank of the Mississippi, has offered hope to endangered animals—the Baird's tapir and Mississippi sandhill cranes, to name only two—by providing a refuge where they can breed undisturbed and eventually boost their numbers in the wild.

The Audubon Center for Research of Endangered Species, scheduled for completion in 1996, provides the research infrastructure for developing new information on advanced breeding techniques, animal behavior, and nutrition, including a cryogenics lab that focuses on frozen embryos.

Add to all of this a cleaned-up Lake Pontchartrain and recycling programs that are in every neighborhood in the New Orleans region, and it's easy to see how technology, environmental research, and health care make a difference in the daily life of every New Orleanian. ◆

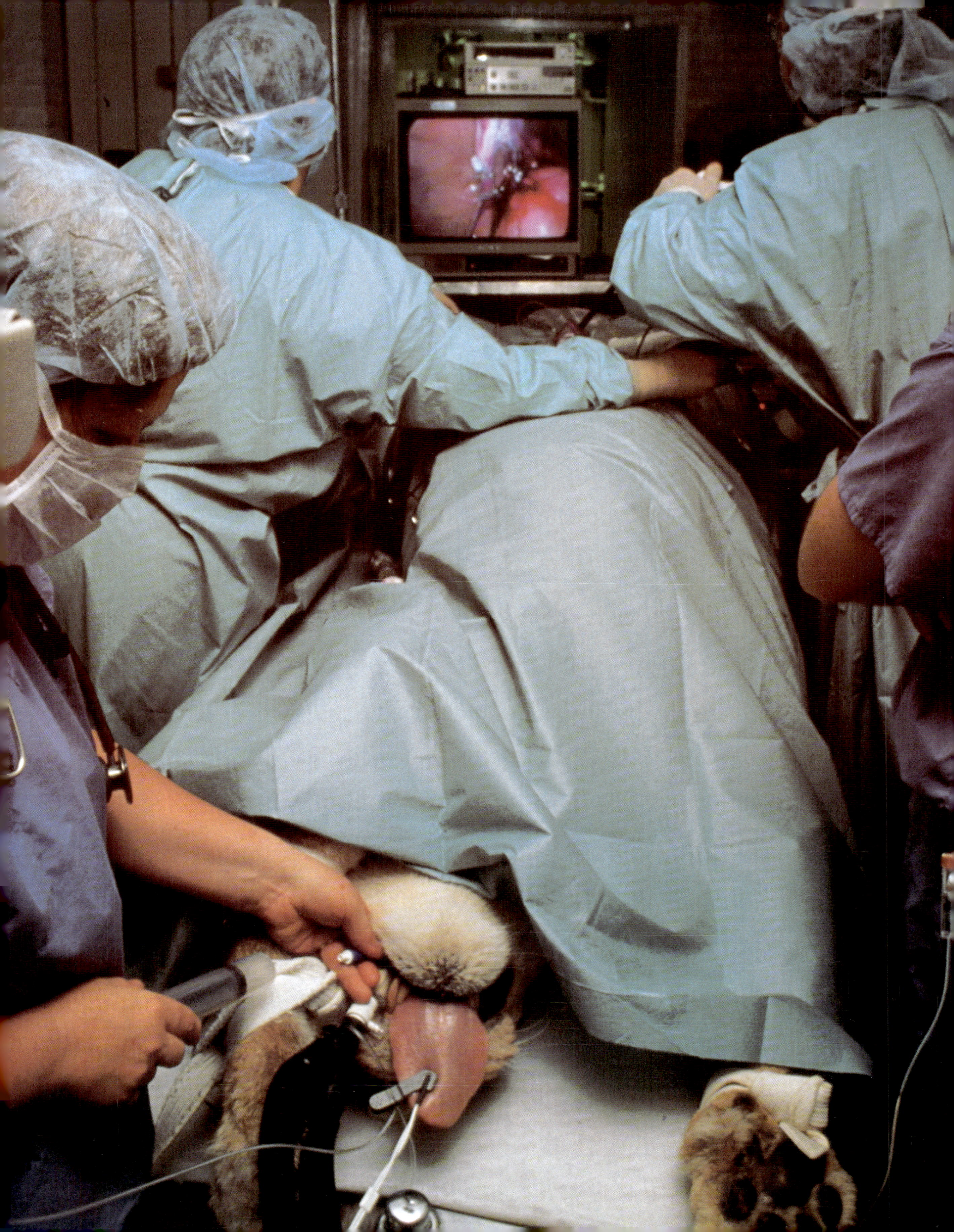

The People of New Orleans

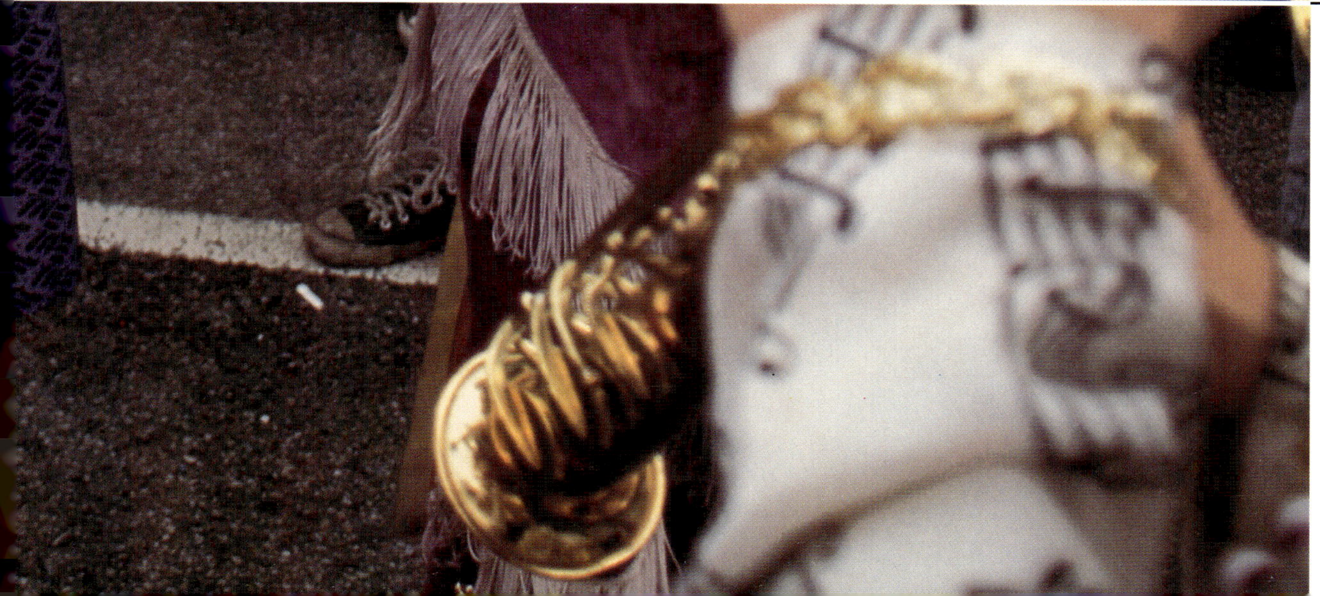

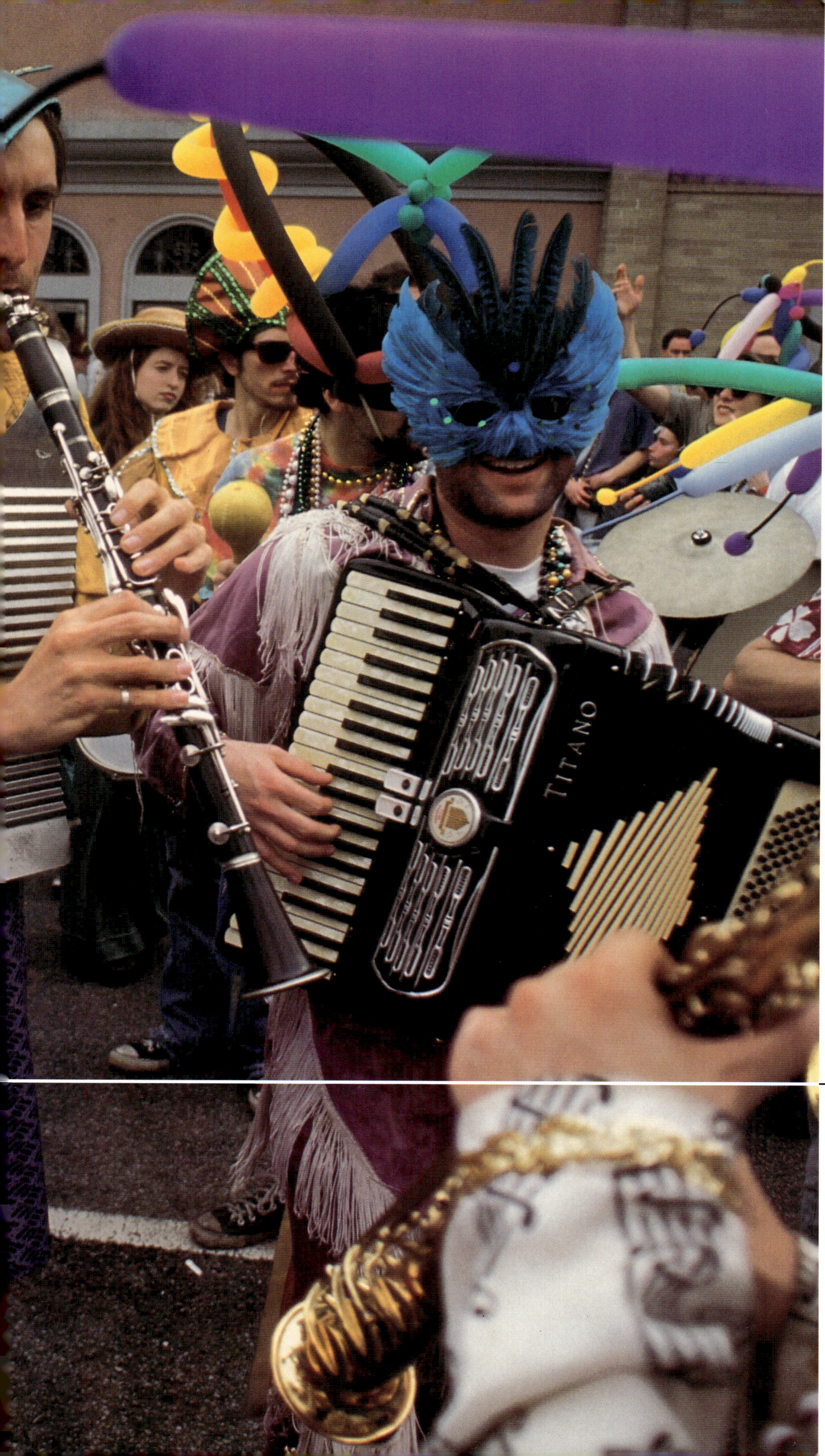

CHAPTER 8

A veteran observer's second rule of life in New Orleans is "There's always a parade." Many of those parades, and the festivals they celebrate, come directly from the rich mix of cultures that has made the city so interesting. Photo by Jackson Hill/Southern Lights Studio.

"New Orleans is not a melting pot.

It's a gumbo. When you combine the

diverse people and neighborhoods of the

city—or the ingredients of the famous

Creole stew—they keep their own different

characters, and draw strength and depth

of flavor from those differences."

from New Orleans' presentation in the
1996 All-American City and Community
Awards finals

The New Orleans region is culturally one of the most diverse in the world. Given its history and its active port, it's no wonder.

Founded by the French on the site of a Native American village, the city was also governed by the Spanish before the Americans gained possession of a thoroughly European Catholic city in the 1803 Louisiana Purchase. At some points during the colonial period, more than 50 percent of the city's population consisted of blacks from West Africa and the Caribbean. About half were slaves and half free people of color.

Those people, black and white, are the original Creoles. The most common definition of the word—applied to everything from shrimp to society—is a person of either race who can trace his or her ancestry to Louisiana, particularly New Orleans, before 1803.

But that is not to be confused with Cajun. The Cajuns, mostly country people who live in the small towns along the bayous of Louisiana southwest of New Orleans, have family roots that lead back to the Acadians. Acadians were expelled from Canada by the British in the mid-1700s, when they refused to renounce their French allegiance and their Catholic religion. The Spanish invited them to southwest Louisiana, where they settled, and some 750,000 of their descendants remain.

Creoles and Cajuns both spoke French in colonial Louisiana, but they might not have understood each other. Isolated in the bayous, the Cajuns retained much of the seventeenth century French of their ancestors, while the urban Creoles' language was closer to that spoken in Paris. Both groups have also earned renown for their food. Cajun dishes, particularly, have moved from southwest Louisiana to spice up palates all over the country, thanks in part to famed chef Paul Prudhomme and his extended family of talented cooks. The distinctive fiddle-and-accordion beat of Cajun and Zydeco music, with lyrics usually in French, has also moved from the bayou to the borders of the mainstream, with bands such as Beausoleil, Steve Riley and the Mamou Playboys, and Rockin'Dopsie and the Zydeco Twisters playing to packed houses around the world—and receiving their share of Grammy nominations.

African-American culture also plays a main role in shaping New Orleans—with its food, music, and rhythms of life. The first Africans were brought from a region near Senegal by French slavers in 1719; in the next dozen years, the French Company of the Indies brought in 7,000 slaves. The Code Noir, established in 1727 by the French, regulated the treatment of slaves. As cruel as its mandates were, the code was less oppressive than similar British-based treatises. Free people of color, often former slaves who came from the Caribbean to New Orleans, were also recorded as among the city's population as early as 1720. By 1860, there were more than 7,500 free people of color in New Orleans, some of them 20 generations removed from Africa and 10 from slavery.

The distinctive fiddle–and–accordion beat of Cajun and Zydeco music, with lyrics often in French, has moved from the bayou to the mainstream. Photo by Jackson Hill/Southern Lights Studio.

(top) In an Italian–American tradition every March 19, a priest blesses a St. Joseph's Day altar laden with foods that altar sponsors have spent days and weeks preparing. The altars raise money for the poor and, after sampling by the devout, the food is distributed to the needy people of the parish. Photo by Jackson Hill/Southern Lights Studio.

Irish–Americans in New Orleans observe St. Patrick's Day by wearing green clothes, drinking green beer, and parading through the streets with green flowers—and kisses—for select spectators. Photo by Jackson Hill/Southern Lights Studio.

From the early nineteenth century, free people of color and slaves would meet at Congo Square (now the site of Armstrong Park), where African ritual and ceremonies were traded, passed along, and kept alive. One example of that tradition continuing to this day—albeit in a more formal sense—is the Amistad Research Center at Tulane University, one of the nation's largest archives of African-American historical materials.

When the French gave New Orleans to the Spanish in 1762, they didn't bother to tell the residents, who weren't particularly happy to discover that they had new rulers. Especially since the Spanish had notably poor taste in wine, a flaw which led to an armed revolt. The Spanish tenure in New Orleans covered only 34 years, culminating when they sold the entire Louisiana Territory to the Americans in 1803. But their heritage lives on in street names and architecture—the French Quarter is really Spanish in era and style, thanks to historic eighteenth century fires which destroyed most of the French buildings.

More than 200 years ago, the Islenos came from the Canary Islands, a Spanish colony just off the African coast, to settle in St. Bernard Parish to fish and trap. Over 500 of them still speak Creole Spanish in a neighborhood that's now a bedroom suburb of New Orleans. About a quarter of the parish's 67,000 residents are of Isleno descent.

In 1809, nearly 6,000 refugees fled to Cuba to escape a slave insurrection in Santo Domingo. But the Spanish wouldn't let them stay, so they came to New Orleans. More than 150 years later, many other citizens fleeing Cuba settled in the New Orleans area, and the city has been a popular destination for Central Americans as well. The Salvadorans in New Orleans would make up one of the largest cites in El Salvador, for example, and Guatemalan, Honduran, and Nicaraguan expatriates also have thriving communities in the region.

Just a year after New Orleans was founded, 250 German farmers arrived, primarily to help the French settlers grow enough food to eat. Most were responding to handbills that promoted south Louisiana as a paradise. It wasn't, as they quickly realized, but they became successful farmers, bakers, and beer brewers in spite of the heat, humidity, and mosquitoes. In a second great wave of immigration, more than 50,000 Germans came into the United States through the port of New Orleans between 1820 and 1850. In fact, in that period, New Orleans was the nation's second most popular destination for immigrants, following New York. In 1860, the city had about 175,000 residents, 40 percent of whom were foreign-born.

Some 24,000 of those were Irish. Though they had been moving to New Orleans since its founding, the Irish influx came after the potato famine of the mid-nineteenth century. A $12 ticket to New Orleans was the way out, and the city's Catholic culture was friendly. But the economy wasn't. Irish were often hired to do jobs that were considered too dangerous for slaves, including digging the New Basin Canal, linking Lake Pontchartrain and the Mississippi River.

The Sicilians were the last large wave of immigrants to come to New Orleans in the nineteenth century. In the 1840s, Sicilian merchants looking to establish a new market for their citrus fruits founded one of the earliest Italian colonies in the United States. Fifty years later, New Orleans

New Orleans, the gumbo culture, is a city of distinct neighborhoods. Photo by Jackson Hill/Southern Lights Studio.

(following page) New Orleans' own Neville Brothers have hit the pop charts as their music has become a familiar part of national culture. Photo by Jackson Hill/Southern Lights Studio.

NEV
BROT

HERS

became a primary destination for their poverty-stricken countrymen, many of whom worked as contract laborers to replace slaves on sugar cane plantations. Some 200,000 New Orleans residents can trace their ancestry to Sicily, making New Orleans the most Sicilian city in America.

Greek sailors settled into the New Orleans community over the years, and immigrants from the former Yugoslavia became oyster fishermen. More recently, Vietnamese immigrants have added their distinctive culture to the city. Many Vietnamese came to New Orleans after the fall of Saigon, finding the climate and the watery landscape much like that of their native land. East New Orleans became a popular neighborhood for Vietnamese families, and a traditional Vietnamese market held there each Saturday morning is an attraction for cooks from throughout the city.

New Orleans, the gumbo culture, is also a city of distinct neighborhoods. According to one study, New Orleans—Orleans Parish alone, not the metropolitan area—has 71 definable neighborhoods. Some are as small as 10 blocks,

People from all neighborhoods come to play on Lake Pontchartrain—in a boat, with a fishing rod or just to relax and observe. Photo by Jackson Hill/Southern Lights Studio.

In any New Orleans neighborhood, you're likely to hear the sound of a trombone or a trumpet. Photo by Jackson Hill/Southern Lights Studio.

some are as large as 50 acres. And 10 neighborhoods are on the list of National Historic Districts, including the Uptown Historic District—with more than 10,000 structures the second-largest in the United States.

In his book *New Orleans Unmasqued*, S. Frederick Starr writes about the power of the neighborhoods, and their singular institutions. "From the Irish Channel to Faubourg Treme, each neighborhood of the Crescent City has its own distinctive character. Some can be recognized by the shade of their native accent, or by the songs the children chant on school playgrounds. Many neighborhood peculiarities are rooted in the life of a particular church or parish, local bar or grocery store."

Neighborhoods are also making headlines—in the best possible way. In defining 10 ways New Orleans has improved over the last 30 years for its 30th anniversary issue in 1996, *New Orleans Magazine* cited a re-emergence of some neighborhoods.

The Warehouse District downtown was the neighborhood for the 1984 World's Fair, which sparked renovation, residential development, and a critical mass of restaurants, galleries, artists, coffeehouses, small hotels, and offices for attorneys, architects, ad agencies, and other professionals. A dozen years later, the Warehouse District has become one of the city's newest residential meccas, with condos selling as quickly as they are built. Thanks to work by the Downtown Development District, there's also a move to encourage residential living on Canal Street, above shops in architecturally distinguished, historic buildings. The residential developments in the Warehouse District, on Canal Street, and in other parts of the Central Business District add to a vibrant, dynamic downtown New Orleans, which has a well-earned reputation as one of the healthiest downtown areas—with one of the broadest mixes of activity—of any city in America.

In headlining a front-page story on a "Bywater Revival," the *Times-Picayune* notes that "artists join blue-collar stalwarts to bring a bohemian sensibility and stability to a neighborhood." In Bywater and elsewhere, neighborhood organizations are joining together all over the city to approach problems from a grassroots basis, whether it's renovating blighted housing, encouraging economic development, or fighting crime. They're succeeding, too. "All the city's neighborhoods are worthy of being saved," writes *New Orleans Magazine*. "The good news is that some of them have been."

A veteran observer's second rule of life in New Orleans is "There's always a parade." Many of those parades, and the festivals they celebrate, come directly from the rich mix of cultures that has made the city so interesting. For example, Irish-Americans in New Orleans—and all the rest of us— observe St. Patrick's Day by wearing green clothes and drinking green beer. But how many other places are there St. Patrick's Day parades where float riders throw the crowds cabbages, brussels sprouts, potatoes, carrots, onions, and, to the occasional favored petitioner, a corned beef?

On March 19, St. Joseph's Day, special altars are featured at dozens of sites throughout the city—from homes to churches to halls. Some are prepared by Italian-American families, some by other devout groups. They honor the patron saint of the family, who delivered Sicilians from starvation in the early 1800s. The dramatic, bountiful altars feature all kinds of intricate, traditional foods—cookies, decorative breads, vegetables, pasta, cakes. A priest blesses each altar, which is then opened to the public for sampling, and an offering is collected. After the celebration, the food is given to the poor. There's also a St. Joseph's parade, with Italian-Americans wending their celebratory way through the French Quarter.

Super Sunday, usually in late March, doesn't have a thing to do with the Super Bowl. It's the time—other than Mardi Gras itself—when the Mardi Gras Indian tribes parade in their spectacular feathers and beadwork. The African-American tradition, which dates back at least a century, also involves rhythms based on West African drumming and dancing. Those beats have become a part of national culture with the popularity of the Neville Brothers—one of whose musical mentors was Jolley Landry, Big Chief of the Wild Tchoupitoulas. The annual Black Heritage Festival is also held in March, with events throughout the city.

Festivals are a constant—and constantly enjoyable—part of life in New Orleans, with food, music, and fun for every taste. From the Spring Fiesta and the French Quarter Festival to the Greek Festival and Carnaval Latino; from Vietnamese New Year to Oktoberfest; from the Swampfest at the Audubon Zoo to the Mirliton Festival or the Tomato Festival or the Gumbo Festival—in New Orleans, we know how to celebrate each other's culture and enjoy our differences. ◆

(left) The neighborhoods of New Orleans, with their schools, playgrounds and porch chats, are in the midst of a renaissance that's attracting attention locally and nationally. Photo by Jackson Hill/Southern Lights Studio.

Super Sunday, usually in late March, doesn't have a thing to do with the Super Bowl. It's the time—other than Mardi Gras itself—when the Mardi Gras Indian tribes parade in their spectacular feathers and beadwork. Photo by Jackson Hill/ Southern Lights Studio.

CHAPTER

9

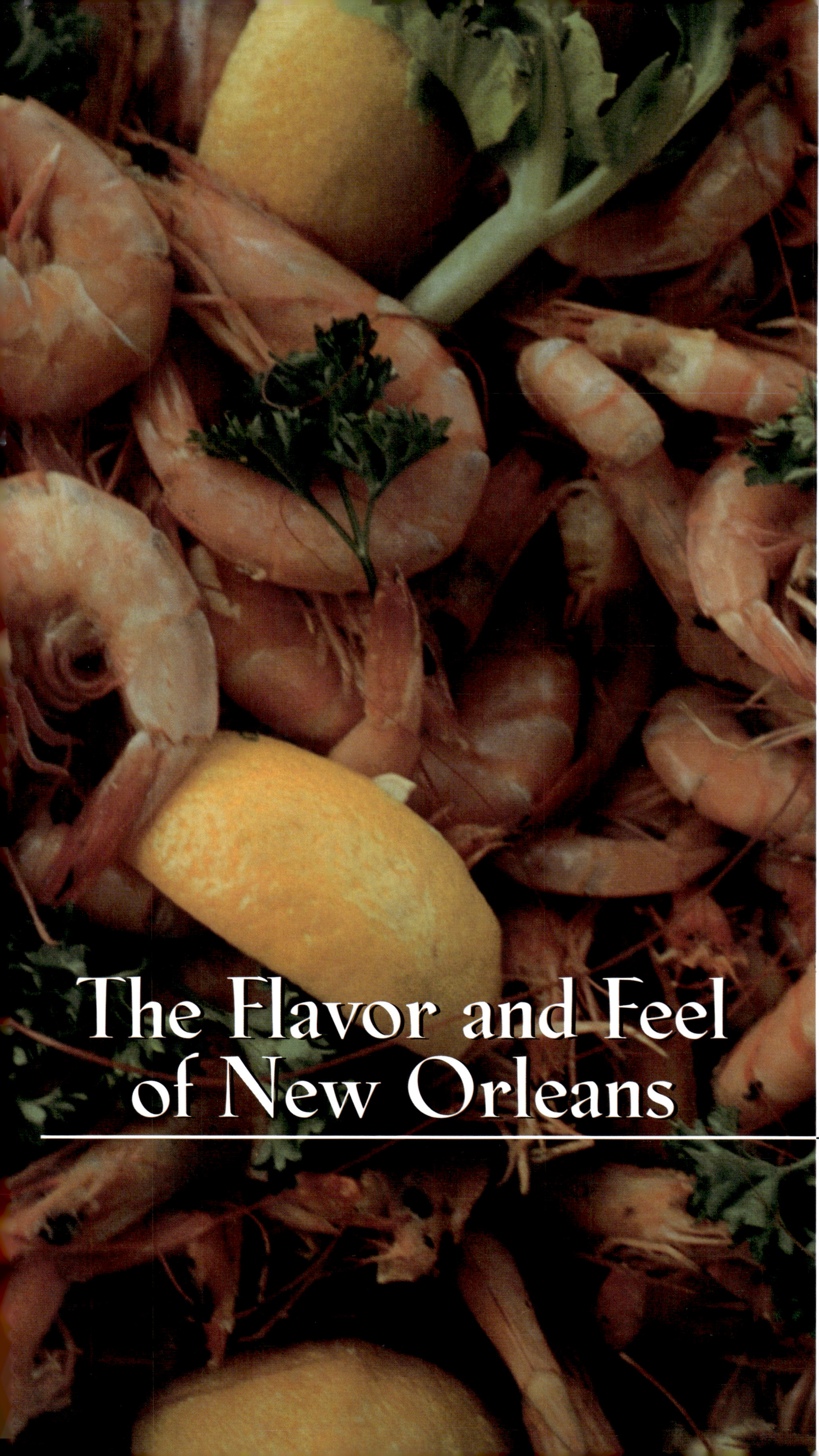

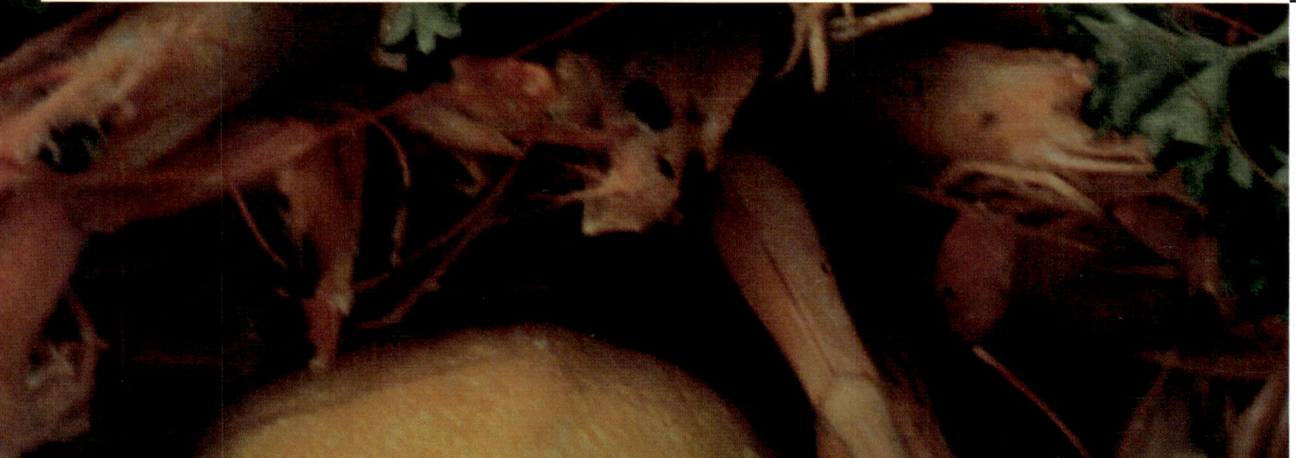

The Flavor and Feel of New Orleans

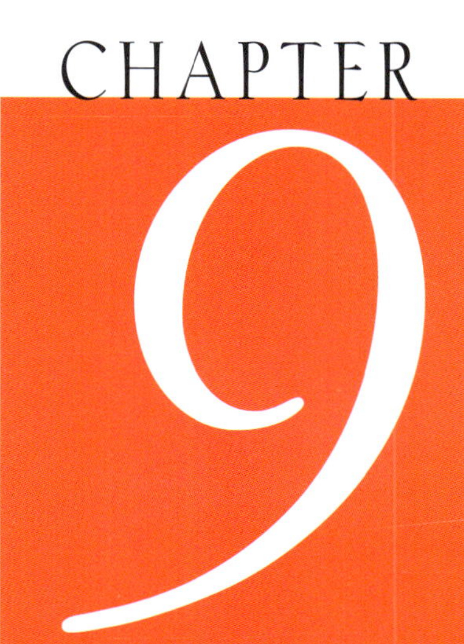

The taste of New Orleans is unlike that of any other city, thanks to common delicacies like big plates of boiled shrimp, spiced just right, with a little lemon on the side. Photo by Michael Varisco/Southern Lights Studio.

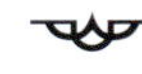

"Eating in New Orleans is not something

you do in order to be able to pursue other

activities, but the reverse. Neither religion, sex,

nor even politics can compete with food as a

topic of conversation. And not just before

dinner as the juices flow, either. Pull back the

chairs after a four-course groaner at K-Paul's

or Dooky Chase's and what will the company

discuss? Food."

S. Frederick Starr in New Orleans Unmasqued

The cast-iron balconies of the French Quarter decorate townhouses, whose tall windows and high ceilings were designed to take maximum advantage of the breezes in an era before air conditioning. Photo by Jackson Hill/Southern Lights Studio.

New Orleanians love their city. They love to think about and talk about and experience the things that give it a flavor and a feel that's dramatically different from Little Rock or Boston or Atlanta or Houston.

Among the most important elements that go into the New Orleans recipe are its distinctive food and architecture—not to mention the streetcars, a moving monument inscribed in the National Register of Historic Places, that will deliver you to shopping or to work every day, for just a dollar.

Food in New Orleans paves the way to greater glory—on earth and beyond. In a panel on food-writing at the 1996 Tennessee Williams Festival, the participants were asked what each of them would offer up to St. Peter to make those pearly gates swing wide. Three New Orleans natives recommended three different dishes that characterize the city's cuisine.

Ella Brennan, the guiding hand of Commander's Palace, mentor to some of the city's most famous chefs (including Paul Prudhomme and Emeril Lagasse), and driving force behind much of the best in the New Orleans restaurant industry, chose a perfectly cooked redfish courtboullion, in a sauce combining fresh Creole tomatoes and spices with the "holy trinity" of New Orleans cooking— onions, peppers, and celery—and served over rice. The Palace Cafe's Ti Martin, Brennan's daughter, would tempt with an oyster po-boy—fresh, crusty French bread as long as your forearm, split and filled with perfectly fried fresh oysters and "dressed," as we say in New Orleans, with lettuce, tomato, and a garlic-kissed mayonnaise. And Lolis Elie, a columnist for the *Times-Picayune* and author of a new book on barbecue in the South, chose his "Auntee Carol's gumbo"—a stew that's packed with okra, seafood, a little sausage, maybe some chicken, and the distinctive seasonings that are the taste of the city.

While New Orleans diners don't always get dishes worthy of St. Peter, the food in the city's eating establishments is consistently good. It's possible to get a bad meal in New Orleans, but it's not likely. You'd probably have to be notably unlucky, or work at it. There are almost 2,000 restaurants in the area. Some are tiny; some seat hundreds. Some are Creole; some are Cajun—and no, it's not the same thing. Many are ethnic, ranging from Vietnamese to African, from Italian to Greek. Some have carefully designed decor; others have Formica-topped tables. Some will give you all you can eat for $5; others have multi-course dinner tabs that reach 10 or 20 times that. But whatever the atmosphere, the size, the flavors, the cost—the food is good. If it isn't, the restaurant doesn't stay in business. New Orleanians see to that.

The experts agree. *Condé Nast Traveler* magazine rates New Orleans food as the best in the world, and the city has more restaurants with more different cuisines rated by *Zagat's Guide* for best value than any other city in the country. Commander's Palace, flagship of the Brennan family restaurants, has been named the top restaurant in America by readers of *Food & Wine* magazine, with more than three times the votes of its nearest competitor. In 1996, it won the coveted James Beard Award for overall excellence, given to the best restaurant in the country.

What makes the New Orleans difference? The culinary heritage is more complex here than any city in the country— with each ethnic group building from and adding to traditional cooking styles. "In each bowl of gumbo served in Louisiana today," writes Bethany Bultman in the *Compass Guide to New Orleans*, "there is French roux, African okra, American Indian file, Spanish peppers, Cajun sausage, and

oysters supplied by Yugoslav fishermen, served over Chinese-cultivated Louisiana rice."

The raw materials are also bountiful. Many flavors of New Orleans are based on seafood, whether it's the shrimp for barbecuing, frying, or remoulading that are caught in the Gulf; the crawfish for etouffe, stew, or eating boiled by the pound that come from the muddy ponds and bayous of Southwest Louisiana; the crabs for gumbo, marinated crab salad, or ravigote from Lake Pontchartrain; the fresh Gulf fish that are blackened, grilled, sauced with meuniere, or court-boullioned; or the oysters for Rockefeller, Mosca, or raw on the half-shell, from the lakes around the region.

Rice is one of the state's top agricultural crops, and it is a staple of the New Orleans cook, though pasta is beginning to rival it as a base for the wonderful sauces and stews. Creole tomatoes and strawberries each have their festivals, and their seasons, to inspire the taste buds. The famous Tabasco sauce is made just down the road, from peppers

People in New Orleans drink more—and stronger—coffee than anyplace else in the nation. Often they love it with chicory, especially when it comes with a beignet from the Café du Monde in the French Quarter. Photo by Jackson Hill/Southern Lights Studio.

grown at Avery Island, and its spark is typical of the fire folks like to add to their food. Some dedicated New Orleanians travel with a tiny bottle of hot sauce, just to make the rest of the world's cuisine tasty to native tongues.

Of course, there's always bread pudding, or banana cream caramel pie drizzled with chocolate for dessert. Sugar is, after all one of the state's main crops. In New Orleans, we know how to use it to dramatic after-dinner effect. And we mustn't forget the coffee. People in New Orleans drink more—and stronger—coffee than anyplace else in the nation. Often we love it with chicory, especially when it comes with a beignet from the Café du Monde in the French Quarter.

Wonderful fresh vegetables, fruits, and herbs are available every Saturday morning at the popular new Cresent City Farmers' Market in the Warehouse District downtown, direct from the local farmers who have grown them. The market

also features cheeses from Louisiana's Chicory Farms, which have earned national renown. Cooking demonstrations with some of the top chefs in the city using fresh market ingredients have become a weekend tradition for many New Orleanians. A bit further afield is an outdoor Saturday Vietnamese market in Eastern New Orleans, where ambitious cooks can find the freshest ingredients (including live poultry) for many Asian dishes.

Perhaps food in New Orleans is so good simply because the audience is so appreciative. People in New Orleans like to eat, and like to talk about eating. It's enough to inspire all kinds of cooks—in a home kitchen or a restaurant environment—to do their best work. Then comes the true reward— they get to eat it.

In *Charles Kuralt's America*, the veteran newsman confesses to a lifelong passion for New Orleans cooking. "I have

Food in New Orleans plays a starring role in festivals as well as day-to-day life and conversation. Photo by Jackson Hill/ Southern Lights Studio.

(following page) In New Orleans, eating is a fabulous indulgence, from seafood to fresh produce to the famous Muffaletta sandwich. The French Market, on the edge of the Mississippi River in the Quarter, is filled with fresh fruits and vegetables, garlands of garlic, freshly poured pralines, and a flea market area where you just might find a real New Orleans bargain. Photos by Jackson Hill/Southern Lights Studio.

been overfed in this city, Lord knows, but I cannot remember ever being poorly fed, and I return frequently to New Orleans, always in anticipation, my eyes, as my mother used to say, always bigger than my stomach...My memories of New Orleans are glazed with remoulade sauce, and happily converge."

Sometimes, we have to walk off all that food. Such strolls can be an opportunity to take in the never-ending variety of New Orleans architecture, which gives the city so much of its distinctive European flavor. "There is no town in America with so much fine old architecture in such a grand assortment of styles and renditions," Jeanette Hardy writes in the *Times-Picayune's Insider's Guide to New Orleans.*

The cast-iron balconies of the French Quarter decorate townhouses, whose tall windows and high ceilings were designed to take maximum advantage of the breezes in an era before air conditioning. Many French Quarter residences (yes, it is still a vital neighborhood, with schools, families, and grocery stores) are built around courtyards, with the attention turned inward to lovely landscaping and dramatic fountains, rather than outward to the street. There is also still a sprinkling of Creole cottages, square four-room structures which date to as early as the 1790s.

The famous long, narrow "shotgun" houses are all over the city. Reputedly named because you could shoot a gun from the front door out the back without hitting a wall, the most basic of the houses have rooms in a straight line, each opening to the other through doors that are parallel. Some "camelbacks" have added second stories set back from the front of the house. Shotgun houses—or shotgun doubles, for two families—are one of the most common styles in New Orleans, in part because they are well-suited to the narrow lots carved out for homes in a city of limited land mass, growing within the immutable borders of river, lakes, and swamp.

The impressive mansions in the Garden District and along St. Charles Avenue were built primarily by Americans who moved to New Orleans in the first half of the nineteenth century. The structures are glamorous even today,

Historic plantations are but a short drive away, lining the Mississippi River and giving glimpses into the antebellum South. Photo by Jackson Hill/Southern Lights Studio.

Many French Quarter residences are built around courtyards, with the attention focused on lovely landscaping and dramatic fountains. Photo by Jackson Hill/Southern Lights Studio.

Another architectural phenomenon unique to the region are the above-ground cemeteries— the "cities of the dead." Tombs in New Orleans have a unique design, resembling tiny windowless houses, many with small porches or elaborate statuary. Photo by Jackson Hill/Southern Lights Studio.

with their leaded glass doors, galleries, wooden beadwork, stained glass windows, and sprawling floor plans. The massive live oaks lining the Avenue, and many other streets, add their spreading branches to the fabled New Orleans charm. They even have their own organization. The Louisiana Live Oak Society enrolls trees that are 100 years old and at least 16 feet in circumference, when measured 4 feet from the ground.

The clanging of the streetcar as it winds its way from Canal Street up to St. Charles and onto Carrollton Avenue, past shotguns and mansions, adds much to the New Orleans architectural ambiance. Itself on the National Register of Historic Places, the streetcar is the oldest continuously operating street railway system in existence. Its history dates to 1835, when the New Orleans and Carrollton Railroad was built to connect the city of Carrollton with downtown. Today

it carries commuters to work, students to school, shoppers to market, and tourists past some of the most beautiful parts of the city. The olive-green cars, with their wooden seats that are simply reversed at the end of the seven-mile line, run 24 hours a day and are part of the Regional Transit Authority (RTA). Recently, RTA added a riverfront line from Canal Street to the French Market, with red and gold cars. The city once had many other streetcar lines, but they were removed with the advent of the bus system. Restoring some of them, particularly the one on Canal Street, is currently under consideration by RTA officials.

Another architectural phenomenon unique to the region are our above-ground cemeteries—our "cities of the dead." Tombs in New Orleans have a unique design, resembling windowless houses, many with small porches or elaborate

of the Moriarty tomb, surrounded by statues representing Faith, Hope, Charity, and Mary Moriarty. The oldest existing cemetery in the city is St. Louis No. 1, established in 1789. Its inhabitants include a cross-section of New Orleanians—Etienne de Bore, who was the city's first mayor and the first to granulate sugar successfully; nineteenth century world chess champion Paul Morphy; Dutch Morial, the city's first African-American mayor, who died in 1989; and Marie Laveau, the infamous voodoo queen of New Orleans. Her tomb is marked with red brick-dust x's and is the site of frequent offerings from tourists as well as practitioners in the city, where voodoo is an important element in the present (and, most likely, the future) as well as the past.

New Orleanians—native or adopted—know that their city is different than any other in the country. That's why they're here. "Imagine growing up in a place like this," writes Jeanette Hardy in the *Times-Picayune* guidebook, "this repository of crumbly bricks, filigreed ironwork, fancy columns, and the legends about them that make history walk and talk in the mind. This is the rich world in which New Orleanians pass their lives. This is what gives them their sturdy sense of place." ◆

The clanging of the streetcar as it winds its way from Canal Street up to St. Charles and onto Carrollton Avenue, past shotguns and mansions, adds much to the New Orleans architectural ambiance. Itself on the National Register of Historic Places, the streetcar is the oldest continuously operating street railway system in existence. Photo by Jackson Hill/Southern Lights Studio.

statuary. Both nature and tradition are responsible for the custom. With a water table barely a foot below the surface, New Orleans just isn't the right place for below-ground burials. In early days, bodies tended to float up, though the introduction of effective drainage methods in the early twentieth century solved that problem. In addition, above-ground burial was the custom in eighteenth and nineteenth century Europe, and the French and Spanish settlers in New Orleans followed those dictates.

There are 42 cemeteries in the metropolitan New Orleans area. One of the most dramatic is Metairie Cemetery, established in 1872 on the 150-acre site of a former race track. Among its more than 7,000 tombs are edifices featuring a pyramid with a sphinx, a Temple of Nike, and a dog with a marble tear falling from its eye. Then there's the 60-foot-shaft

Naturally New Orleans

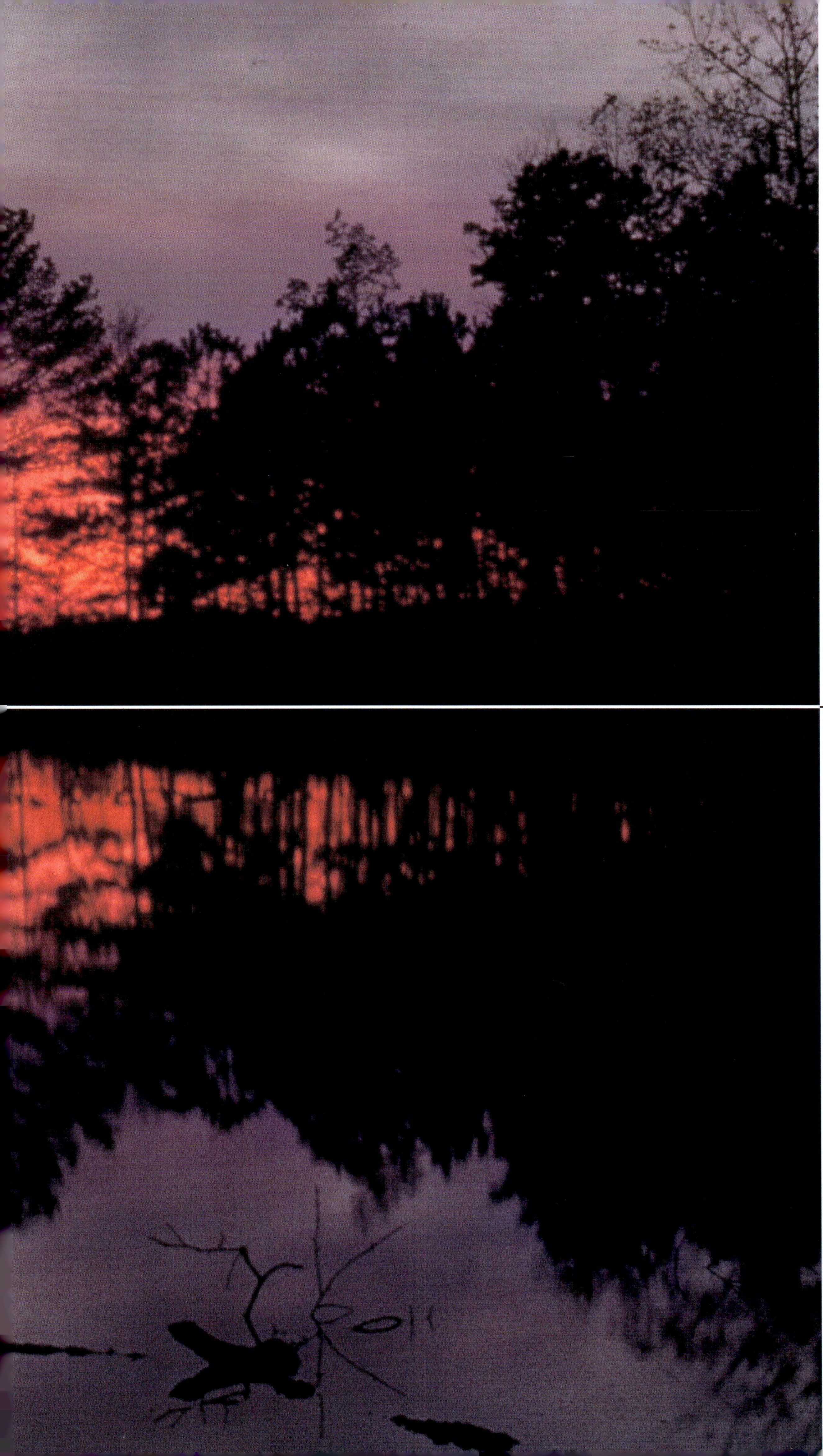

CHAPTER 10

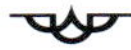

The sunsets over Lake Pontchartrain are among the natural gifts that enrich everyday life in New Orleans. Photo by Jackson Hill/ Southern Lights Studio.

Lagniappe: A much–used New Orleans term for a little something extra. There's a lot of lagniappe in this city.

That little something extra that makes living in New Orleans different—and more entertaining— than life in some other places extends to our vast array of recreational resources in sports, parks, and the natural environment.

It's the excitement of a Saints NFL football game or a Rolling Stones concert in the monumental Superdome. It's the soft thump of bat and ball connecting in the swing of a six-year-old Little League player, to the relieved cheers of parents and friends. It's the opportunity to relax quietly in our parks in the midst of the distinctive natural life of the area—alligators and live oak trees, herons and bayous—or to drop a fishing line and catch dinner. It's the chance to show out-of-town friends a slice of life gone by in the stately plantation homes that jostle for space with oil companies and grain elevators along the banks of the Mississippi River just outside the city.

The distinctive profile of the Louisiana Superdome highlights the skyline of the city, and the enthusiasm contained within its walls for hundreds of major events each year could probably power New Orleans. With a capacity of 85,000 people for festivals and 76,791 in expanded football seating, the Superdome itself covers 13 acres and is located on a 52-acre site that has revitalized the Poydras Street corridor, the heart of the downtown office district. It has hosted an incredibly wide variety of visitors, ranging from the Rolling Stones to Pope John Paul II, from the 1988 Republican Convention to the 1996 world premiere of Disney's animated movie *The Hunchback of Notre Dame*. It is the site of the biggest indoor concert crowd in history (87,500 for the Stones in 1981), the biggest charitable event (12,000-plus playing Bingo for the Lions Eye and Ear Hospital Fund) and the largest single session and total attendance at a political convention (1988 Republican National Convention).

Super Bowl XXXI comes to the stadium in 1997. It's the eighth Super Bowl to be played in New Orleans, a record for any city, and the fifth to take place in the Superdome. Before then, more than $20 million will be spent on renovations, including new movable seating and improvements to meeting rooms and concession stands. Other sports highlights include the Bayou Classic, pitting Grambling University against its arch-rival Southern University every Thanksgiving weekend; the NOKIA Sugar Bowl Classic, which is slated to host the national collegiate football championship game in 1997; and periodic visits from the men's and women's NCAA Final Four or regional tournaments. Many of these events have been attracted with the help of the Greater New Orleans Sports Foundation.

Extravaganzas hosted by the arena draw national attention to New Orleans. And the building itself, an engineering tour de force, gets its share. The Superdome is one of the top sightseeing attractions in the South, with an annual attendance of more than 75,000 for its daily tours.

The Dome is home to the New Orleans Saints, the city's professional football team, and the Tulane Green Wave footballers. In 1994-95, 1,372,770 people went through the turnstiles at the Superdome, more than 60 percent of them to attend sports events. Over 560,000 fans went to pro football games, while 191,000 cheered on college football and some 64,000 came to high school games. Almost 26,000 people enjoyed basketball and nearly 20,000 attended baseball.

A prime concert, entertainment, and convention venue as well as a sports arena, the Superdome in 1994-95 played host to more than 140,000 music-lovers, over 300,000 people who came for family shows like Barnum & Bailey Circus and the Kids Fair & Expo, and almost 65,000 convention attendees. In its 20-year life, the arena has had a total economic impact of more than $4.5 billion. "There was a great deal of controversy about spending $165 million to build a dome in 1975," writes Dr. Timothy P. Ryan, University of New Orleans business school dean who conducted an economic impact survey of the stadium. "In a one-week period in 1990 during the Super Bowl, more than that—$237 million, to be exact—was brought into the city of New Orleans to support local business, pay salaries, and create tax revenues. It is hard to imagine a better return on investment."

In 1993, the state legislature appropriated $215 million for sports development, including the money for Dome renovations, $84 million for a new sports arena behind the Superdome, to house Tulane basketball and potential pro teams in hockey, basketball, and boxing, as well as a concert venue; $6 million for renovations to the Saints training camp; and $7 million for an Olympic Volleyball Training Center at Bayou Segnette State Park.

An additional $20 million is slated for a 15,000-seat stadium in Jefferson Parish to be the new home of the New Orleans Zephyrs, the city's minor league baseball team. Only one step below the major leagues, the team is the AAA baseball club for the Houston Astros.

College sports also keep fans excited. Tulane Green Wave teams are Division I-A of the NCAA, with football, baseball, men's basketball, and women's basketball, in particular, each having a loyal contingent of supporters. The UNO Privateers keep the hoops hopping and the bats slamming on the lakefront campus. Xavier, Loyola, and Dillard universities also field competitive intercollegiate teams. High school sports, Little League, and programs sponsored by the New Orleans Recreation Department mean virtually every night of the year some sort of team is playing some sort of competitive game somewhere in the Greater New Orleans region.

The Superdome and its sports offerings anchor one end of Poydras Street; the other end opens to a sweeping view of the Mississippi River from the balconies of Riverwalk shopping center, on the site of the 1984 World's Fair. In the 1980s, New Orleans stopped turning her back on the river that was the reason for the city's founding and opened her heart to its charms. It's a dramatic environmental change. From the Convention Center; from the Aquarium of the Americas, its plaza, and the adjacent Woldenberg Park; from the Moonwalk near Jackson Square; from the Riverview area of Audubon Park; and from many hotels and high-rise office buildings in the city—the mighty Mississippi and its endlessly fascinating traffic are again a focal point for urban attention.

New Orleanians have also been paying a little extra attention to their distinctive natural environment, cleaning and restoring some of the treasures that nature has bestowed on the city. Lake Pontchartrain is cleaner than it

The Superdome is home to the New Orleans Saints, the city's professional football team. Photo by Jerry Ward.

A *magnificent annual display of holiday lights and ornaments called Celebration in the Oaks attracted 400,000 people to City Park in 1995. Photo by Jackson Hill/Southern Lights Studio*

has been in decades, though swimming is still off-limits.
Every January, discarded Christmas trees are dumped wholesale into some of the most delicate marshlands, to help them
hold the line against further erosion. All parts of the area are
involved in recycling paper, plastic, aluminum, and glass.
The city's Parkway Partners program organizes businesses,
schools, and volunteer groups to befriend New Orleans
neutral grounds (median strips to the rest of the world). The
Partners also sponsor community gardens, which help build
New Orleans neighborhood spirit while they yield delicious
produce for individual consumption or sale at the weekly
Cresent City Farmers' Market.

Green is a point of pride in New Orleans, thanks in part
to its impressive parks. The city was ranked the sixth green-
est metropolitan area in the country by the 1994 Metro
Green Index, a survey based on eight environmental criteria.

City Park, a former sugar plantation with more than 1,500
acres, is the fifth largest urban park in the U.S. It is home to
more than 22,000 live oak trees, the largest collection of
mature live oaks in the world, and it operates the largest

*The red-and-gold cars of the Riverfront streetcar line link Canal Street with
Esplanade, as they clang along the edge of the French Quarter.
Photo by Jackson Hill/Southern Lights Studio.*

*(following page) City Park is home to more than 22,000 live oak trees,
the largest collection of mature live oaks in the world. Photo by
Jackson Hill/Southern Lights Studio.*

Jackson Square in a rare quit moment. The park, in the heart of the French Quarter, is surrounded by street entertainers such as jugglers, clowns, magicians, balloon artists, musicians, and the many artists who set up their easels on the sidewalk and render instant portraits of passing tourists. Photo by Jackson Hill/Southern Lights Studio.

Magazine Street—the Street of Dreams— features art, antiques, bookstores, coffee bars, and fine restaurants. Photo by Jackson Hill/Southern Lights Studio.

municipal tennis and golf facilities in the South. In the last 10 years, City Park has undergone a major revitalization, developing a showpiece botanical garden, a new Pavilion of Two Sisters in the botanical garden designed to house receptions and special events, a magnificent annual display of holiday lights and ornaments called Celebration in the Oaks, which attracted 400,000 people in 1995, a 700-variety orchid collection, and a renovated nineteenth century carousel. The New Orleans Museum of Art, at the entrance to City Park, has also dramatically enlarged its space. The park is a virtual Art Deco monument, thanks to the sculptures of New Orleans artist Enrique Alferez and the bridges and structures built by the Works Progress Administration in the 1930s. It also contains popular golf courses and two stadiums—Pan American and Tad Gormley, the site of the 1992 Olympic Track and Field tryouts. Storyland in City Park, a children's fairy tale theme area featuring 26 larger-than-life exhibits, was recently rated as one of the nation's 10 best playgrounds by *Child* magazine.

The 385-acre Audubon Park, on the streetcar line across from Tulane and Loyola universities, is home to the renowned Audubon Zoo. It was founded on the site of the World Industrial and Cotton Exposition of 1884. The front of the park, on St. Charles Avenue, is a popular place for the walkers, joggers, skaters, and bikers who move at varying speeds under the shade of the live oak trees at virtually every hour of the day, past picnickers, frisbee throwers, sunbathers, and the cacophony of ducks and birds who inhabit the lagoon and its islands. There's also a golf course and a tropical plant conservatory. The middle part of the park, facing Magazine Street, houses the zoo. The back area, between the zoo and the river, has athletic fields and a spectacular view of the Mississippi. A favorite attraction is the ZooCruise, which runs from the zoo to the aquarium downtown, giving riders an up-close view of the river at work.

When the ZooCruisers disembark, they are on the borders of Woldenberg Park, a linear green space along the river beside the Aquarium of the Americas. In addition to a fine view of the water, the park features colorful sculpture, a bandstand with frequent concerts, the occasional festival, and the Monument to Children, erected by the New Orleans Council for Young Children in 1996.

In addition to Audubon Park, the zoo, the aquarium, and Woldenberg Park, the Audubon Institute also operates the Louisiana Nature Center in eastern New Orleans. Its 86 acres include woods, wilderness, wetlands, trails, a natural history museum, a planetarium, and the Judith W. Freeman Astronomy Center.

The 31-acre Louis Armstrong Park, just outside the French Quarter, is named for the famous jazzman who was a native son. It encompasses Congo Square, a Sunday gathering place for slaves in the eighteenth and nineteenth centuries and the fount of some of the music that inspired jazz; and the Black Music Hall of Fame and Museum, as well as WWOZ, a community radio station devoted to New Orleans music. Plans for further development are scheduled to be unveiled soon.

Jean Lafitte National Historical Park in Barataria, about half an hour from downtown New Orleans, is a coastal wetlands preserve with hardwood forests, cypress swamps,

and freshwater marshes. It offers a variety of distinctive
Louisiana flora and fauna, including alligators, wild iris,
herons, and muskrats. The park is also a center for studying
the history and culture of the region. Jean Lafitte National
Historical Park has a branch in the French Quarter, with a
folklife and visitor center and tours to introduce New Orleans
culture to visitors. The third branch, in Chalmette, preserves
the 164-acre battlefield where American forces, led by
Andrew Jackson defeated the British in 1815 at the Battle
of New Orleans.

Five state parks are located in the greater New Orleans
region, including Fairview/Riverside in Madisonville,
Fontainebleau in Mandeville, Bayou Segnette in Westwego,
St. Bernard in Violet, and Grand Isle State Park in the town
of Grand Isle. Lafreniere Park, while not a state park, is a
popular recreation, festival, sports, and concert spot in
Jefferson Parish.

Plenty of opportunity for driving tours to plantations
and bayous, swamp tours, and plain old good fishing and
hunting—not to mention water sports—lies just outside the
city in every direction. Weekend escapes to a fishing camp
or a duck blind or a Greek Revival bed and breakfast help
sustain and renew the energy, flexibility and creativity that
New Orleanians just naturally draw on to power the
region's renaissance. ◆

*The numerous parks in New Orleans are
a popular place for the walkers, joggers,
skaters, and bikers who move at varying
speeds under the shade of the live oak trees
at virtually every hour of the day.
Photo by Jackson Hill/Southern
Lights Studio.*

*Jean Lafitte National Historical Park in Barataria, about half an hour from downtown New Orleans, is a coastal wetlands preserve with hardwood forests,
cypress swamps, and freshwater marshes. Photo by Jackson Hill/Southern Lights Studio.*

Our Recipe for the 21st Century

New Orleans is a city that

knows how to survive, adapt, and

flourish. It's been true for almost

300 years—and those historically

proven skills will carry us into a

successful 21st century renaissance.

The seeds for growth are already in place. More industries than ever—technology, information services, textiles and garments, chemicals and plastics, medical devices, and other areas—are taking a hard look at the competitive advantages the New Orleans region offers. Then they're choosing to move here, providing jobs for our residents. Our strong infrastructure in health care and higher education is part of the attraction. So are our thriving port, our proximity to Latin America, our ethnic diversity, and progressive changes in state and local government policies. More visitors than ever come to New Orleans for work and for play. Like our residents, they enjoy a distinctive culture—food, art, music, festivals, architecture, traditions, people—that no other city in America can match.

Perhaps the best metaphor for such a diverse, flavorful, nourishing city is a gumbo. It's the metaphor used by more than 100 representatives of the region in 1996, when New Orleans was a winner of a coveted All-American City and Community Award. They came up with the recipe for the New Orleans difference—the spirit that nurtures our sparkling renaissance.

Creating The Spirit of New Orleans—A Prize-Winning Recipe from a City Famous for Its Flavors

◆ Start with a group of **diverse people**,
community activists and citizens willing to work together to solve the varied problems of a region that's about 33 percent African-American and 60 percent white, with significant Hispanic and Asian-American populations, as well.

◆ Add a generous scoop of **imagination**
to visualize what the city can be when we address its needs.

◆ Throw in a pinch of **ingenuity**,
for a city built on a swamp that has addressed problems creatively for almost three centuries.

◆ Mix with lots of **initiative**,
to help build coalitions, energize civic activists, bounce back in the face of challenges, and focus on solutions that will work in the real world.

◆ Stir in **innovation**
in raising friends and funds to carry out our plans.

◆ Season with **inspiration**,
the deep spirituality that underlies so much of the energy for change in the region.

◆ Whip up **involvement**,
of 2,500 civic and business groups and hundreds of thousands of people at every level of every community, in organizations that span the block or encompass the region—people of all backgrounds, ethnic and economic, who love New Orleans and will not give up until we have made her a better place.

◆ Carefully measure out **impact**,
to make sure that efforts are effective in addressing specified projects and that outcomes are visible and concrete.

◆ Fold together and marinate in a seven-parish region.

For best results, taste daily. Serves 1.5 million.

Visitors and residents alike love the distinctive New Orleans flavor—that mix of energy, caring, focus, and *joie de vie*. It's a recipe—and a revitalization—unmatched anywhere in the world.

LYKES
CANAL PLACE

New Orleans' Enterprises

The Marketplace
RIVERW
MARKETPLACE
FESTIVAL ON THE MISSISSIPPI

Louisiana
TOMAT

Creole
OES

In almost rhymthic tandem with a bustling slice of downtown New Orleans, the DoubleTree Hotel glows at night across a skyline altered by progress.

"We really are in the kind of location where a great deal of recent development activity has occurred," says Robert (Tico) Bevier, CHA, general manager of the DoubleTree. "And it has taken place during the same time that our hotel has undergone extensive renovations."

Since the late 1980s, the immediate vicinity surrounding the DoubleTree has seen the expansion of the massive and much-used Morial Convention Center; the opening of the $40 million Aquarium of the Americas, with more than 10,000 fish from all over the Americas; and the building of the airy 16-acre Woldenberg Riverfront Park adjacent to the aquarium.

The hotel's International Ballroom, at 5,500 square feet, offers an elegant setting for up to 700 people on the DoubleTree's sixteenth floor, which looks out over the sweeping vista of the nearby Mississippi River and the ancient rooftops of the French Quarter below.

But the DoubleTree, since taking over management, in 1986, has become even equally regarded for what, as well as where, it is. With 363 guest rooms, including twelve suites, and over 20,000 square feet of flexible meeting space, the DoubleTree is today one of the city's most popular convention and business group destinations, scoring an occupancy rate that has been over the 76 percent mark for the past two years.

"Our hotel is about 60 percent group-driven," explains Kevin G. Wooldridge, director of sales and marketing with the DoubleTree, "and 60 percent of that number are people coming here from other parts of the country for conventions, while the remaining 40 percent is composed of local or in-house business groups."

Among those in recent years who have called the DoubleTree home are the U.S. Tennis Association, the Motorola Corporation, the American Dental Association, and the American College of Cardiology.

One of more than 100 DoubleTree hotels across the country, the DoubleTree in New Orleans, at 300 Canal Street, is located at the former site of the International Hotel, which opened in the mid-1970s. Upon becoming the DoubleTree in 1986, the hotel began extensive renovations that have averaged about $500,000 a year. They adroitly converted an unused cavernous two-story lobby space into some additional 3,000 square feet of prefunction space, and then started in on the rooms. Indeed, Wooldridge estimates that the hotel annually redecorates at least 75 rooms.

The ultimate effect complements the hotel's modern, sleek design with the latest interior decorations in furniture, carpeting, and drapes. But even such amenities as the rooms' ironing boards and coffeemakers are also regularly replaced, helping to account, altogether, for the more than $13 million the DoubleTree has spent on its ongoing renovations during the past decade.

With a staff of more than 220 people, the DoubleTree emphasizes the small details that can later loom large in memory: free freshly baked chocolate chip cookies for a guest's first night and a guarantee that breakfast is served hot and quick—in less than 5 minutes—or it's free.

Further luxuries include the hotel's Chicory Rotisserie and Grill, which features the type food Louisiana is known for around the world, and the Chicory Lounge, with the kind of drinks that can only be mixed in New Orleans.

The hotel's International Ballroom, meanwhile, offers an elegant setting for up to 700 people on the DoubleTree's sixteenth floor, which looks out over the sweeping vista of the nearby Mississippi River and the ancient rooftops of the French Quarter below.

But the hotel's singular strength remains its business and convention facilities that include nearly twenty meeting spaces of varying sizes, including the International Ballroom at 5,500 square feet, the Crescent Ballroom at 2,385 square feet, and the Madewood Room with 2,380 square feet.

The DoubleTree also offers an audio visual service that includes projectors, monitors, microphones, computer displays, and large screens, all an integral part of any contemporary conference.

"The convention-goer and the business groups remain as one of our principal target groups, which is why so much of our hotel space is geared towards them," explains Wooldridge. The hotel has also provided the hospitality for larger conventions, such as the National Association of Television and Program Executives, which frequently meets at the nearby Morial Convention Center.

The attention to marketing and customer satisfaction has paid off for the DoubleTree. In the past five years the hotel's gross operating profit has increased steadily to the point where it has become number one out of the more

than 100 hotels that the DoubleTree Hotels Corporation manages nationally. Not incidentally, the hotel company itself, purchased two years ago by baseball commissioner Peter V. Ueberroth, is today the sixth largest hotel company in the world.

And because New Orleans is now rated as one of the top three cities in the country as both a convention and tourist destination, the DoubleTree only expects to grow. "The larger national company is right now growing very quickly," explains Wooldridge, "but so is our own hotel locally, which makes for a very exciting environment for all of us to work in."

Since becoming the DoubleTree, the hotel has also strived to increase and improve the recreational attractions that are today required and expected by guests. Besides a spacious outdoor fourth-floor swimming pool—perfect for the bountiful sun that visits New Orleans most of the year—the DoubleTree also provides a complimentary fitness center with Stairmaster, treadmill, and Universal station equipment on the third floor.

Rates at the DoubleTree vary upon seasonal availability—during the month-long carnival season surrounding Mardi Grass, for example, prices across the city increase. But rates at the DoubleTree generally range between $129 and $210 for guest rooms. For the larger suites, prices range between $250 and $350, all the way up to $2500 for the exquisite 2,200 square-foot Penthouse Suite, which offers, among other treats, a piano, fireplace, and panoramic view of the city.

With 363 guest rooms, including twelve suites, and over 20,000 square feet of flexible meeting space, the DoubleTree, at 300 Canal Street, is today one of the city's most popular convention and business group destinations.

Those rates, coupled with the DoubleTree's strategic marketing, has pushed the hotel's occupancy rate past the overall city average of 72 percent. In 1994, the DoubleTree led New Orleans with one of the highest occupancy rate at 80 percent. In 1995, the rate was only marginally smaller, but nonetheless vibrant, at 77 percent.

And sales director Wooldridge says he expects more of the same in the immediate years to come. "We are fortunate as a hotel in that we know where our customer base is and how to cultivate them to visit us," he says. "Now our primary task is to make sure they are satisfied when they stay here." ◆

It should come as no surprise that the Hotel Inter-Continental New Orleans, housed in a stylish steel, granite, and chrome structure near the downtown corridor of Poydras Street, which is heavily populated with some of the city's most powerful oil and gas and law firms, gets most of its business from those same companies.

"We have purposely sought them out," says Leland Lewis, general manager. "For the past five years our goal has been to increase and make permanent our market share of the business group and local corporate markets, and I think we are all proud to say we've done it."

Indeed, today the hotel gets at least 60 percent of its occupancy from the local corporate sector as well as the national association market, playing host in any given year to such professional organizations and groups as the American Heart Association, the Pittsburgh Conference,

The Hotel Inter–Continental's location at 444 St. Charles Avenue, in the midst of the dense Central Business District on the city's famous streetcar line, has 482 guest rooms including 25 plush suites.

Stairs and escalators lead from the ground level to a spacious second–floor lobby with indirect lighting, potted palms and displays of modern art. The mahogany wood panels and marble floors and panels accentuate the hotel's sleek elegance.

Computer Associates International, Inc., the Eli Lilly Company, Pan American Life Insurance Company, and Tulane University's Continuing Education Program—an annual conference series bringing together heavyweight regional education, law, and business interests.

Hotel Inter-Continental's location at 444 St. Charles Avenue, in the midst of the dense Central Business District on the city's famous streetcar line, gives it an undeniable aesthetic quality that is buttressed by the flowing fountains and multilingual staff members greeting visitors upon entering the fifteen-story building. The hotel's real attraction for business remains the facility itself.

Opened in 1984 on the site of the Old St. Charles Theatre, which in the 18th century was said to compare as a premiere opera house with its counterparts of the day in Milan and Vienna, the Hotel Inter-Continental has 482 guest rooms, including 25 plush suites. On its fourteenth floor, otherwise known as the Governor's Floor, are 28 deluxe guest rooms and six luxurious suites, including two of the hotel's six unique environmental rooms offering special water and air filtration systems.

But for convention and business group visitors, the hotel's greatest feature is its meeting capabilities.

"We have two entire floors of meeting space," says Lewis. "There is enough room on these floors for any reasonably sized business group or conference." The hotel's 21 designated rooms include the Executive Conference Center, built in 1988 and housed in the adjacent Pan American Life Insurance Building. It is uniquely joined to the hotel by a ground-level atrium and has a maximum seating capacity of more than 240.

The hotel's sterling meeting room showcase, however, is its third-floor Grand Ballroom, an 8,330-square-foot space overlooking St. Charles Avenue that has seen the likes of governors, U.S. senators, and captains of major U.S. industries.

Owned jointly by the Pan American Life Insurance Company and the Inter-Continental Hotels Corporation, headquartered in London, Hotel Inter-Continental New Orleans is one of more than 175 properties spanning some 47 countries around the globe.

With nearly 300 employees and room rates that range from $180 to $2,000, depending upon seasonal availability and room size, the hotel is not, continues Lewis, "one of the largest hotels in New Orleans or hotel networks in the U.S. But we have tried to position ourselves as the leading first-class hotel company in the country."

To that end, the Hotel Inter-Continental is smartly supported by its Veranda restaurant, a place of dining variety on the second floor, where the cuisine includes a melange of European, Creole, and American dishes, winning the restaurant a long list of prestigious industry awards. There is also the lunch-oriented Pete's, on the hotel's ground level, where casual attire mixes nicely with a New Orleans of the 1900s motif. The food offerings run from salads to nouveau pizzas bearing the names of the Buffalo Chicken and the Crescent City, to name just two.

The hotel's Lobby Lounge offers live jazz from Wednesday to Saturday evenings, and also serves drinks, sandwiches, and snacks.

With the hurried and frequently harried meeting traveler in mind, the Hotel Inter-Continental also offers the SweetCar, located on the ground floor of the building. It offers an imaginative array of homemade pastries, cakes, freshly baked bread, coffees, and light meals for quick-moving visitors.

Other hotel amenities include a rooftop swimming pool open daily from 7 a.m. to 10 p.m., which is, not incidentally, not far removed from the herb and spice garden the hotel's Veranda restaurant maintains. On the fifteenth floor is the fitness center, complete with Lifecycles, treadmills, free weights, and a universal weight machine. The hotel also offers a wide variety of in-house guest services, harkening back to the classic big-city hotels of tradition. They include a hair and beauty salon, shoeshine service, valet parking, laundry facility, and business center complete with fax machines and computer terminals.

The sum of Hotel Inter-Continental's many parts sometime seems to exceed its whole. Harder to qualify is the hotel's breezy elegance, nicely represented by the warm mahogany-paneled wall space making up much of the Grand Ballroom, various corridors, and second floor reception area.

A fifth-floor courtyard sprouting an unexpected mosaic garden bloom and original wind sculptures adds to an atmosphere of both class and tranquility.

With an annual occupancy rate in the 70 percent range, Hotel Inter-Continental has found its niche, explains Lewis. "There are many different market segments a hotel today can cater to: the individual traveler, the leisure traveler, and

The Hotel Inter–Continental's sterling meeting room showcase is its third–floor Grand Ballroom, a 8,330–square–foot space overlooking St. Charles Avenue that has seen the likes of governors, U.S. senators, and captains of major U.S. industries.

the convention traveler," he said. "We, of course, welcome all of those here. But our niche has become the group market and the local corporate market."

Its placement adjacent to bustling Poydras Street, which leads in one direction to the mammoth Morial Convention Center or in the other direction to the Louisiana Superdome, is also a Hotel Inter-Continental asset. "We are right in the middle of many of the things people come to New Orleans for," says Lewis. "And that, as it turns out, is good for all of us." ◆

The Windsor Court Hotel

English tea is delicately served each afternoon at the hotel, a ritual that somehow seems all the more appropriate given the presence of the many exquisite oil paintings created by such royal artists as Reynolds, Huysman, and Gainsborough.

Like an improbable Westerner in a distinctly Latin culture, the Windsor Court Hotel of New Orleans, with its magisterial ties to England of olde, distinguishes itself in a city bathed in the culinary and musical cultures of the Mediterranean, Africa, and Latin America.

"It is true, we are different. We have a strong investment in tradition and custom," explains John A. Cardona, director of sales and marketing at the Windsor Court, which was opened in the spring of 1984 by James J. Coleman, Jr. of the prominent family of New Orleans. "Mr. Coleman for years wanted to build a deluxe residential-style property in the city," Cardona continues. "But it wasn't until he opened the Windsor Court that he got what he had dreamed of."

Indeed, from it's inception, the Windsor Court has visually attracted attention, standing out in the otherwise grey Central Business District skyline with it's rose-colored granite exterior, while it's interior has magically evoked a time and place from a distant, historic past.

The tradition of careful service, reminiscent of the classic English inns, is also seen in the professional demeanor of the roughly 500-member Windsor Court staff. "Everyday we have an operations meeting at 5 p.m. with the guest relations director, the maitre d', the front office manager, and the concierge, among others, and we go down the list of people expected to arrive that day," says Cardona.

The end result of such meetings is that when Dr. Simmons walks through the Windsor Court's front glass doors, he is not greeted by a bellman with the more generic salutation: "Welcome to the hotel," but instead confronts a bellman he knows, who remarks: "Welcome back, Dr. Simmons, it is nice to see you again."

Windsor Court's emphasis on such niceties has not gone without results: the hotel's occupancy rate for 1995 was 70 percent, a healthy figure in the industry, especially given that the average rate for a suite at the Windsor Court is nearly $350, compared with a citywide rate average of $130.

With meeting rooms bearing the titles of the Library, the Gallery, La Chinoiserie, and the Boardroom, and looking every bit as good as they sound, the Windsor Court is also unique by it's clientele: small business groups and the corporate traveler are the hotel's principal guests, while New Orleans social clubs, debutantes, and Mardi Gras balls receive special space and consideration in the Windsor Court's meeting facilities.

The hotel's furnishings represent rich themes going back to the seventeenth century and can be found in each of the Windsor Court's 319 accommodations.

English tea is delicately served each afternoon at the hotel, a ritual that somehow seems all the more appropriate given the presence of the many exquisite oil paintings created by such royal artists as Reynolds, Huysman, and Gainsborough. The hotel's furnishing's, meanwhile, represent rich themes dating back to the seventeenth century and can be found in each of the Windsor Court's 319 accommodations.

The hotel's famed Grill Room features an extensive menu steeped in the dishes of Africa, Asia, and India—indeed, the foods of the world. For that reason, among a plateful of others, the Windsor Court, owned by Sea Containers Ltd., was honored last year by Conde Nast Traveler Magazine as the number one hotel in America for 1995—one of the grandest tributes in the national hotel industry. ◆

Synonymous with the very latest in wireless communications, Radiofone offers the largest coverage area in the metro New Orleans area for paging and cellular telephone services.

The company traces its roots to 1921, when New Orleans husband and wife Thomas and Loretta Garvey founded the New Orleans Doctors' Exchange, the first telephone answering service in the city.

In 1958, two of their sons—Larry and Don—started a radio paging enterprise that featured the first beep paging service in New Orleans and the second in the United States. Radiofone was officially established in 1960, when a mobile telephone service was added to the already flourishing paging service.

When the company debuted, paging units worn by Radiofone customers weighed two pounds. Today, they weigh just over two ounces, and come in a variety of colors, shapes, and sizes.

Among other distinctions, Radiofone's paging service was the first in the country to allow beepers to be dialed from the telephone network (direct dial paging). In 1978, it was only the second paging service in the United States to offer a wide-area paging capability. Today, through a subsidiary company, Beepers Unlimited, Radiofone customers have access to paging services covering 18 states.

Radiofone was also a local and regional pioneer in cellular telephone service. In 1984, the company installed the first non-wireline cellular telephone system in the southeastern United States, out-engineering systems proposed by such companies as Western Union Telegraph Co. and Mid-America Cellular Systems.

Radiofone's cellular system was judged "superior"—the highest rating—by the Federal Communications Commission, which grants permits for cellular radio systems.

Radiofone's cellular operations offer uninterrupted cellular services from New Orleans to Baton Rouge, with an increased service range anticipated as cities complete cellular systems. Radiofone is equipped to handle hundreds of calls at any given moment—so there is never a wait for an available phone line. Every call is private, and even long-range calls suffer no loss of sound or clarity.

On the cellular equipment end, Radiofone customers can select from a variety of telephone styles and designs, including some as small as a wallet and as portable as a pager.

A staff of in-house engineers lead the cutting edge of technological developments in communications, assuring Radiofone consumers the best possible service and equipment on the market. Consequently, Radiofone carries only the four top product lines in the world in paging and cellular equipment.

Radiofone offers competitive prices for all its services and a sales staff ready to help clients tailor a plan to suit their specific communications needs, from the businessman or woman needing constant communication capabilities, to the homemaker, who may need cellular or paging services only occasionally.

Radiofone's 12 retail stores, located in a five-parish area, feature fully staffed customer service desks and the complete array of available equipment from which to choose. Their sales consultants can be called to the job site to make repairs or answer any service-related questions.

Locally owned and operated for nearly 40 years, Radiofone prides itself on being a tireless and responsive corporate citizen.

In 1995 alone, the company sponsored or co-sponsored 77 galas, 187 golf tournaments, 58 road races, 3 telethons, 77 fairs and festivals, and 41 public service announcements for nonprofit organizations.

Radiofone is also a participant in the national Life Page program, furnishing 350 pagers to area hospitals for use by individuals awaiting organ transplants. The company provides an additional 11 cellular phone banks, tents, and trailers to non-profit organizations for use during their functions.

Headquartered in Metairie, Radiofone and its 12 retail stores employ over 750 individuals from across the metro New Orleans area. Customer satisfaction on every transaction, whether a page, cellular call, or call for service, is the cornerstone of its operations. ◆

In a city thriving on social and business interactions Jennie McNeill Enterprises, L.L.C., is making magical meetings come true.

From their spaciously modern corporate offices on General Meyer Avenue, on the Westbank of New Orleans, Jennie McNeill, CMP and her staff daily create and coordinate conventions, sporting events, fund-raisers, and unique themed events that bring people together to enjoy delectable food, delightful entertainment, and the opportunity to make business contacts in a relaxed and stimulating atmosphere.

Considering the rave reviews that her company has received for its planning, coordination and execution of special events, it should come as no surprise that McNeill's client roster has included the American Bar Association, the Republican and Democratic Parties, and dozens of national and international businesses and corporations.

What does come as a surprise is Jennie McNeill's relative youth in the industry; the company began operations in 1994 after McNeill realized early successes organizing special charity and business events.

McNeill targets one event in particular as the catalyst for her career; in 1992 she organized a tennis tournament to benefit cancer research after her mother was diagnosed with breast cancer. Over the years having raised over $80,000.00, the expanded "Crescent City Tennis Cancer Classic" is now held annually among the open vistas of City Park.

The planned events coordinated and supervised down to their finest detail by Jennie McNeill and staff are as varied and numerous as the clients she serves. "I very much enjoy using my knowledge, contacts, and experience," states McNeill, "to create a memorable function that fulfills the needs of my client."

But McNeill, whose client base is nearly 90 percent out of the city, state, and country, has not limited her company to destination management services. She stresses openness, flexibility, and diversity, and has expanded her corporation to offer meeting planning services and a series of motivational seminars designed to increase corporate productivity through quality management, time management, and improvement of organizational skills.

In 1995 she completed her degree as a Certified Meeting Professional (CMP), a distinction shared by only one percent of meeting planners worldwide. Her talented and dedicated staff includes computer consultants, one based out of California; a director of meeting planning, who is also a CMP; a director of events and promotion; non-profits events staff, special events assistants and college interns.

As a member of the New Orleans Metropolitan Convention and Visitors Bureau, The Chamber (serving on both the Executive Committee and Education Council), Meeting Professionals International (serving as a faculty member and working to establish a Louisiana Chapter), American Society of Association Executives, Hotel Sales and Marketing Association, and Professional Convention Management Association, among many other business and professional organizations, McNeill is particularly well-positioned to respond to the special needs of her corporate and private clients.

And whether the event is a simple business seminar here in the United States or abroad, or an elaborate cocktail reception with a unique theme, McNeill's goal remains the same—to make it easy and elegant bringing people together. ◆

Jennie McNeill, CMP·and her staff daily create and coordinate conventions, sporting events, fund-raisers, and unique themed events that bring people together to enjoy delectable food, delightful entertainment, and the opportunity to make business contacts in a relaxed and stimulating atmosphere.

For over 155 years, royalty, presidents, and celebrities, along with the most discerning palates of New Orleans, have flocked to Antoine's restaurant to enjoy a world-class dining experience.

The Crescent City's most revered gastronomic institution, Antoine's is in its fifth generation of uninterrupted, family-operated service.

Founded in 1840 by Frenchman Antoine Alciatore and in its present location on St. Louis Street since 1868, the restaurant blends the best of the French dining tradition with Louisiana culinary excellence and ingenuity. Its present proprietor is Bernard R. Guste, the founder's great-great-grandson.

Antoine's most famous dish, Huîtres en Coquille à la Rockefeller—Oysters Rockefeller—was created in 1899 by Jules Alciatore, one of Antoine Alciatore's 18 children and the restaurant's second-generation proprietor. Oysters Rockefeller was named in reference to the richest American family in the world at the time due to the extreme richness of the oyster sauce.

Another popular dish, Pompano en Papillote—pompano baked in a paper bag with shrimp and lump crabmeat in a white wine sauce—was created by Jules Alciatore in honor of a visiting French balloonist. The guest was served fish around which a paper bag was fashioned to resemble an inflated gas balloon. More practically, the bag, which marked New Orleans' first use of that culinary technique, helped to retain the flavor of the fish while cooking.

The Antoine's menu is an à la carte listing of specialty items such as Crevettes Ravigote, Les escargots à la Bordelaise, Gumbo créole, Bisque de crevettes, Salade de légumes, Pommes de terre soufflées, Filet de truite Pontchartrain, Filet de bocuf nature with Marchand de vin sauce and Café brûlot diabolique—hot spiced coffee with brandy. When serving the latter, the restaurant's lights are dimmed so guests can enjoy the sight of blue flames leaping from the liqueur.

In addition to peerless cuisine, Antoine's has one of the finest wine cellars in the country, boasting a standing stock of 17,000 to 23,000 bottles, the oldest one dating from 1895.

Courteous service in a quaint, understated atmosphere is the restaurant's hallmark. Decorated simply, yet elegantly with paintings, old photographs, white-linen covered tables and solid tableware, there are no disturbing influences such as music, dancing, or garish art to detract from the dining experience.

Besides the main dining room, Antoine's has 15 other dining rooms available for banquets and parties of 2 to 200 guests. One is the 1840 Room, which is the original family dining room created to celebrate the 100th Anniversary of the restaurant. The room contains portraits of the founder and his wife. Another is the Rex Room, whose walls are adorned with Mardi Gras memorabilia.

Waiters, who are required to serve a ten-year apprenticeship before they are eligible to become waiters, take orders without the aid of paper and pencil. Many of the restaurant's staff of 130 have been with the restaurant for more than 20 years.

Another Antoine's tradition is its menu. Printed in French and English, and used at both luncheon and dinner, the same menu has been in use at the restaurant for over 100 years. ◆

Founded in 1840 by Frenchman Antoine Alciatore and in its present location on St. Louis Street since 1868, Antoine's restaurant blends the best of the French dining tradition with Louisiana culinary excellence and ingenuity.

Courteous service in a quaint, understated atmosphere is Antoine'e hallmark. The restaurant is decorated simply, yet elegantly with paintings, old photographs, white–linen covered tables, and solid tableware.

Since its 1995 opening, the New Orleans Courtyard by Marriott has offered business and leisure travelers an option they never had before: moderately priced accommodations in the heart of downtown New Orleans.

Conveniently located in the Central Business District on historic St. Charles Avenue, the 140-room-hotel is one block from the French Quarter, two blocks from Bourbon Street, and just minutes away from such attractions as the Aquarium of the Americas, the Ernest N. Morial Convention Center, and the Superdome.

Managed by Marriott International and owned by a partnership of local businessmen, the six-story New Orleans Courtyard is a re-creation of the old Verandah Hotel, which stood at the site from 1839-1855. The new hotel, which overlooks the St. Charles Avenue streetcar line, repeats its antecedent's ornate iron trellis balcony and Greek-Revival-style architecture.

The Courtyard family of hotels debuted in 1983 when Marriott International saw the need for moderately priced lodging designed around the special needs of business travelers. Clean and comfortable rooms, friendly service, and fast check-in and check-out were among their primary concerns, according to surveys.

The New Orleans Courtyard, now one of more than 300 of its kind in the United States and the United Kingdom, features such guest-room amenities as a large work desk, separate seating area with sofa bed, two telephones in each guest room, remote control television with cable programming including free HBO, CNN, and ESPN, complimentary in-room coffee maker and tea service, and shower with water massage.

The New Orleans Courtyard also boasts a whirlpool spa, mini-gym, guest laundry services, and dinner delivery from local restaurants. Its restaurant offers a large breakfast buffet seven mornings week, and its airy Streetcar Lounge features a full-service bar, complimentary bar snacks and a menu offering "a taste of Louisiana flavor," including hot seafood plates and po-boys sandwiches.

The New Orleans Courtyard also offers special in-house services that make it easy to conduct business at the hotel. There are two conference rooms accommodating groups of up to 50, convenient fax and copy services, and audiovisual and catering service upon request.

"Local businesses tell us the Courtyard concept is just what they were looking for," said New Orleans Courtyard General Manager Charles Glanding. "We offer virtually all the amenities you would expect from a luxury hotel without the costly overhead of a large, multi-departmental staff."

Upon entering the hotel's airy lobby, guests are greeted by a friendly desk staff that will personally assist them with anything from directions to baggage. The hotel's interior uses cast iron columns salvaged from the old hotel to punctuate the soaring, six-story atrium space that serves as the new hotel's "courtyard."

Membership in the Courtyard Club—the chain's frequent travel program—offers such perks as fax usage to anywhere in the United States, free accommodation for spouses when accompanied by a member, free local calls, and morning newspapers delivered to your door. Other services include express reservations, advance room requests and express check-in and check-out. Members accumulating 12 paid nights at any Courtyard hotel receive either a free-night certificate for future stays or 1,750 frequent flyer points on participating airline partners. ◆

The New Orleans Courtyard offers spacious rooms with a comfortable sitting area.

OPEN
COME ON IN'
BROWSERS
WELCOME

New Orleans' Waterways

CHAPTER 12

Bisso Towboat Company, Inc.

❦

A Dixieland band, a promenade of local civic and business leaders, and the panoramic backdrop of the sweeping Mississippi River helped usher in the christening of the *Scott T. Slatten*, a triple-screw 5,200 horsepower tugboat in the spring of 1995, much as it did the twin-screw, 3,600 horsepower *Allison S.*, the year before that, and the same-sized *Liz Alma* in 1991.

"And we've got another one in the making, scheduled for delivery in October 1996," says Scott Slatten, vice-president of operations for the Bisso Towboat Company, Inc., of New Orleans. "Business has been good for us in the past few years, and we're hoping it stays that way for many more years to come."

The tugs, which cost between \$2 and \$3 million to build, are painstakingly produced and crafted by the shipbuilders of the Main Iron Works Company in Houma, Louisiana, where it takes about 10 months to go from concept to completion on their way to the waters of the Mississippi.

Tug Liz Alma *assisting the 96,687 DWT Tanker* Stena Concertina.
Photo by Jim Bonner.

Tug Scott T. Slatten *assisting the 84,395 DWT Tanker* Ventares *into repair berth.*
Photo by Jim Bonner.

Once there, they join a regular Bisso fleet of some 18 tugboats and 2 pushboats that mostly assist ships in and out of the massive grain, coal, and oil terminals along the river between the Gulf of Mexico and Baton Rouge.

"Everybody figures that all of the river work takes place right here in New Orleans," explains Slatten. "But that's a fallacy. I'd say that no more than 20 percent of our business is in the actual Port of New Orleans area. The rest is below and above the city, where the big oil, coal, and grain terminals and chemical plants operate."

Slatten should know: since 1890 his family's business, founded by the legendary Captain Joseph Bisso, and reorganized in the 1960's by Cecilia Bisso Slatten and Captain Billy Slatten, has been negotiating the river's waters, providing an essential tug service to several hundred regular clients.

Between Baton Rouge and the mouth of the Mississippi as it spills into the Gulf of Mexico are dozens of anchorage points for the always-working Bisso fleet in such places along the river's edge as Burnside, St. James, St. Rose, New Orleans, Myrtle Grove, and Empire, in the swampy state bottom.

"We contract with the shipowners and operators to provide them with a regular towing service for their ships when they come into the river," continues Slatten, "which means we have to be ready to do that work at any of a variety of locations up and down the river."

With more than 140 full-time employees, and representing agents across the globe in Great Britain, Norway, Germany, and Japan, the Bisso Towboat Company also provides a much-in-demand variety of derrick and lineman services, not to mention its busy barge operation.

Each of the intricate Bisso vessels are equipped with state-of-the-art navigational and radio communications systems that are operated on an around-the-clock basis. The company also offers floating derrick cranes with capacities of up to 60 tons.

Located at the end of Walnut Street, where the mostly tree-lined, historic uptown thoroughfare meets the Mississippi River, the Bisso company has also emphasized staying competitive within its industry, continuously modernizing and maintaining its growing fleet on a yearly basis, and becoming in the process one of the industry's growth leaders in the Deep Gulf South.

It is the Bisso tugboats, however, that have the greatest public profile as they travel on the water with their trademark yellow and black-striped stacks. And it is also the Bisso Towboat Company that frequently does the heavy lifting when, for example, the *Andros Chryssi*, the largest vessel to ever travel up the river came through the area, it was the Bisso Towboat Company that won the assignment to help maneuver the 1,100-foot-long, 282,883-ton oil-tanker through what can oftentimes be the treacherous bends and turns of the Mississippi River as the mighty tanker motored through.

Tugs Allison S. *and* Liz Alma *towing the dredge ship* Wheeler *stern first to the U.S. Army Corps of Engineers Dock. Photo by Jim Bonner.*

"We get a lot of big projects like that," continues Slatten, "and I think the reason for that is not only because we are the oldest operating tugboat service in this region, but also because we are the most reliable."

And that reliability factor, intangibly important in an industry where cargo can costs billions of dollars and whether or not it is delivered might determine the success or failure of any number of business enterprises, may be the central reason for Bisso's growth in the 1990's, a time that has seen an uneven economic performance for many other businesses in the local maritime industry.

"We've seen steady growth for the last four or five years now," says Slatten, "and we want to keep it that way. When you have explosive growth, it makes it that much harder to pay attention to all of the little details, which sometimes means you are not giving your customers the fullest possible service. That's not at all what we want to do."

With more than $10 million invested in a new construction program in the 1990s as part of its ongoing efforts to add to the Bisso fleet, the company is expecting future growth for the rest of the decade to remain steady-as-she-goes. "Our past and present have been good," says Slatten. "But the future, for us, looks even better." ◆

Tugs *Captain Joseph Bisso,* Bill S., *and* Captain Billy Slatten *turning the largest vessel ever to sail up the Mississippi River, the 1,100-foot-long, 287,416 DWT Tanker* Andros Chryssi. *Photo by Jim Bonner.*

International–Matex Tank Terminals

Shown left to right are James J. Coleman, Jr., chairman; James J. Coleman, founder; and Thomas B. Coleman, chief executive officer of International–Matex Tank Terminals. Photo by David Spielman.

From above, spanning along the river's edge, they look like so many mushrooms of varying sizes and color, a field of prehistorically large vegetation in neat uniform clusters.

On earth, the visual sensation is nothing if not stronger: along both the west and east banks of the Mississippi River, there are dozens of them; the steel-shrouded tanks of New Orleans' International-Matex Tank Terminals that daily store the fuels and fluids that make America grow.

"Our specialty is liquid logistics," says Thomas B. Coleman, IMTT's chief executive officer, from the company's corporate headquarters in New Orleans. "We store, blend, and throughput every imaginable liquid commodity from chemical and petroleum products to vegetable oils and fertilizers."

IMTT's customers range from the largest corporations in the world to small local distributors. The service they provide is evidenced by IMTT's mission statement "to exceed the expectations of our customers."

Founded by James J. Coleman, a well known attorney and civic leader, over 50 years ago in a small location in Avondale, Louisiana, with just 7 tanks, IMTT has now grown to be the nation's second largest terminal operation with close to 30,000,000 barrels of tankage and a staff of over 500. Their terminals serve the maritime gateways to North America: the St. Lawrence Seaway, New York Harbor, Chesapeake Bay, the Mississippi Valley, and the San Francisco Bay area. In addition to IMTT, the Coleman family runs myriad business ventures from hotels, office buildings, and parking to managing the U.S. Strategic Petroleum Reserve. ◆

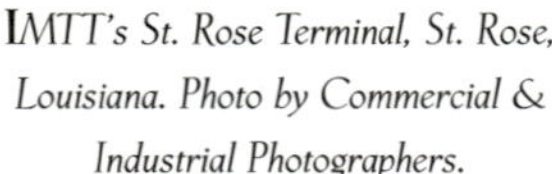

IMTT's St. Rose Terminal, St. Rose, Louisiana. Photo by Commercial & Industrial Photographers.

Cooper/T. Smith became more internationally competitive when it built floating derrick cranes. These cranes are the workhorses of the business and are used for heavy lifts and mid-stream operations.

Cooper/T. Smith Corporation is the parent company to one of America's oldest and largest stevedoring firms. The corporation, headquartered right here on the Gulf Coast, has offices in 38 ports and owns 37 satellite companies.

The roots of Cooper/T. Smith's stevedoring history run deep, reaching back to 1840 when Terrence J. Smith, a plucky Irish immigrant, created the New Orleans based company of T. Smith & Sons, the strongest stevedoring and tugboat company in the United States Gulf.

While Terrence Smith was developing his business in New Orleans, an industrious Scotsman named Angus Cooper was launching his own stevedoring enterprise. Thus was the beginning of three generations of strong, steady growth in a multifaceted maritime service company.

In 1983, T. Smith & Sons merged with Cooper Stevedoring Company to form Cooper/T. Smith Corporation, the parent company for a multitude of service companies that support the all encompassing maritime organization. Today the company is headed by sole owners Angus R. Cooper, II, chairman, and David J. Cooper, president.

Angus Cooper and David Cooper credit their success to the demanding requirements laid down by both their father and grandfather, who enforced a "roll up your sleeves" approach to stevedoring.

"In the summers during high school and college, David and I did everything imaginable on the docks," Angus Cooper II recalls then continues, "Our management style is hands-on. We believe in being out on the cranes and tugboats learning about things for ourselves."

David smiles and adds, "Our father felt it was important for us to work every long, dirty, painful job the company had. It was a great way to learn about the business—all first-hand. We learned what to expect—both from our equipment and our people—and we learned what our customer expects too."

The company became even more internationally competitive when it built floating derrick cranes. These cranes are the workhorses of the business and are used for heavy lifts and mid-stream operations. Industrial innovation such as this has established Cooper/T. Smith as one of the major stevedoring companies of the world.

Cooper/T. Smith has the equipment and ability to handle any type of cargo. Breakbulk materials like steel and aluminum, bulk products such as grain and coal, and containerized cargo are handled on all three coasts of the United States.

Today Cooper/T. Smith has grown from a small enterprise into a progressive, innovative, and multi-port corporation employing thousands. The 37 affiliate companies include warehousing, insurance, terminal operations, barge fleeting, push-boat operations, and floating terminals.

Cooper/T. Smith has earned international respect for its efficiency and expertise in working ships' cargo at both ocean ports and inland waterways. This respect is maintained by the leadership of Angus and David Cooper and their proven ability, imagination, attachment to the waterfront, and "hard hat" determination which has built Cooper/T. Smith into a major player in the worldwide maritime industry.

Crescent Towing

Crescent Towing has been a part of the New Orleans community for more than half a century. From the purchase of their first tug in 1942 to the custom design of the *Ervin S. Cooper,* they have enjoyed a well-earned reputation for superior service.

More than just a source of raw engine power, the strengths of Crescent Towing extend past the water's edge to include a superior performance and safety record, quality equipment, proficient captains and crews, plus highly-trained service and support operations.

In New Orleans, their 24-hour, 365-day-a-year services provide docking, undocking and towing, from the mouth of the Mississippi River to Baton Rouge, with additional vessels permanently stationed in the Industrial Canal.

Crescent Towing also operates tugs in the Ports of Mobile, Alabama, and Savannah, Georgia. ◆

The Margaret F. Cooper tugboat of Crescent Towing busy at work on the Mississippi River.

Intermarine, Inc.

Intermarine, Inc., is a world leader in the carriage of "project cargo"—typically heavy and cumbersome equipment associated with major construction projects, power generation plants, mining operations, oilfield development, chemical plants, and other industrial concerns.

Founded in 1990 by marine transportation veteran Roger Kavanaugh, Intermarine is headquartered on the 47th floor of One Shell Square in Downtown New Orleans. The world's fastest growing carrier of project cargo, the company's annual revenues now exceed $150 million, up from $5 million, its first full year of operation.

Since its founding, Intermarine has earned a reputation for performing time- and cost-efficient voyages of overdimensional, hard-to-handle equipment to all corners of the world. With most of its business focusing on deliveries to the north coast of South America, the Caribbean, and the Far East, the company logged 213 voyages in 1995, carrying nearly 2 million revenue tons of cargo.

Intermarine acts as the managing agent of two vessel operating companies—Industrial Maritime Carriers (USA), Inc., and Industrial Maritime Carriers (Bahamas), Inc.,—which together form one of the world's largest charterers of multipurpose vessels. Ships chartered by the companies range from small, 3,000-ton coaster vessels to 24,000-ton multipurpose heavy-lift ships.

Intermarine manages Industrial Maritime Carriers (USA) Americas service, which specializes in transporting project and liner cargoes from the United States and Mexico to Latin America and the Caribbean Islands. Boasting a minimum

An over dimensional project cargo loads onto an Industrial Maritime Carries, Inc. vessel in New Orleans.

of 15 sailings per month and service base ports of Houston, New Orleans, Point Lisas, Guanta, Maracaibo, Puerto Cabello, Santa Marta, Cartagena and Barranquilla, Intermarine is the leading carrier of breakbulk, containerized and project cargoes to the area.

Intermarine manages Industrial Maritime Carriers (Bahamas) Pacific Rim service, which offers four to five sailings per month from the U.S. Gulf and East coasts to the Pacific Rim, an area comprising about 40 percent of the world's trade. Base ports are Houston, Philadelphia, Busan, Shanghai, Xingang, Dalian, Qingdao, Hong Kong, Manila, Singapore, Jakarta, Surabaya, Bangkok, Map Ta Phut and Laem Chabang. This service is also the leading carrier of project cargo in the trade.

Intermarine's quick ascent in the shipping world is largely credited to its expertise in safely and quickly transporting individual pieces of cargo as heavy as 650 metric tons and as long as 200 feet. In addition to heavy project equipment, the company is also a major carrier of resins, steel, forest products, containers, and a variety of general cargoes.

Flexibility and personal attention to clients' special needs are company hallmarks. Instead of confining customers to a rigid shipping schedule and a set fleet of vessels, Intermarine addresses their project cargo needs on a case-by-case basis. Upon learning of the cargo job at hand, Intermarine will find exactly the type of vessel to meet the specific need. If the vessel type is not available within Industrial's fleet of approximately 36 vessels, they will charter the appropriate vessel to accommodate the customer's schedule and technical needs. Once the cargo arrives at its port of call, Intermarine oftentimes arranges land-based or barge services to complete the movement to final destination, no matter how remote.

Intermarine employs about 70 individuals with 50 in its headquarters in New Orleans and 20 in Houston, its largest cargo load center. Industrial Maritime Carriers (USA and Bahamas) offers weekly sailings to the Caribbean, South America and the Far East and is the U.S. Gulf's largest and most frequent carrier of breakbulk, heavy-lift and general cargo. ◆

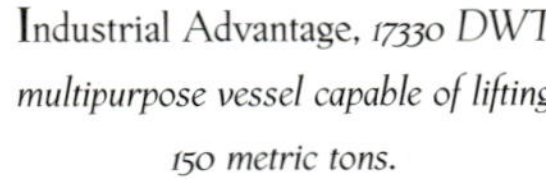

Industrial Advantage, 17330 DWT multipurpose vessel capable of lifting 150 metric tons.

Natural Resources

McDermott International, Inc.

Though it is today one of New Orleans' largest companies, with 23,000 employees in locations around the world, McDermott International, Inc., traces its heritage to the East Texas oil fields, where in 1923 R. Thomas McDermott received a contract to build 50 wooden drilling rigs for a wildcatter. McDermott, who was 24 years old, asked his father, J. Ray McDermott, to supervise construction of the rigs and named the company after him.

Over the years, the company established itself, first in Texas and later in South Louisiana, where in the late 1940s, oil and gas companies were exploring the potential of fields under the waters of the Gulf of Mexico. McDermott, which had floating equipment used in marshland development, helped the producers develop these fields by pioneering the construction and installation of platforms and pipelines, beginning in 1947 when the company installed its first offshore platform in 20 feet of water.

By the 1970s, offshore fields had become a primary source of hydrocarbons, and J. Ray McDermott & Co. was providing its services in every major offshore oil and gas province in the world. As the company realized greater

J. Ray McDermott, McDermott International's marine construction subsidiary, is a leader in development of deepwater oil and gas fields in the Gulf of Mexico. The company installed this platform for Shell in over 2,800 feet of water.

B&W brought McDermott other new product lines, such as environmental and boiler-cleaning equipment. It also brought McDermott the highly precise technologies required to manufacture nuclear products. Since the 1950s, B&W had been a leader in the development of nuclear power and an important part of the U.S. Navy's nuclear program. By the time it joined McDermott, B&W supplied products and services to the electrical power industry and other industries throughout the world.

The acquisition of B&W changed McDermott dramatically. To reflect both the diversification brought by its new products and its growing worldwide presence, J. Ray McDermott changed its name. In 1983, the company that had started out in the East Texas oilfields became McDermott International, Inc. Corporate headquarters continued to be located in New Orleans, as they had for some years, but the company had spread far beyond its Gulf of Mexico roots.

Over the next 12 years, McDermott continued to grow and diversify. In the early 1990s, it acquired Delta Catalytic Corporation, one of the largest engineering, procurement, construction, and maintenance companies in Canada. Delta Catalytic brought McDermott expertise in engineering of large-scale onshore industrial projects for oil and gas production, refining, and power generation; managing construction of these projects; and maintenance management of industrial facilities.

In 1995, McDermott International took a step forward by reaching back in its history. The company created a new subsidiary from its marine construction business and called it J. Ray McDermott, S.A., reviving the name the company first bore over 70 years earlier. The new company merged with Offshore Pipelines, Inc., a Houston-based company, to form one of the world's largest marine construction companies. In the Gulf of Mexico, where the original J. Ray McDermott installed its first platform in 20 feet of water, the new J. Ray

Babcock & Wilcox, a subsidiary of McDermott International, is one of the world's leading suppliers of power generation equipment to plants like this one near Orlando, Florida.

success, it expanded the role it played in the supply of the world's energy needs by the acquisition in 1978 of The Babcock & Wilcox Company. B&W traced its history to a partnership formed in 1867 by George Babcock and Stephen Wilcox, who in that year had patented a boiler design. The boiler was very successful and was the beginning of a line of equipment that played an important part in the electrification of the United States and the rest of the world.

A *molten sulphur carrier built by McDermott Shipyard in Morgan City, Louisiana.*

McDermott is today working in depths beyond 3,000 feet.

Including J. Ray McDermott, McDermott International operates in five units. Two of those units are made up from Babcock & Wilcox: the B&W Power Generation Group and the B&W Government Group. The B&W Power Generation Group builds and services equipment for utilities and industries. In the 1990s, the group has consistently been the leading supplier of power generation equipment to the world, relying on joint ventures in China, Indonesia, India, and Egypt to supply those growing markets. The group is also a major supplier of environmental equipment to U.S. and international utilities.

The B&W Government Group is the sole supplier of nuclear fuel and reactor components to the U.S. Naval Reactors Program, and it is establishing itself in other government and commercial markets. It is involved in the operation of a number of government-owned sites, including the Strategic Petroleum Reserve, which has sites throughout Louisiana and Texas.

The two other McDermott units, the Engineering and Construction Group, and the Shipbuilding and Industrial Group, capitalize on the company's existing expertise to expand its capabilities into new markets. Engineering and Construction includes Delta Catalytic, now called Delta Hudson, and oversees McDermott's operations in the former Soviet Union, which include an interest in an oil and gas development and joint ventures for onshore and offshore engineering and construction. The Shipbuilding and Industrial Group operates a bustling shipyard in Morgan City, Louisiana, and a yard in Vera Cruz, Mexico.

But the McDermott story contains more than buiness and technical success. It is also a story of community support. For years, McDermott has quietly supported the community, giving to civic causes, the arts, and education. The Audubon Zoo and the Aquarium of the Americas, the New Orleans Museum of Art, the Louisiana State Museum, the Louisiana Children's Museum and the planned National D-Day Museum have all benefitted from McDermott's support. As have local colleges and universities such as Tulane, Loyola, Xavier, and the University of New Orleans and local public schools. McDermott's support of these and other institutions and causes earned it the Business at its Best Award from The Chamber/New Orleans and the River Region in 1994.

In 1996, McDermott put its community support into more prominent view when it joined Freeport-McMoRan to sponsor the New Orleans stop on the PGA Tour. The Freeport•McDermott Classic draws thousands of people to the city each year and puts millions of dollars into the city's economy. But most importantly, it contributes hundreds of thousands of dollars each year to children's charities in the community.

Building on its long business history and record of community support, McDermott International is proud to be part of what makes New Orleans a great place to live and work. ◆

McDermott's offshore fabrication yard in Morgan City, Louisiana.

Shell Companies of Louisiana

❧

Shell companies have operated in Louisiana for over 70 years, both onshore and offshore. Today nearly 5,500 Shell employees are engaged in a wide range of business activities associated with finding, developing, and producing oil and gas, transporting these raw materials, converting them into transportation fuels and a wide range of petrochemical derivatives, and, finally, marketing gasoline and other light oils into both wholesale and retail markets. Over the years Shell has become the biggest producer of oil and gas in the Gulf of Mexico while conducting one of the most significant, state-of-the-art oil refining and chemical manufacturing operations in the state. Accompanying these business successes, Shell companies and employees have achieved an equally notable record of giving back to their communities.

Employees annually give thousands of hours of themselves to community projects that improve the quality of life where they live and raise their families. Much of this volunteer effort is organized under the Shell Employees and

At Shells' Norco Refining Company employees regularly transform up to 300,000 barrels of crude oil and feedstocks daily.

At Shells' Norco Refining Company employees regularly transform up to 300,000 barrels of crude oil and feedstocks daily into such products as heating oil, aviation fuel, and automotive gasoline. To do this, up to 6,000 railcars, 22,000 trucks, 1,700 barges, and some 100 oceangoing vessels transport Norco's products to locations around the world. The Norco facility uses enough water annually to meet the normal demands of about 100,000 homes. Its electrical needs would serve up to 40,000 homes while daily fuel usage would satisfy the needs of roughly 600,000 homes. The facility also provides the essential intermediate chemical derivatives needed to make tires, furniture, tennis shoes, plastic food containers, and many other items.

In the Gulf of Mexico, Shell Offshore, Inc., is the industry leader in oil and gas production. Activities in the Gulf account for about 40 percent of Shell's overall production of oil and gas. Its nearly 2,000 employees are responsible for the average daily production of about 175,000 barrels of crude oil and 1.2 billion cubic feet of natural gas. Shell has been operating since the late 1940's in the Gulf where it is the largest leaseholder with about 3.5 million acres presently under lease.

These unique achievements haven't been limited to Shell's business pursuits. While involved in numerous community programs, the Shell companies' and employees' most noteworthy involvement has been in their support for public education. Substantial company and employee resources have been channeled into area public schools over the years through participation in the Partners in Education

Shell employees participate in numerous educational activities in many schools throughout the state.

Retiree Volunteerism Effort (SERVE), United Way campaigns, Junior Achievement programs, and education outreach.

The Shell family in Louisiana includes Shell Offshore, Inc., Shell Pipe Line Corp., and major affiliates of Shell Oil Products Co., and Shell Chemical Co. with many facilities extending from New Orleans to Baton Rouge.

programs throughout the region. Shell companies have also helped pioneer the school-to-work initiative. This program puts area students and teachers directly into the workplace to keep classroom curriculum current with the needs of the workplace.

The Shell-sponsored "Say YES To A Youngster's Future" program is a National Urban Coalition program which focuses on female minorities emphasizing the sciences and mathematics.

The Louisiana Alliance for Education Reform project helps create a process within local communities to focus resources, influence, and action toward progressive school change. These partnerships are operational in several parishes with plans to expand to other parishes.

The River Parishes Education Initiatives program encourages parental and community involvement, promotes business/education partnerships, and supports school-to-work initiatives by effectively communicating with the community at large.

These are a few of the educational programs that the Shell companies and employees are actively involved and have a major impact.

The Shell companies and their employees are proud of their record of accomplishment in helping to improve the quality of life in their communities. The nearly eighty years of vigorous participation in this undertaking has made Shell an integral part of communities in which it operates. ◆

Shell's most involved ongoing community effort centers around the Partnership In Education (PIE) program, bringing together hundreds of Shell employees for such things as one-on-one tutoring and mentoring.

Shell Offshore's Auger Tension Leg Platform.

Texaco

The Star Shines Onshore And In The Gulf Of Mexico

One of the numerous companies that has come to symbolize the dynamic might and endurance of Louisiana's important oil and gas industry is Texaco, whose presence in the state since 1902 leaves it well positioned for growth into the next century.

Texaco's 1995 revenues surpassed $36 billion while production of oil and natural gas continued to increase for its New Orleans-based operations. Playing a major role in the rejuvenation of the entire industry, the 1,400 employees assigned to the onshore and offshore divisions of Texaco Exploration and Production Inc. (TEPI) successfully implemented a plan for growth.

Using three-dimensional seismic imaging (3-D) to explore mature fields in South Louisiana, Texaco more than doubled its drilling activity on state leases in 1995 alone. This new drilling produced more than 2 million barrels of oil and some 40 billion cubic feet of natural gas, not to mention the creation of hundreds of new jobs as a result of the increased activity. The state also benefitted in increased royalty, severance and sales tax payments while millions of dollars flowed to local governments.

In the deep blue waters of the Gulf of Mexico, Texaco has discovered oil and natural gas reserves once only imagined. Texaco has been able to visit these new ocean depths utilizing 3-D seismic and patented vertical cable seismic technology.

In 1995, Texaco drilled three rank wildcat wells in deepwater, which is defined as water depths of 1,300 feet or greater. All three were discoveries. The Petronius Prospect, drilled in 1,754 feet of water 130 miles southeast of New Orleans, has reserve estimates of approximately 100 million barrels of oil equivalent.

The Gemini Prospect, located 90 miles southeast of New Orleans in 3,393 feet of water, was drilled through a thick layer of salt before hitting hydrocarbon zones. Texaco's third discovery in deepwater, the Fuji Prospect, rests in nearly 4,000 feet of water 150 miles southwest of New Orleans. The exploratory well at Fuji established significant hydrocarbons and Texaco continues to explore other areas of the two dozen clustered leases that comprise the prospect.

This rig in 3,400 feet of water drilled Texaco's Gemini Prospect in 1995.

Texaco believes the new frontier of deepwater is just beginning and plans to increase its drilling activity offshore. At a recent offshore lease sale, Texaco added to its extensive portfolio when it successfully bid on 125 leases. These new leases, coupled with an exclusive contract for a deepwater drilling rig, well-position Texaco to conduct exploration and drilling activities in the vast Gulf for several years to come.

When Texaco's employees aren't searching for oil and gas, they are likely to be found volunteering to better their communities. At Texaco, volunteering *is* energy. Whether it's picking up trash on beaches, tutoring school children or planting trees on the city's neutral grounds, the "Shining Stars" at Texaco make a difference.

Texaco also provides needed funding for a host of educational, environmental, and civic projects. The company also has a rich history of contributing to arts and culture organizations, including the ballet, symphony, and opera.

With strong earnings and a superior workforce, Texaco is poised to enter the next century as vibrantly as it began the last. ◆

Texaco's "Shining Stars" volunteer their time for a variety of community projects, including this tree planting event at Cypress Island Preserve. Texaco donated the property to the Louisiana Nature Conservancy.

Employees at Star Enterprise's Louisiana Plant in Convent.

The Louisiana plant, which is very condensed by refining industry standards, occupies 600 acres and has a refining capacity of 225,000 barrels per day. In 1995, the Louisiana plant was recognized as a Star Worksite, the highest safety award granted by the Occupational, Safety, and Health Administration (OSHA) under its Voluntary Protection Program (VPP).

With the ability to be a major supplier of quality petroleum products, Star Enterprise and Texaco announced early in 1996 a new Global Brand Initiative, a worldwide marketing effort to capitalize on Texaco's legendary name and reputation. As part of the initiative, an exciting new design for Texaco outlets has been developed featuring brighter color schemes and completely redesigned food and fuel service areas.

Star Enterprise is also pursuing joint ventures with another industry that is automobile-driven: the national food industry. Such co-developers include McDonald's, Burger King, Blimpie's, Dunkin' Donuts, Baskin-Robbins, and Taco Bell, to just name a few, and will provide customers the added convenience of multiple services at selected gasoline retail facilities.

Highlighting these developments is Star Enterprise's decision to serve as the Official Petroleum Sponsor for the 1996 Summer Olympic Games and the Official Petroleum Supplier for the 1996 Olympic Torch Run.

With gasoline sales increasing at an average of 1.4 percent since the creation of Star Enterprise in 1989, current projections estimate that the company's future growth will continue, marked by the strong, steady performance that has already made Star Enterprise a major player in the industry. ◆

History was made when Star Enterprise was established in January 1, 1989. Its creation as a joint venture partnership between subsidiaries of Texaco, Inc., and Saudi Aramco was a bold move that significantly enhanced the energy interests of both companies. Under the terms of the partnership, Star Enterprise has access to 600,000 barrels per day of crude oil produced in Saudi Arabia, which ensures a dependable supply of oil for the company well into the 21st century.

With assets of more than $4 billion, Star Enterprise manufactures, distributes, and markets petroleum products under the Texaco brand name in 26 Eastern and Gulf Coast states, plus the District of Columbia. Headquartered in Houston, Star Enterprise's major assets include three refineries located in Convent, Louisiana; Delaware City, Delaware; and Port Arthur, Texas. Other assets include product distribution terminals and a distribution network of nearly 9,500 Texaco brand stations within the 26-state region. Together, these assets have generated over $47 billion in revenue between 1989 and 1995.

For its part, the Louisiana plant, located at the base of Sunshine Bridge in St. James Parish, proudly represents Star Enterprise's newest and most modern, fully integrated refinery. The plant's employees, numbering approximately 500, work to convert crude oil into Texaco brand CleanSystem³ gasolines, aviation fuel, diesel fuel, furnace oil, fuel oil, and liquefied petroleum gas. Since 1994, the Louisiana plant has also been a manufacturer and supplier of premium diesel fuel for cars and trucks.

Star Enterprise's Texaco Star 21 in Houston is a prototype of the new facilities design introduced by the Texaco Global Brand Initiative Program in March of 1996. By the year 2001, Texaco outlets all over the world will feature this new look.

The Louisiana Land and Exploration Company

Founded in 1926, The Louisiana Land and Exploration Company (LL&E) is today one of the oldest and largest independent oil and gas exploration and production companies based in the United States. LL&E is headquartered in New Orleans and its capital stock is traded on the New York Stock Exchange (symbol: LLX).

Since its creation LL&E has played a prominent role in the development of oil and gas as a major industry in Louisiana and the world. LL&E's founders pioneered many of the techniques in oil field geology and engineering that paved the way for the discovery and extraction of oil and gas not only by LL&E but by other industry producers.

LL&E's fee ownership of more than 600,000 acres of land in southern Louisiana provided the springboard for its future prosperity. By leasing these lands to others for exploration and production and by retaining a significant royalty interest in the hydrocarbons discovered, LL&E grew into a major royalty company.

During the early years LL&E's operations were concentrated in southern Louisiana. In the early 1960's, realizing that its south Louisiana production would not provide the necessary base for future growth, LL&E's leaders expanded the company's exploration efforts for its own account. LL&E was an early participant in the exploration of the Outer Continental Shelf of the Gulf of Mexico, acquiring its first leases there in 1962. The 1970 discovery of the Jay-Little Escambia Creek Field in Florida firmly established LL&E as a working interest producer, and in 1971 LL&E's revenues from working interest production exceeded those from royalty production for the first time.

Today oil and gas exploration and development remain the primary business for LL&E. However, LL&E's operations are no longer confined to southern Louisiana and the Gulf Coast region. LL&E now has division or district offices in Houston, Denver, and London, England.

In the United States, LL&E continues to be an active participant in exploration and production operations in south Louisiana. Over 3.5 billion barrels of oil equivalent have been produced from LL&E's fee land ownership. The latest oil field technology, particularly 3-D seismic has enabled the company to rejuvenate many of the old producing fields in this region as well as generate a large number of new drilling prospects that could not be identified with previously utilized technology. In the Gulf of Mexico, LL&E owns an interest in 133 leases covering over 580 thousand gross acres and 96 producing platforms. In Wyoming, LL&E has a significant interest in natural gas reserves at the Madden Field that will produce into the next century.

The LL&E Tower in downtown New Orleans, headquarters office for the Company.

LL&E's international exploration program includes drilling in high potential areas such as Algeria shown here.

Over 60 percent of LL&E's domestic hydrocarbon reserves are natural gas, making this company an important player in an expanding industry. Approximately 40 percent of LL&E's proved reserves of oil and natural gas are located outside the United States, in the United Kingdom and Dutch sectors of the North Sea, Colombia, and Indonesia.

In addition to its international production operations, LL&E is actively exploring for new hydrocarbon deposits in several exciting world-class oil and gas basins in Algeria and Tunisia in North Africa and Venezuela in South America.

LL&E takes an active role in the civic, cultural, educational and political affairs of the community. Its employees formed a Volunteer Action Committee to coordinate the time and talents that employees donate each year ensuring the success of a wide variety of institutions devoted to the education, health, and general welfare of Louisianians. Whether it's teaching a Junior Achievement Class to fifth graders, refurbishing a community center for Christmas in October, or providing leadership through Board participation in over 25 different local organizations, LL&E employees are making a difference in their community. LL&E was recognized for these community efforts in 1995 when it received the Chamber's "Business at its Best" Award.

LL&E has long been a champion of environmentally sound techniques of mineral extraction in the sensitive wetlands of Louisiana, realizing that these fertile nursery grounds are very valuable to the world's food chain and to the survival of many species that contribute to the quality of life on this planet. More than 35 years ago LL&E recognized that these wetlands were being severely impacted by a combination of saltwater and coastal erosion. Since then, LL&E has been engaged in cooperative programs with federal and state soil conservation and wildlife protection agencies to slow down the pace of coastal erosion. Currently, LL&E is engaged in numerous educational projects designed to acquaint the general public with the value of Louisiana's wetlands to the nation as a whole and the forces that are threatening these wetlands.

As a result of many years of thoughtful, creative management, The Louisiana Land and Exploration Company is today respected by shareholders and the financial community and, at the same time respected by civic and environmental activists as a corporate good neighbor, dedicated to preserving and enhancing the environment in which it operates. ◆

The expanding use of 3–D seismic technology in south Louisiana has resulted in the rejuvenation of this mature producing region.

LL&E has become a significant player in the exploration and development of the Gulf of Mexico where it operates over 50 platforms.

L&L Oil Company, Inc.

L&L Oil Company, Inc. in metropolitan New Orleans, is the Gulf Coast's largest supplier of diesel fuel and lubricants to the oil and gas exploration and production industry. L&L has also emerged, with the decade heading toward a new century, as one of the newest, yet potentially busiest environmental cleanup enterprises in the central region of the Gulf South.

L&L's full service facility in Morgan City, Louisiana.

"It is ironic, because it is a service we started doing only in more recent years because of the new regulations required by the Oil Pollution Act of 1990," says Frank L. Levy, owner and president of the company his father Leon Levy and partner Lee Adams (the L's in the L&L) created in 1956. "But it has really taken off for us because of our strategic locations along the Louisiana coast and the quality of the people employed at these facilities."

Certified and approved by the U.S. Coast Guard for their spill response capabilities, L&L has also, in the past three years, moved into the frontier region of recycling and pollution control. "A big problem in this country today is what happens to used oil and filters," continues Levy. "So we are now deeply involved in both used oil and filter recycling, finding new uses for both."

Tote tank of bulk lubrication oil being sent for delivery to an offshore drilling rig.

Of course, even with the company's new emphasis on environmental services, the company's primary mission remains pretty much what it was four decades ago when it and the Gulf's oil and gas industry were nascent: To be the premier petroleum product supplier in South Louisiana providing its customers the best buying experience in the industry. It started in the southeast corner of the state and has grown to include the entire Louisiana coast and Southeast Texas. "We are very optimistic about the future activity in the Gulf of Mexico," says Levy. "With the new technology in deepwater drilling and 3-D seismic, activity levels are at their highest levels in years."

L&L's operations include its corporate headquarters in the New Orleans suburb of Metairie, a dozen marine fuel docks, three inland terminals, thirteen towboats, twenty barges, and a large fleet of trucking equipment.

The variety and quality of L&L's facilities and employees, however, is also equalled by its resiliency, a resiliency that in many ways reflects the changing economics and challenges of the region itself. As the oil and gas business boomed in the 1970s, L&L happily surged along with it. But when that boom fizzled in the 1980's, L&L smoothly found other work as well. "We began to do more government contracting then," recalls Levy. "Those were the years of the big Reagan buildup of the military. We became the major supplier of diesel fuel in this area for the U.S. Navy and the Corps of Engineers, and really came out of the decade in decent shape."

Thanks to very hard work and some strategic acquisitions, L&L now has a stellar client roster that lists some of the region's most important exploration and drilling firms, including Shell, Mobil, McDermott, BP, Texaco, Kerr McGee, Amoco, Diamond Offshore, Noble, Rowan, Sonat, Falcon, and Marine Drilling. L&L expects to deliver on the promise of its current anniversary celebration motto: "Forty years of success and just beginning."

"We are certainly just beginning when it comes to environmental cleanup work," says Levy. "And we intend to do more of that kind of thing, along with the work we have always done traditionally. We are still here, as always, to deliver petroleum products to the varied industries of South Louisiana." ◆

Main Pass sulphur mine offshore Louisiana
in the Gulf of Mexico.

The Freeport-McMoRan companies have vast world-wide interests in copper/gold mining in Indonesia, sulphur mining in the Gulf of Mexico, the production and sale of phosphate fertilizers, oil and gas operations, real estate assets, and other interests.

Freeport-McMoRan Copper & Gold (FCX) is today one of the world's largest and lowest-cost copper and gold producers, operating principally through its majority-owned subsidiary, P.T. Freeport Indonesia Company, and enjoying revenues that in 1995 neared the $2 billion mark. FCX has discovered the world's largest single gold reserve and the third largest open-pit copper reserve of any mine in the world. FCX has been mining in Irian Jaya, Indonesia since 1972.

Even with an increased mill output of some 125,000 metric tons of ore per day, the FCX reserves are expected to last for at least another 45 years giving the world vast supplies of copper, gold, and silver.

Freeport-McMoRan, Inc. (FTX), through its majority-owned affiliate, Freeport-McMoRan Resource Partners (FRP), is one of the world's largest and lowest-cost producers of integrated phosphate fertilizers. In 1995 its revenues neared $1 billion. The company's sulphur dome in the Gulf of Mexico, the Main Pass mine, is not only the first major Frasch sulphur discovery in North America in a generation, it is also a reserve expected to last for at least the next 30 years. FRP also had over 6 million barrels of proven oil reserves at its Main Pass mine at the end of 1995.

McMoRan Oil & Gas Co. is an independent oil and gas entity primarily engaged in the exploration, development, and production of oil and natural gas properties located principally in the offshore Gulf of Mexico and onshore Gulf Coast area. FM Properties is principally engaged in the development and mar-keting of certain real estate in the Austin, Dallas, Houston, and San Antonio, Texas areas.

All of this is good news for New Orleans, due to Freeport-McMoRan's corporate generosity, which has surpassed the $80 million mark since the com-pany relocated its headquarters from New York to New Orleans in 1985.

On an annual basis, Freeport-McMoRan gives to a stunningly wide array of programs in the arts, education, human services, and environment, reflecting the concerns of company employees and the personal commitment of chairman James R. Moffett, recipient of the prestigious Horatio Alger Association of distinguished Americans Award for his work in helping disadvantaged youth.

In 1995 alone, the company gave more than $755,000 in educational gifts; nearly $500,000 for arts and cultural projects; more than $3.8 million for a variety of health and human services needs; and over $2.1 million to civic organizations.

Freeport-McMoRan is also a principal supporter of the Environmental Research Consortium of Louisiana, a partnership that includes Tulane, Xavier, Louisiana State University, and the University of New Orleans, dedicated to the preservation of the planet through the sharing of resources and ideas.

Other environmental projects include the Nature Conservancy, the Freeport-McMoRan Audubon Species Survival Center, and the Audubon Institute Office of Environmental Policy. The corporation is also experimenting with new ways to fight coastal erosion, a major Louisiana concern.

Nearing the next century, Freeport-McMoRan will continue to focus on improving its reserves and production for the benefit of its shareholders while at the same time realizing its corporate citizenship responsibilities both in the United States and overseas. ◆

James R. Moffett, Chairman and Chief Executive Officer of Freeport–McMoRan Copper & Gold Inc. and Chairman of Freeport–McMoRan Inc.

Lubriport Laboratories, Inc.

Lubriport Laboratories, Inc., is an independent testing facility offering state-of-the-art analysis of fuel oils, lubricant oils, and other petroleum-based products.

Southeastern Louisiana's only independent, full-service, oil testing lab, Lubriport, serves clients from throughout the Gulf South region and from as far away as Alaska, Japan, and Honduras.

The majority of Lubriport's customers are from the petroleum and marine industries, whose daily operations depend on the safe and efficient operation of boating and drilling machinery, countless engines, hydraulic systems, air compressors, cranes, and other equipment with lubrication or fluid-power systems.

The use of oil analysis as an important preventive maintenance tool is the foundation of Lubriport's operations. Using the wrong type of fuel or lube oil, or continually using an oil that is well past its prime, can have disastrous effects on the life of an engine or part.

Routine oil analysis can alert clients to growing contamination levels or the acceleration of mechanical wear and oil deterioration, both of which can cause failures down the line.

With just a small sample of oil, Lubriport chemists can detect such problems as seawater or antifreeze leaking into a lubricating oil, wear or corrosion of bearings, the presence of excessive soot in engine oil or a diesel fuel that is contaminated or poor in quality.

Lubriport's employees: standing left to right, top row: Paula Clark, Andrea Laurie, Nora King, and Pam Talley; middle row: Evonne Friloux, Floyd Friloux, Jr., and Anne S. Friloux; Great Danes: Angus, Bella, and Hoda. Photo by Roger Gibson Photography.

Lubriport Laboratories, Inc., is an independent testing facility offering state-of-the-art analysis of fuel oils, lubricant oils, and other petroleum-based products. Photo by Roger Gibson Photography.

Using Lubriport's services is simple: samples of oil can either be mailed or brought to the company's lab at the corner of Airline Highway and Maria Street, near New Orleans International Airport.

The samples—an average of 100 per day—go through a battery of tests to determine quality and contamination levels. Among the many pieces of laboratory equipment helping Lubriport's chemists diagnose and predict oil-based problems are an emission spectrometer, which detects and measures the presence of up to 20 metals in a given oil sample; an infrared spectrometer, which helps in the identification of unknown samples; and a number of other machines gauging such factors as oil viscosity, acidity, cleanliness, and sulfur content. Lab results are generally available to clients in two to three working days; same-day service can be arranged.

Established in 1982 by owner/operators Floyd and Anne Friloux, Lubriport has grown from a three-person business operating out of a trailer-size lab, to a seven-employee operation serving over 100 regular customers out of a 32,000 square-foot laboratory complex.

While most petroleum-based businesses experienced economic lows during the 1980s, Lubriport enjoyed steady growth as offshore industries began to pay more attention to preventive maintenance.

"Before, if an engine failed, companies would say, 'So what. We'll buy another one.' Cost is not a problem," said Floyd Friloux. "Our services became more important to them when the industry began to slow down. They could afford an inexpensive oil analysis, but they couldn't afford to buy another half-million dollar engine," Friloux said, noting that personnel cutbacks in the oil fields also led industry leaders to use Lubriport as an integral part of their preventive maintenance program.

One of Lubriport's most popular services is its evaluation of oil change intervals for every type of machinery. Frequent oil changes often are deemed unnecessary upon laboratory analysis of samples, much to the surprise of clients.

"Today, especially for industries dealing with high volumes of waste, it is often more expensive to dispose of old oil than to buy new oil. We help them safely get the most out of the oil they have," Friloux said.

In addition to industry, Lubriport's oil-testing services are available to recreational boaters, car owners, small business owners or anyone who wants to get reliable performance out of their fuel and lube oil systems. ◆

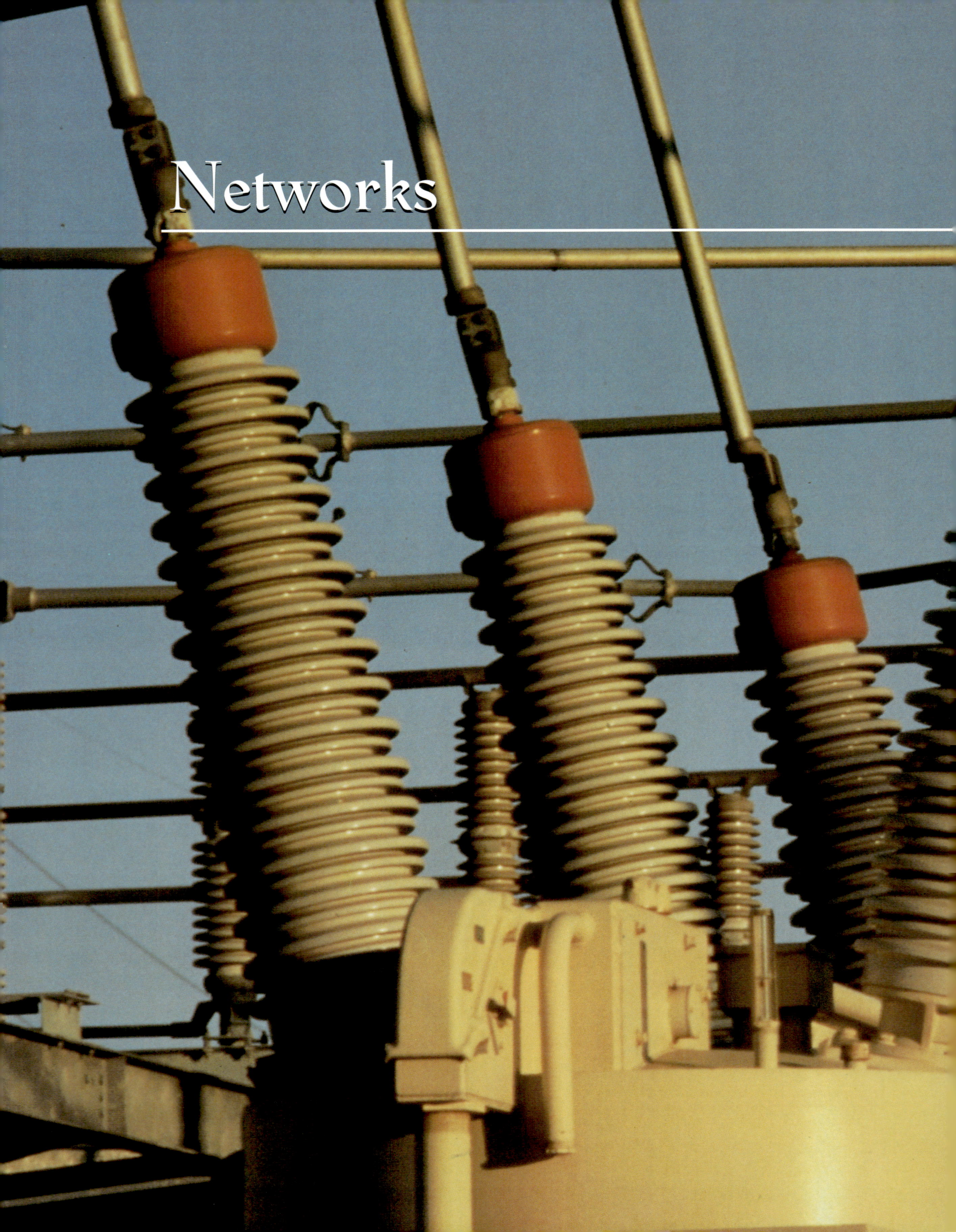
Networks

CHAPTER 14

WWL-TV

WWL-TV is the Spirit of Louisiana. Powerhouse station Channel 4, the CBS affiliate, is woven deep into the fabric of Greater New Orleans and its surrounding parishes. It's a unique station in a unique city, thanks to its people, some of whom have been covering New Orleans for three decades; its commitment to award-winning news coverage, at 26 hours a week more than any other local station; its roots in the historic French Quarter, and its impressive record of contributions to the community. To coin a phrase made famous by Frank Davis, WWL-TV's on-air fishing expert, resident chef, and featured personality, the station is "Naturally N'Awlins." At a time when newscasts around the country are becoming more and more similar from market to market, WWL-TV is different, because it reflects the fabric and flavor of its distinctive city.

That difference has made WWL-TV, a subsidiary of A.H. Belo Corporation, into a national broadcast legend. Consider a few examples of the station's strength. In May, 1996, from the time it signed on the air every day to the time it signed off, the station had as many viewers as the ABC, NBC, and Fox affiliate stations combined. WWL-TV is probably the only station in the country with those kinds of ratings. It's also the number-one CBS affiliate in the top 100 markets in the country and the top affiliate of any network in the nation's 50 biggest markets in the share of the audience it attracts. The New Orleans market leader for more than two decades, WWL-TV is consistently ranked among the nation's top five local stations year after year.

The station is about more than outstanding numbers, however. It's about a legacy. The letters WWL have been part of the New Orleans broadcast scene since 1922, when the Gulf South's first AM radio broadcast traveled over the air

Investigative ace Bill Elder keeps a sharp eye on local government.

from a physics lab at Loyola University. The CBS affiliation is also stable in a time of frequent change—WWL-AM joined the Columbia Broadcasting system in 1935.

It's also a story of people—people who have spent decades working in and caring about New Orleans. It's a team that knows the city, in a way that's increasingly rare in television stations across the country.

General Manager J. Michael Early celebrated 35 years in that post in 1996, having built one of the most impressive franchises in television history. The eloquent commentaries of Phil Johnson have been a New Orleans institution for 36 years, earning him the title as longest-running editorialist on American television, along with a prestigious Sigma Delta Chi award. His trademark signature—literally a flourish of his pen—has often been a driving force for needed change, while supporting the good things about New Orleans. Anchorman and Investigative Reporter Bill Elder, who has been a part of the station for 30 years, reported a 31-part series on drug rehab fraud that received a coveted George Foster Peabody Award in 1995. In awarding WWL-TV its fifth Peabody, the judges cited the series as "investigative reporting of the highest caliber, marked by courage and intensity."

Johnson and Elder are joined by nine other on-air personalities who have each spent more than a decade working with the WWL-TV powerhouse. They are the voices that viewers of southeastern Louisiana trust year after year— Meteorologist Dave Barnes, Action Reporter Bill Capo, Resident Chef/Fishing Expert/"Naturally N'Awlins" Reporter Frank Davis, Sports Director Jim Henderson, Anchorwoman Angela Hill, Morning Co-Hosts Eric Paulsen and Sally-Ann Roberts, Hurricane Consultant Nash Roberts, and Weathercaster Don Westbrook.

There's always something good "In the Kitchen" with Resident Chef Frank Davis.

The experienced hands have been joined by new faces like Hoda Kotb, recently voted favorite female news anchor in the market; News Anchor Dennis Woltering, widely respected for his political knowledge and journalistic skills; and Essayist Ronnie Virgets, whose distinctive pieces explore the special corners of South Louisiana. The result: multifaceted, in-depth journalism that ranges from hard-hitting investigative series to the best cooking tips in town, from the most relied-on weather forecasting in an area subject to flooding and hurricanes to prime time political debates.

Viewers continue to take notice of WWL-TV's commitment to quality news. While local newscasts in most cities compete in a tightly contested ratings race, every edition of WWL-TV's Eyewitness News (5:30 a.m., 6 a.m., noon, 5 p.m., 6 p.m., 10 p.m.) outperforms all news competitors' shares combined. WWL-TV devotes over 26 hours of air time every week to news programming, produced by one of the most-honored news departments in America. In addition to the five prestigious Peabody Awards, WWL-TV's Eyewitness News has earned the coveted National Edward R. Murrow Award twice in the last decade. The award, which signifies the country's best overall local news operation, is rarely presented to stations in medium-sized markets. Such a station winning not one but two Murrows is unprecedented.

But the market leader in news isn't resting on its laurels—not for a minute. In 1996, the station instituted a 5:30 a.m. newscast to answer the needs of a growing commuter market. WWL-TV was the first station in the country to launch a two-hour morning newscast, which continues to have one of the highest local ratings of any morning newscast in the nation. It was also the first in the nation to meet viewer need for news on demand by introducing a local news around-the-clock cable channel, with either a simulcast or a rebroadcast of WWL-TV's most recent local news telecast. NewsWatch on Channel 15, now available in the five parishes of metropolitan New Orleans, is a national model for television stations across the nation launching similar viewer services. The station has also earned fame and viewer loyalty for its live broadcasts. WWL-TV's series of prime-time *Forums on Our Future* brings together people from all over the viewing area to discuss approaches to problems of crime, neighborhoods, or other timely issues. Every Mardi Gras, the station takes to the streets for four hours of live continuous coverage of the nation's favorite spectacle—with the colorful parades, outrageous costumes, flying beads, and exuberant spirit that characterizes Carnival. With an overwhelming share of Fat Tuesday viewership, Mardi Gras with WWL-TV is one of southeast Louisiana's favorite traditions.

WWL-TV, Channel 4 is a catalyst for positive change in New Orleans, with hands-on efforts that extend far beyond the charming courtyards and historic walls of the station buildings on the edge of the French Quarter. Staff members are deeply involved in the community because they are committed to making the area become an even better place to live.

The neighborhoods of New Orleans are an architectural treasure—and if our neighborhoods are strong, our city is strong. To help improve Treme, just across South Rampart Street from the station, WWL-TV staff worked together in 1995 to renovate a Creole cottage. After investing hundreds

Angela Hill's warmth and credibility have made her a local broadcasting legend.

WWL-TV's French Quarter courtyard provides an interview setting for Anchor/Reporter Sally-Ann Roberts.

of hours in sanding, caulking and painting, the house was another success story for Christmas in October, a grassroots, community-based effort spearheaded by the Preservation Resource Center to reclaim New Orleans neighborhoods one house at a time. And the WWL-TV staff had such a rewarding time, they plan to renovate another Treme home as part of Christmas in October each year.

As part of a program sponsored by the Metropolitan Area Committee and Orleans Parish Public Schools, the station is a Partner in Education with two elementary schools—McDonogh 15 in the French Quarter and Craig School in Treme. While the schools are separated by only

six blocks, they are worlds apart in terms of resources to enhance education. Station employees collected hundreds of children's books to create a library at Craig, for example. They also provide teacher materials and act as role models for students at both schools.

To help children continue to learn outside the classroom, WWL-TV has created two permanent, interactive community exhibits. A scaled-down, hands-on news studio, WWL-TV's KidWatch draws thousands of small visitors—and their parents—downtown to the Louisiana Children's Museum, where they trade roles as camera operators, reporters, and anchors. At WeatherWatch, a part of Kenner's Daily Living Science Center in the suburbs, young weatherwatchers can track hurricanes, while learning the concept of latitude and longitude. Other educational outreach projects supported on an ongoing basis include the Zoomobile, which brings the acclaimed Audubon experience to children who are unable to visit the zoo, and Van Go, an art museum on wheels that visits area schools.

WWL-TV also helps New Orleans celebrate—and everyone knows we have celebration down to a fine art. It was the first station to put its name on a stage at that annual rite of spring, the New Orleans Jazz & Heritage Festival. The stage has grown from the size of a flatbed truck into the major Jazzfest venue at the fairgrounds, featuring high-visibility acts like the Neville Brothers. The station is the mainstage sponsor for Jeff Fest, held every October in Lafreniere Park. And it was the organizing force behind Celebration in the Oaks, a holiday event that brings thousands of visitors to City Park to see the world's largest collection of live oaks sparkle with over a million festive lights. Celebration in the Oaks, now in its tenth year, has become a southeast Louisiana holiday tradition.

Through two popular TV campaigns, WWL-TV continues to celebrate the unique strengths of the New Orleans area. "Louisiana Made, Louisiana Proud"; begun in 1990, has showcased more than 70 local companies whose stories range from the rice fields of Acadiana to the wharves of the mighty Mississippi. Because people can't get enough of South Louisiana, and its food, music, and culture, WWL-TV celebrates the region with the Emmy Award-winning "Spirit of Louisiana" on-air promotional campaign. This high-profile campaign uses music videos to highlight the extraordinary range of styles and talent growing out of Southeast Louisiana—gospel, rhythm & blues, salsa, Cajun—a dozen spots and styles. It has also encompassed a tribute to the region's flourishing arts scene and showcased the talented students at NOCCA.

In mid-1996, footage from the spots—edited into *The Spirit of New Orleans: A Winning Recipe from a Community Famous for its Flavors*—played a key role in helping New Orleans win a coveted designation as one of 10 All American

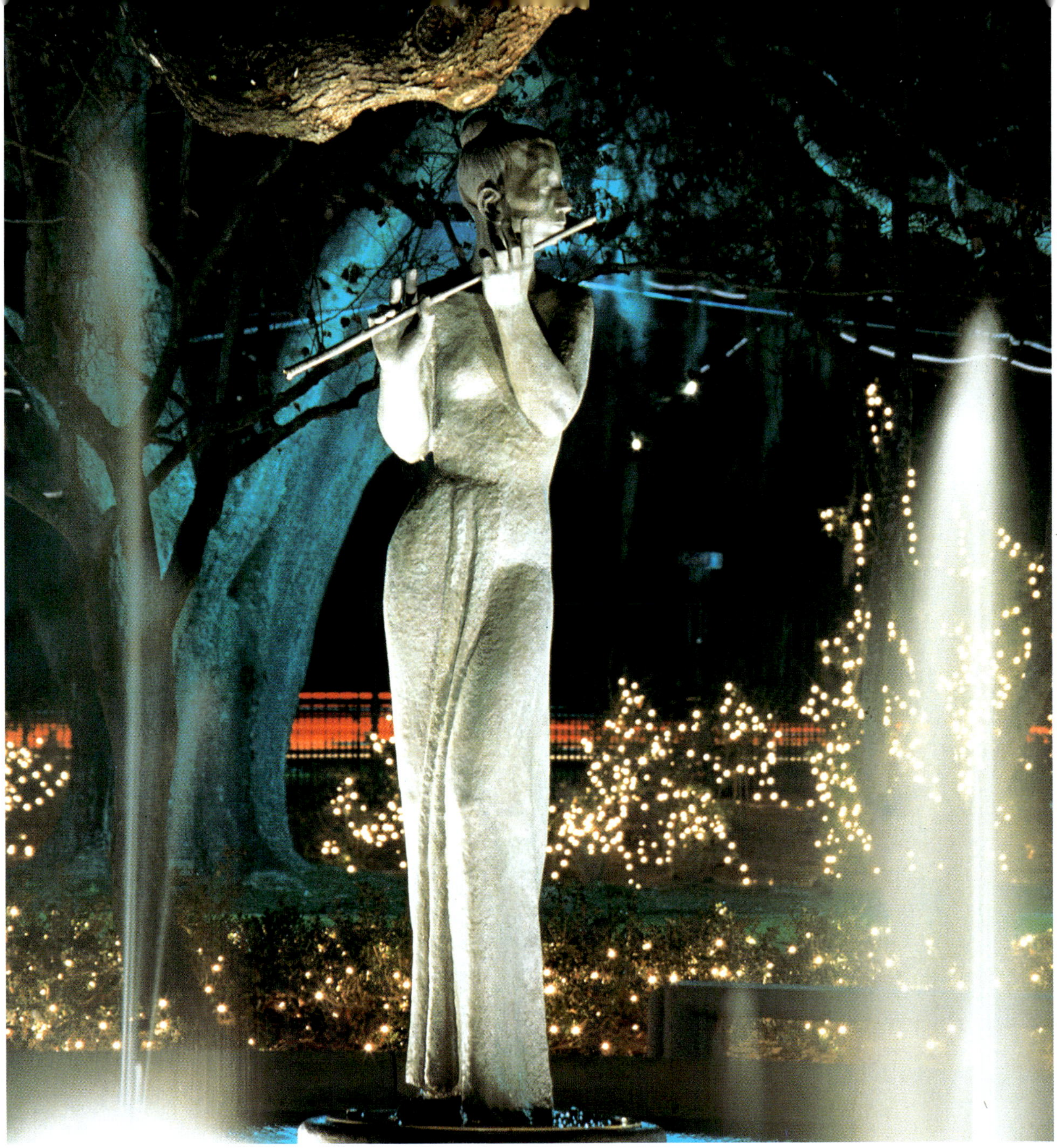

City Park glows with holiday spirit during the station-sponsored "Celebration in the Oaks."

Cities. "The spots hold up a mirror and reflect what's good about where we live," says Station Manager Jimmie Phillips. "That's why people like them so much."

Because of the new demands of digital technology, the next few years will see WWL-TV move to a new facility, most likely away from their historic French Quarter location. The buildings are now part of the station's unique New Orleans feeling, but they don't provide the space for a digital conversion required by high-definition television. Even now, officials are scouting sites for a station that will feature the newest in technology while maintaining and expanding the family feel for which the station is famous.

WWL-TV is an institution in New Orleans—and for New Orleans. "The story of WWL-TV is woven into the fabric of our southeast parishes, which form a rich tapestry of many colors," says WWL-TV's own brochure. "It is also a story of steady dominance in a fragmenting media world, of courageous reporting in tabloid-driven times, of the greater community good over individual gain. But most of all, it is a story of spirit—the spirit we've been entrusted to reflect back to the people of Louisiana."

The WWL-TV spirit, legendary in the nation, is an indispensable part of everyday life for hundreds of thousands of people in Louisiana. ◆

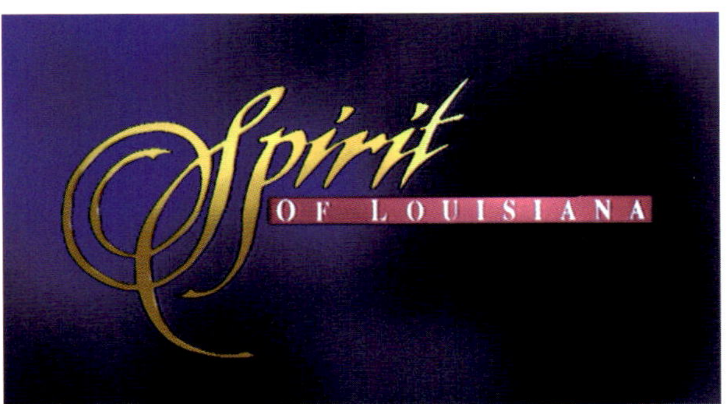

Entergy Corporation

Although officially less than 10 years old (it adopted the name Entergy Corporation in 1989) this mighty and vastly expanded New Orleans company reigns at the pinnacle of an intricate family tree with roots extending back through most of the last century, even as the company reaches forward.

Entergy is the former Middle South Utilities, the holding company for Arkansas Power & Light, Louisiana Power & Light, Mississippi Power & Light, and New Orleans Public Service. The New Orleans subsidiary was at one time the sole owner and operator, beginning in 1922, of New Orleans' historic streetcar line.

"But today, we're moving into an era of advanced technology and increasing competitiveness in the industry," says Entergy's Chairman and President, Ed Lupberger. This bold, but nonetheless uncertain time will be marked by the kind of change that comes fast. So fast that a company "flexible enough to anticipate changes and adapt to them," Lupberger explains, "will be the company that thrives."

Entergy, upon its inception, sent immediate signals throughout the local business community and national energy industry that it was prepared to thrive.

Those signals, watched intently by financial analysts, were received in a variety of forms that included Entergy's functional reorganization, acquisition of Beaumont, Texas-based Gulf States Utilities Company and its expansion into the energy services, telecommunications, and independent power project markets. As this was being accomplished, operating profits rose annually at double-digit rates for most of this same period.

In 1993 the company moved its local employees onto the 16 floors of the modern, marble building it now occupies—a building near New Orleans' government corridor that includes City Hall and the Louisiana Supreme Court, among other public institutions.

But Entergy's most important move, noted earlier, came on New Year's Eve 1993 as Entergy completed a historic $2.3 billion merger with Gulf State Utilities, Inc. The merger increased the company's assets to more than $22 billion, and expanded its market beyond the Louisiana, Arkansas, and Mississippi customer base it already served, into the Southeastern reaches of Texas.

Meanwhile federal legislation, in the form of the Energy Policy Act of 1992, opened the doors of the world to Entergy, allowing it and other U.S. energy companies to expand business and pursue projects far from home.

As a result, Entergy's worldwide business investments by 1995 totaled more than $950 million and today includes projects in Pakistan, Peru, Argentina, and a joint-venture company considering projects in Brazil. They are also engaged in negotiations on power projects in Chile—an emerging Latin American economic colossus—and have acquired an Australian power distribution company, CitiPower, Ltd., that serves some 233,000 customers in Melbourne's central business district and inner suburbs.

The Entergy Building is a 28-story granite edifice located in the heart of New Orleans' modern business district. It is home to the worldwide energy company's corporate staff of some 1,200 professionals.

"Electricity is a fundamental building block for any country hoping to improve its infrastructure," says Lupberger, "an essential component that lifts nations from their second and third world status to the level of industrialized economies."

In return, Entergy records profits and a healthy pattern of growth. The electric energy growth rate internationally has been near the 6 percent level. A powerful figure made even more so, says Lupberger, when compared with U.S. domestic growth rates: "In the U.S. the domestic energy growth rate is probably in the 1 to 2 percent range. So, obviously, a 6 percent growth rate is an enormously positive indicator of an expanding market."

But their overseas efforts in far-flung corners of the world are also designed to eventually reward the company's expanding customer base back home. By owning and operating an energy distribution system in Argentina or a generation facility in the Andes Mountains of Peru, Entergy learns more about energy efficiencies and economies, strategies and procedures it can apply to its U.S. operations.

Entergy's power development includes investments in the privatization of Argentina's electric energy infrastructure, as well as in an international consortium formed to develop power along the Hub River near Karachi, Pakistan.

Says Lupberger: "There is no question that the international profile of Entergy is growing and it will continue to grow for the foreseeable future."

That type of investment and operational activity has helped to shape Entergy's corporate portfolio, which features operating revenues in excess of $5.9 billion with a net cash flow of more than $1.5 billion—one of the largest cash flow reserves for an energy company in the nation.

At the same time, the fall 1995 edition of *Entergy Investor Facts*, a company publication, shows that operating expenses in early 1995 declined by nearly 4 percent even as commercial and industrial sales moved up 3 percent and 2.2 percent respectively. Total sales in electric energy have increased for Entergy by some 4.2 percent.

With more than 2.4 million retail customers domestically, the company has also emerged as a positive corporate citizen, largely under Lupberger's direction.

Among Entergy's many educational support programs is the Save Our At-Risk Students, designed to encourage the interests of younger students in subjects like math and science, and the Camden-Fairview Mentoring Program, which helps students control anger while working towards conflict resolution.

Other Entergy-supported initiatives include the tutoring of poverty-line at-risk children in Mississippi, a buddy system linking troubled children with disabled children in Arkansas, and a family Mentoring project in Louisiana called Families Learn Together, that brings together students, their families, and teachers for learning in a community environment.

Such community involvement has won for Entergy the praise of any number of civic and political leaders while also infusing the company with the spirit of a mission. "We know that while the 'bottom line' and the numbers, investments, and projects are important, so is the community in which we work and live," says Lupberger. "Giving something back to that community is a very important part of the kind of corporation we are." ◆

Located across the Mississippi River, in the New Orleans suburb of Gretna, the Entergy Command Theatre monitors information technology systems serving Entergy's 112,000-square-mile service area.

BellSouth

BellSouth's long tradition of providing reliable, affordable telephone service in the Greater New Orleans area has prepared the corporation to be a major player in today's rapidly evolving telecommunications industry.

This tradition of service began in 1879—only four years after the invention of the telephone—when BellSouth's predecessor, Cumberland Telephone Company, began providing telephone service in New Orleans.

Today, BellSouth is a $17.9 billion corporation, providing voice, data, video, and wireless communications; directory advertising and publishing; and information services to more than 25 million customers in 16 countries worldwide.

The company provides local telephone service to customers in nine Southeastern states, including Alabama, Kentucky, Florida, Georgia, Mississippi, North Carolina, South Carolina, and Tennessee, in addition to Louisiana.

BellSouth also provides local and long-distance wireless service to more than 2.5 million customers in the United States and more than .5 million customers in Latin America, Western Europe and Australia.

The company will also soon provide Personal Communications Service, the new generation of wireless services, to customers in selected areas of the Southeast.

In the midst of the explosion of the telecommunications industry in the global marketplace, BellSouth remains focused on meeting the individual needs of each of its customers.

"Our customers demand excellent service, value for their money and a telecommunications system they can rely on—and that is exactly what our employees strive to give them 24 hours a day, 7 days a week," said Elton R. King, president of BellSouth's Louisiana operations. "We understand our customers' needs, and we continue to develop products and services that improve their quality of life and enhance their businesses. In fact, our product development team has more than 70 new product ideas in the pipeline."

Innovative services such as MessageLink, CrisisLink(sm) and ZipCONNECT® give customers greater control, flexibility, and mobility. MessageLink service provides a stand-alone voice mailbox and a paging notification option for transitional customers, university students, and people who work at home. Customers can change their greeting or retrieve their messages from any touch-tone telephone at any time of the day or night.

CrisisLink(sm), a service unique to BellSouth, enables businesses to design alternative routing of voice, data, and video communications in the event of floods, hurricanes, or other emergency conditions.

ZipCONNECT® service allows businesses with multiple locations to route calls from a single telephone number to the appropriate branch or outlet. This creates efficiencies for businesses by allowing them to advertise a single telephone number or to consolidate operations during nontraditional working hours.

"BellSouth is well-positioned to provide our customers any number of advanced, sophisticated services over our existing telecommunications network," King said. "Fiber-optic cable and computer-based switching—which allow customers to transmit extremely large quantities of data very quickly—are already in place in New Orleans, and form the backbone of this area's telecommunications infrastructure."

BellSouth services such as SynchroNet® service and MegaLink® service allow customers to send information over the network in a matter of seconds. Banks and other businesses that have a need to transmit data quickly rely

BellSouth's customer service representatives are trained to recommend the services that best meet your personal and business telecommunications needs. Photo by Jackson Hill/Southern Lights Studio.

Network architectures such as ISDN (Integrated Services Digital Network) provide cost efficient ways to access services such as video conferencing through a personal computer. Photo by Jackson Hill/Southern Lights Studio.

on these services to help them run their businesses in the most cost-efficient and effective way possible.

The cost efficiency of one of BellSouth's most advanced network architectures, called ISDN (Integrated Services Digital Network), makes advanced telecommuting, telemedicine, and distance learning applications more widely accessible.

"The availability of ISDN, which combines voice, data, and video services, is important because it provides access at lower speeds," King said.

Distance learning, for example, can be made possible by transporting advanced classes on a particular subject through these special communications circuits from a university in another part of the nation to New Orleans.

This high-speed signal can then be divided into lower speeds and redistributed within the Greater New Orleans area. ISDN makes these classes available to any school anywhere at a greatly reduced cost.

Physicians have also used ISDN to send and receive patient X-rays and video images while communicating with other physicians at remote locations.

ISDN's availability allows physicians to communicate from a hospital, their offices, or even their homes. Healthcare specialists, as well as any other business that has multiple locations within a metropolitan area, can benefit from this capability.

"Customers today are also extremely mobile, and they want to be able to keep in touch with their homes or offices from their car or any other remote location," King said. "They also want the ability to choose one company to meet all their communications needs, and BellSouth intends to be that company."

The Telecommunications Act of 1996 allows BellSouth to provide long-distance, electronic commerce, and video services in addition to the services the company has traditionally provided.

Many of these new services will be provided as soon as the requirements outlined in the federal legislation are met.

"BellSouth is excited about the new opportunities created by the Telecommunications Act of 1996 and our ability to provide one-stop shopping for our customers," King said. "We have a tradition of service to this community, and we intend to be our customers' carrier of choice for all their telecommunications needs in the future." ◆

Customers can learn more about BellSouth by accessing the company's Internet page at www.bellsouth.com. Photo by Jackson Hill/Southern Lights Studio.

BellSouth and its predecessors have been providing excellent service to telephone customers in the New Orleans area since 1879. Photo by Jackson Hill/Southern Lights Studio.

Louisiana Gas Service

A Division of Citizens Utilities Company

Community is more than just a concept at Louisiana Gas Service—it is a living, pulsating spirit leading the company on to greater customer service and corporate success.

LGS, located on the Westbank of the Mississippi River in Harvey, is a company which values, above all, its relationships with the 265,000 customers it serves across the state.

The utility's services have been adapted over the years to meet the needs of customers in its diverse service area, a territory which includes the suburban growth-sprawl areas surrounding the city of New Orleans, the rapidly expanding subdivisions of the North Shore of Lake Ponchartrain, the city of Monroe, and the many smaller and medium-sized communities in 39 parishes spread throughout the state.

To ensure that the needs and wants of all customers are continually met and exceeded, LGS regularly surveys its customers for input and ideas. The management and staff want to determine what products and services customers most desire and their level of satisfaction with those already in place.

LGS' sense of community also extends to the dozens of charitable, civic, and volunteer efforts providing social and medical services to citizens throughout the company's service area. LGS is a loyal corporate contributor to a number of organizations and its 600 employees regularly participate in the United Way and other community support programs.

In 1995, LGS presented $90,000 in customer contributions to the Louisiana Association of Councils on Aging for distribution to lower-income and handicapped customers who needed help paying their gas bills. Additionally, LGS made a company donation to help defray administrative costs of the program.

This sense of community also prevails within LGS' work environment. In systematic fashion, LGS encourages and trains its employees to excel, allowing them a voice in company policy, priorities, and the overall work environment. Increased employee involvement and impowerment at all levels of the corporate structure encourage employee participation, growth and ownership.

LGS is a division of Citizens Utilities, a diversified public utility supplying telecommunication, electric, gas, water, and wastewater services to more than 1.6 million customers in 20 states, stretching across the U.S. from the industrial northeast and midwest to the Deep South and the western plain states.

Like its Louisiana division, Citizens Utilities is growth-driven, with assets increasing from $2.6 billion in 1993 to

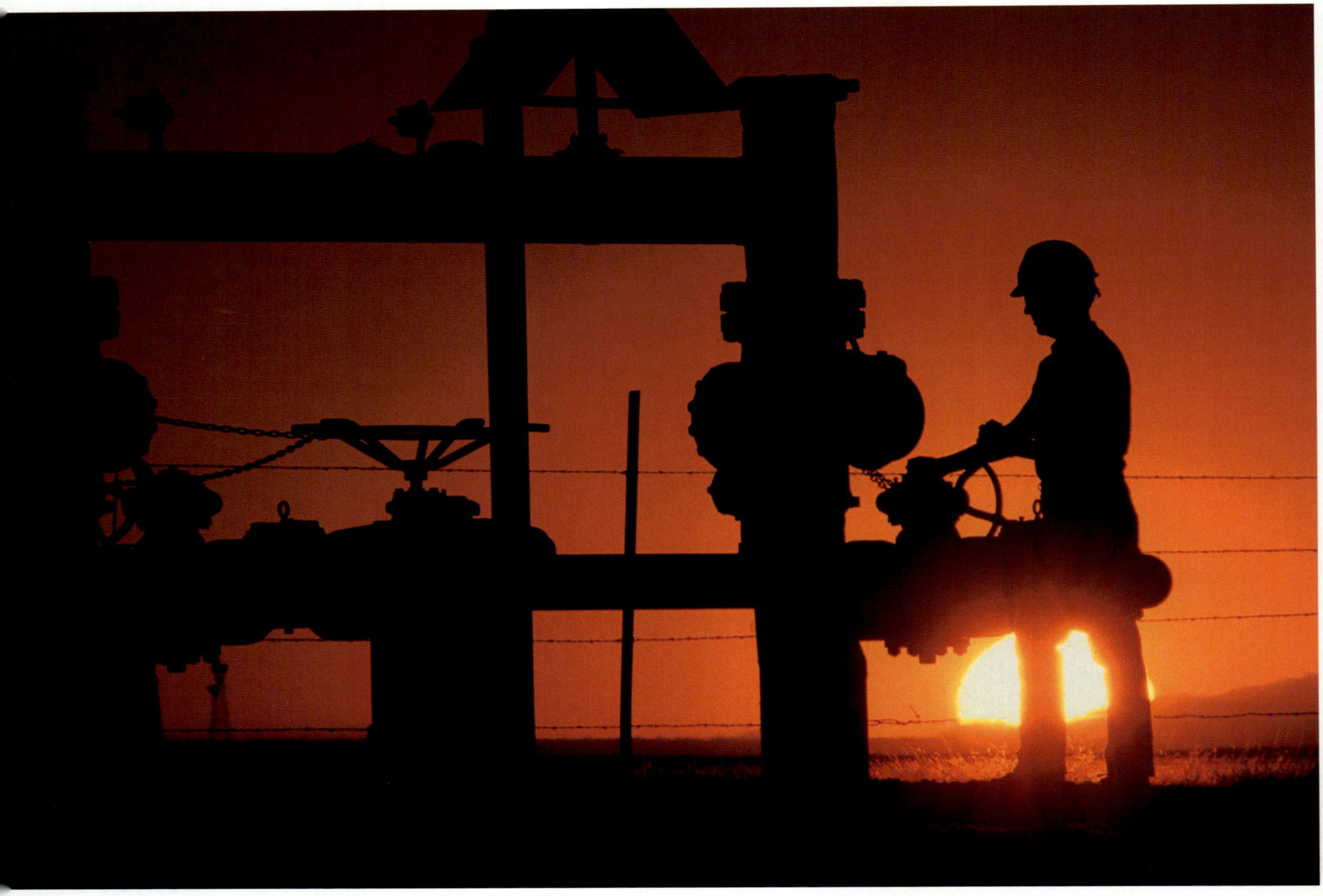

electricity in Arizona, Vermont, and Hawaii; water and/or wastewater treatment services in Pennsylvania, Ohio, Indiana, Illinois, Arizona, and California; and natural gas services in Colorado, Arizona, and Louisiana.

Typical of Citizens Utilities dynamic growth is LGS, where volume output for the company totaled more than 83 billion cubic feet in 1995. With revenues exceeding $153 million, LGS is part of Citizen's Energy Sector, which includes sister operations in Arizona, Colorado, Hawaii, and Vermont. Together the natural gas services in Arizona, Colorado, and Louisiana account for 19 percent of all of Citizens' revenues.

Citizens Utilities is banking on the future growth of Louisiana, evidences not only by the $13.4 million LGS invested in property, plant, and equipment but also in the development of its Geographic Information System (GIS), a state-of-the-art automated mapping and facilities information system designed to reduce operational expenses by as much as $100 million over the next two decades. The GIS technology will be deployed throughout the Citizens' gas operations during the years 1997 to 1999.

nearly $4 billion in 1995. During the same three years, net income for Citizens has risen from $126 million to $160 million, while the company's overall customer base has expanded from just over 1 million to today's approximately 1.6 million.

Also like LGS, Citizens Utilities derives much of its growth by providing diversified utility services to a mostly suburban and rural customer base that has more than tripled in growth over the last several years and is expected to see even greater growth in the decades to come.

Among its many services, Citizens Utilities provides telecommunications services in New York, West Virginia, Tennessee, New Mexico, Arizona, Utah, Montana, Nevada, Idaho, Washington, Oregon, California, and Louisiana;

Another innovation is the Louisiana Gas Management System (GMS), which brings together the gas supply, accounting, marketing, and service dispatch groups of LGS through the division's local data network. This coordinated program ensures the accurate buying, dispatching, and selling of natural gas supplies, even in a time of increased natural gas consumption.

Constantly striving to improve its customer service through the latest product innovations, technological advances, and employee involvement, LGS, as is all of Citizens Utilities, is bullish about its future, determined that as its grows and improves internally, its many customers will reap the benefit of improved services. ◆

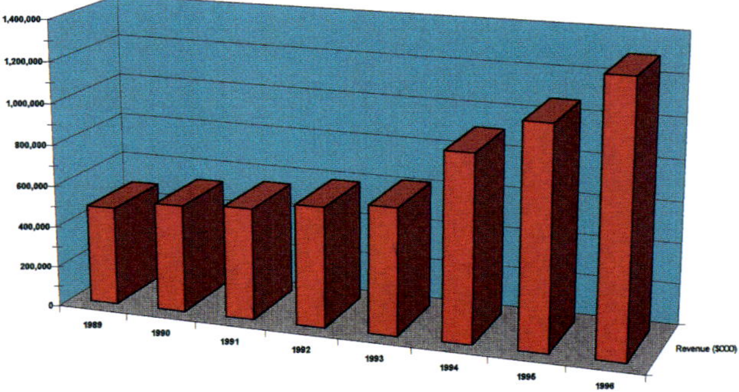

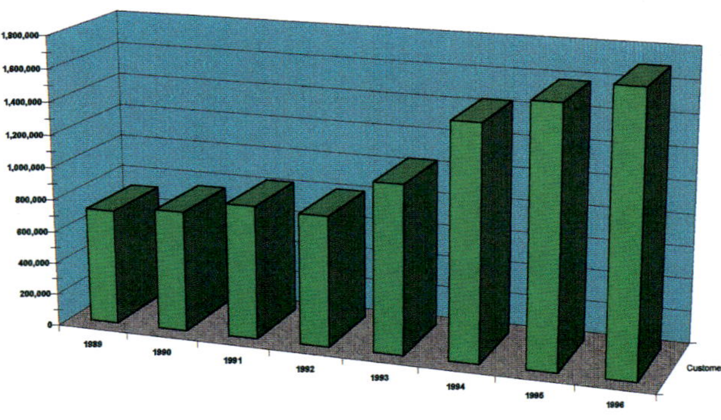

When the political and economic leaders of nearly 30 North, Central, and South American countries gathered in New Orleans for a much-heralded Summit of the Americas to discuss trade and the softening of borders, they came and went through the New Orleans International Airport, giving tribute once again to New Orleans' self-described status as the Gateway to the Americas and the airport's vital role in it.

Home to more than a dozen major national airlines and three international carriers, the airport's history can be traced back to the late 1930s, when city leaders began searching for a site to accommodate the increasing air needs of a growing city. They purchased 648 acres in the City of Kenner for a new airport. The airport today encompasses over 1,600 acres. It is a center of international trade and commerce, and is perhaps the most important link between New Orleans and its neighbors to the south, as well as the rest of the world.

In 1995, the airport serviced more than 8.2 million passengers on its many national and international airlines.

In 1995, the airport serviced more than 8.2 million passengers—up from 6.7 million only two years before. Freight and express tonnage, meanwhile, now stands at more than 54,000 tons as the total number of takeoffs and landings at the airport have increased from 126,000 in 1993 to more than 160,000 in 1995, at the same time that the average number of daily flights went up from 347 in 1993 to 439 in 1995.

With an economic impact of more than $1.5 billion and as the generator of more than 10,000 jobs in the metro New Orleans area, the New Orleans International Airport is by any measure a major factor in the city's plans for its fortunes and future.

As such, the airport's capital facilities program—the ongoing expansion of its infrastructure and facilities—seems to never end. Between 1980 and 1990, for example, the airport totally rebuilt it's baggage make-up and claim areas, built a 3,000-car garage and extended a runway.

New concourses, cargo aprons, access roads, runway repairs, and apron development account for project work so far in the 1990s, all designed to increase both the airport's service abilities and amenities for passengers and cargo. In fact, over $100 million will be expended in 1996 alone in construction.

Altogether the New Orleans International Airport has been undergoing a capital facilities program of $650 million over 10 years that New Orleans Mayor Marc H. Morial has called essential if the city itself expects to grow. "This growth is greatly dependent upon air service," Morial said. "One third of our domestic visitors and virtually all of our international visitors come to New Orleans by air. The style and convenience of our airport leave the first and last impressions of our city."

Located just 15 minutes from downtown New Orleans, the airport is also a sleek and handsome facility providing, through the terminal's many restaurants and gift shops, such New Orleans staples as cafe au lait, beignets, Cajun cuisine, Mardi Gras souvenirs, and other Louisiana handicrafts.

Concluding the century that gave birth to air flight as it enters the next century of supersonic international connections, the New Orleans International Airport is graduating from being the Gateway to the Americas and now Links the Americas to the World. ◆

A primary engine driving the economy of the city and state with an annual economic impact of $2.7 billion, the Ernest N. Morial Convention Center in New Orleans is one of the five largest convention facilities in the United States. The Morial Center currently offers some 700,000 square feet of contiguous space in seven ground-level halls; a 118,000 square-foot lobby area; 83 second- and third-level meeting rooms seating 50 to 4,000 people; and two spacious ballrooms.

Built to replace the obsolete Rivergate Exposition Hall, the convention center's first phase of construction was completed in 1984. After serving as the Great Hall for the 1984 World's Fair, the building officially opened in January 1985 as the New Orleans Convention Center. Renamed the Ernest N. Morial Convention Center in 1992 in honor of the late mayor who spearheaded its construction, the facility quickly earned a world-class reputation for quality and service in the exposition industry.

Strong growth in conventions and trade shows triggered two additional phases of construction, the latest of which is targeted for completion in 1999. With "Phase III," the Morial Center will be the most marketable convention center in the nation, with an unparalleled 1.1 million square feet of contiguous exhibit space on one level in 12 separate/combinable halls.

Since its opening, the Morial Center has consistently proven to be an economic catalyst for residents of the metro area. In 1995, events at the center were linked to more than 34,000 jobs locally. In that year, more than 90 major conventions and trade shows attracted over 640,000 delegates, creating a statewide economic impact of $2.7 billion—based on spending in hotels, restaurants, shops, entertainment centers, and other venues.

In its first 11 years of operation, the Morial Center attracted 4.3 million convention delegates, produced a statewide economic impact of $14.5 billion, and generated some $926.6 million in new statewide tax revenue, of which $384.2 million was channeled into Greater New Orleans. In addition, the building's construction and bustling operations are credited with spurring the ongoing transformation of New Orleans' historic Warehouse District from a virtual urban wasteland into a flourishing mixed residential-commercial neighborhood.

The Morial Center's proximity to the French Quarter, the Mississippi River, the Aquarium of the Americas, shopping districts, nightspots and thousands of first-class hotel rooms make it a perfect package of facilities and attractions for conventions.

The facility is also known for its exceptional in-house food and beverage services. Its exclusive contractor, ARAMARK, offers superb New Orleans and Louisiana cuisine under the direction of award-winning chef Leon West. ARAMARK's offerings range from convenient exhibit booth service, to themed evening events, to seated meals for 10 to 10,000 people. The convention center's 400-seat Atrium Restaurant/Lounge, which features casual fare, and Ma Maison, which offers guests an elegant, white-glove dining experience, showcase its varied culinary options under one roof.

The Morial Center is governed by an 11-member board: the Ernest N. Morial New Orleans Exhibition Hall Authority, a political subdivision of the state. The facility is managed by New Orleans Public Facility Management, Inc. ◆

The Morial Convention Center occupies a key part of the City's landscape and its success helped usher in many new developments in the Warehouse District since the colossal Center opened 11 years ago. The facility is a very short walk to the French Quarter, the Mississippi River, hotels, restaurants, and other tourist attractions.

The Earnest N. Morial Convention Center has earned a world-class reputation for quality and service in the exposition industry.

World Trade Center of New Orleans

The World Trade Center of New Orleans is a private, nonprofit organization dedicated to generating wealth and jobs for the city and state through international trade, port development, and related activities.

Headquartered at the riverfront in the 33-story World Trade Center Building, WTC New Orleans traces its ancestry to two predecessor organizations: International House, founded in 1943, and the International Trade Mart, founded in 1945. As such, it was the first of what are today over 300 world trade centers in 90 countries. WTC New Orleans also was a founding member of the World Trade Centers Association, which was created in New Orleans in 1968.

Boasting 2,000 corporate and individual members, WTC New Orleans conducts a variety of trade promotion and educational programs designed to bolster the city's and state's position in international trade, investment, tourism, the maritime industry, banking, and other trade-related areas.

Classes on importing and exporting, international conferences, trade shows, foreign language courses and seminars on doing business in specific countries are among its many educational and business-enhancing programs.

WTC New Orleans members also have opportunities to participate in organized committees on international business, transportation and governmental affairs that recommend policies and projects benefiting Louisiana.

WTC New Orleans helps to coordinate international trade missions of Louisiana business, tourism, port, airport, and government leaders focusing on specific commercial objectives. Conversely, countless national and international dignitaries, including presidents, ambassadors, secretaries of state, foreign leaders and business executives, have visited WTC New Orleans over the years as speakers, honorees, and conference participants.

In addition to offering educational and increased commercial opportunities to the state's businessmen and women, WTC New Orleans members and their spouses are eligible

to receive a wide range of membership benefits.

Members receive full privileges in the Plimsoll Club, a dining and entertainment venue on the 30th floor of the WTC Building, and reciprocal access to all World Trade Centers and their facilities around the globe.

Members also receive reduced rates for enrollment in international trade seminars, training courses, luncheon briefings, and beginning, intermediate, and advanced courses in Spanish, French, and other languages. Members also can join NETWORK, an electronic trading, communications, and information service linking subscribers to other World Trade Centers and their members.

WTC New Orleans also publishes the *Louisiana International Trade Directory*, the most complete source of current information on Louisiana's international business community. The Directory contains 170 pages of more than 2,000 detailed listings of exporters and importers throughout the state and numerous international trade organizations and suppliers of trade-related services. The Directory is also available on 3 1/2-inch IBM-formatted HD diskettes. ◆

Industry & Development

As a new century of space exploration approaches, led by the soon-to-be built International Space Station, New Orleans continues to play a major role in America's access to space.

In the 1960's, the National Aeronautics and Space Administration (NASA), took control of the sprawling Michoud facility in eastern New Orleans for the express purpose of designing and assembling large space vehicles. In a few short years, the facility came to play a vital part in the developing national space program, helping power no less than six Apollo lunar landing missions.

That adventure eventually gave birth to the country's Space Shuttle program, which in turn, provided a mission for Lockheed Martin Manned Space Systems: to design and construct the External Tank for NASA's Space Shuttle program, a mission that has seen it build to date more than 75 External Tanks, with current contracts for the completion of a total of 120 set to run until the year 2,000 and beyond.

"Currently there is no ready replacement for the Space Shuttle system, so there is every likelihood that NASA will continue to fly the Shuttle well beyond the year 2000, until 2010 or even 2020," says Marion A. LaNasa, Jr., communications chief with Lockheed Martin in New Orleans. "The possibility is just as good that we will continue to build External Tanks for at least that long."

Measuring 154 feet long and a hefty 28 feet in diameter, the External Tank is by far the largest single component of the technologically complex Space Shuttle system. With a fuel capacity of some 535,000 gallons, the tank is also intricate: composed of more than 480,000 individual

The Space Shuttle Columbia clears the tower at the Kennedy Space Center with the aid of the External Tank designed and constructed by Lockheed Martin Manned Space Systems. Photo courtesy of NASA.

parts that include, among other things, about 38 miles of electrical wiring, 1,000 feet of insulated sleeving, and 7,000 feet of safety wiring. The ET, as it is called, has remained relatively unchanged over the years. Today, however, it is undergoing design changes to reflect the needs of the shuttle itself, which was first launched into Earth's orbit in April

The External Tank is transported from the production building to the port facility for shipment by barge to the Kennedy Space Center for launch.

of 1981 and more than 70 times since.

The External Tank's latest change calls for reducing its weight for shuttle launches beginning in December of 1997. "We are in the process of using a new aluminum-lithium alloy to reduce the weight of the tank by about 7,500 pounds," says LaNasa, "which will result in an equal increase in the Shuttle's payload. The weight savings is critical to the launch of International Space Station components."

But pinpointing which 7,500 pounds can go out of the tank is no simple task, continues LaNasa. "It is an area of very fine maneuvers. Nothing on the tank is overweight, it is all pretty much made up of many intricate parts, which means you have to examine very carefully what stays, what can go, and what can be transformed into something else."

Because the External Tank is the only non-reusable component part of the Shuttle, a new one must be constructed for each succeeding Shuttle flight. Produced at the rate of seven a year, the External Tank is made up of many component parts produced by a wide variety of subcontractors across the country.

But the actual assembly of the tanks always takes place inside the vast, spacious compound located on more than 840 acres at the NASA Michoud Assembly Facility some 15 miles east of downtown New Orleans on an airy vista of land surrounded by water and trees.

With more than 200,000 square feet of laboratory space housing some $63 million of technologically proficient equipment, Lockheed Martin Manned Space Systems is also a major New Orleans employer providing work for upwards of 2,400 people. In 1995, it generated a local payroll that exceeded $138 million, making it one of the largest employers in the Gulf South.

The site is also an historic one: in the 1960's it served as the final assembly facility for the Saturn-Apollo rocket that put man on the moon for the first time in the summer of 1969.

Not until 1973, in fact, was the facility geared for the almost exclusive production of the External Tanks it has since made famous.

Today the sweeping facility houses a materials testing lab, a comprehensive chemicals analysis lab, and a main through-aisle in the facility's 43-acre production building that is more than a quarter of a mile long. "It is not an assembly line in the traditional sense of a factory," explains LaNasa. "When you deliver one tank every seven weeks that is not what most people would consider to be a typical production line. But it is certainly very much a high-tech line where an extreme level of precision is required to build a tank that has half a million separate parts."

With a past etched in the triumphs of NASA and the nation's exciting space adventure, Lockheed Martin Manned Space Systems' future was made more clear in the spring of 1995 after the $10 billion merger of the Lockheed company with Martin Marietta.

Since then there has been a renewed emphasis on efficiency and bringing new non-NASA work to the facility. "We are also building pressurized helium tanks that have been used for advanced communications satellites," says LaNasa.

But, overwhelmingly, the Lockheed Martin Manned Space Systems' mission and NASA's remain one—to explore the earth's horizon into the darker reaches beyond us, into the galaxy of the surrounding universe. "As long as they want to go up into space, we'll be there with them," says LaNasa. "That's our reason for being here." ◆

Technicians complete the final cleaning inside a liquid oxygen tank.

Measuring 154 feet long and 28 feet in diameter, the External Tank is by far the largest single component of the technologically complex Space Shuttle system.

With its flourishing plant operations on over 800 acres along the banks of the Mississippi River, Cytec Industries has emerged as a major industry player and important community participant, reflecting both the company's significance to the local economy as well as its commitment to its neighbors and the environment.

Cytec Industries Inc. is a vertically integrated, specialty chemical company that serves a wide range of industries, including water treatment, paper, chemical and polymer processing, coatings, plastics, mineral processing, oil drilling and recovery, aerospace, textile, and automotive.

In 1952, Cytec purchased the square mile of largely unsettled land it occupies today, attracted by the direct access to transportation on the Mississippi River, easy connections to natural gas pipelines and the major refineries of the state operating above and below the facility. The history

An archeological dig on the Fortier facility attracts thousands of students each year.

of the site is rich: once owned by the King of Spain and granted to Eugene Fortier in 1776, the land remained in the Fortier family until 1934. Their legacy is remembered by the very name of the facility today—the Fortier plant.

In the years since, Cytec has become an important participant in the local economy—it currently employs more than 650 employees with an annual payroll that exceeds $30 million. Each year, the Fortier plant pays up to $4.6 million in state and local sales and property taxes. Furthermore, in any given year, the plant spends more than $280 million for goods and services based in Louisiana.

The Fortier plant manufactures a variety of chemicals used in many consumer products through out the world, including sulfuric acid, used in water treatment systems and car batteries; ammonia, used in household cleaners and fertilizers; melamine, used for fire resistant clothing, building products, plastic laminate countertops and furniture foam; acrylamide, used in paper manufacturing and water treatment; and acrylonitrile, used in such items as synthetic rubber, synthetic fiber, and high- performance plastics.

A final product, methyl methacrylate (MMA), is not only a component of greenhouses, plastic automotive parts, and eyeglasses, it is also an integral part of the massive tank

walls containing thousands of fish at the Aquarium of the Americas' permanent exhibit on the New Orleans riverfront. The Fortier plant also is a major producer of methanol, a gasoline additive that can substantially reduce the average car's exhaust emissions.

With an annual production capacity of more than 4.3 billion pounds, Fortier's environmental concerns are paramount. In recent years, the company has invested more than $250 million for improvements which, while actually increasing the productive capacity of the Fortier plant, has also reduced SARA TRI emission by up to 80 percent. As a result of its environmental efforts to reduce emissions, Cytec in 1995 was presented a Certificate of Appreciation by the Environmental Protection Agency, followed by the EPA's Excellence in Pollution Prevention Award in 1996. Fortier's strong environmental record has also earned it the prestigious Environmental Excellence Award for Underground Injection, from Region 6 EPA.

One major environmental project at the Fortier plant is sulfuric acid regeneration, where state-of-the-art technology has come into play to recycle waste sulfuric acid, resulting in a 75 percent reduction of deep well releases. Fortier has also reduced air emissions by more than 40 percent in the 1990s and water emissions by 13 percent.

Safety is also a top priority at the plant, evidenced by the ambitious Fortier program for promoting safety awareness and training for all employees. The effort has been so successful that Fortier has been recognized by not only the National Petroleum Refiners Gold Award and Meritorious Award but also with the National Safety Council Award for Best Safety Performance and the OCAW Union Safety Award for Outstanding Performance.

The company's concern for public safety can be seen in the highly regarded Emergency Response and Incident Management (ERIM) team, composed of highly trained Fortier employees who provide swift and effective emergency response if an incident occurs while products are being transported anywhere in the U.S. or Canada.

Continuous process improvements, such as using computers to help run and monitor Cytec's processes allowed the plant to double production while at the same time reduce SARA TRI emisssion to the environment by 75 percent.

Fortier management formed a community advisory panel, known as CYCAP, made up of local community leaders and neighbors. CYCAP's mission is to open and maintain a dialog with neighbors and local citizens about plant operations and to answer any concerns centering around the plant's effect on the local environment.

Fortier has also increased its public profile and participation in the community through its support of a growing number of programs and organizations designed to facilitate education, the arts, and the environment, while providing needed civic and social services. Among other ongoing efforts supported by the Fortier plant is the annual archaeology dig, during which thousands of school children tour the Fortier site, which was the Orange Grove Plantation during the 18th century. Since the beginning of its participation in the program in 1989, the Fortier site has been visited by more than 12,000 students, who through the active dig learn what life was like on an 18th century plantation and also get the opportunity to visit a world-class petrochemical facility.

The company is a prominent sponsor of the Louisiana Wildlife & Fisheries Museum, hoping to spark the interest of more children in science and the environment. The museum, which promotes education through teacher programs, field trips and a variety of seminars on topics such as ecological preservation, recently changed its name to the Cytec Industries Louisiana Wildlife and Fisheries Museum. In addition, the critically acclaimed PBS series *NOVA* and *Bill Nye The Science Guy* are underwritten locally by Cytec Industries' Fortier plant.

Fortier employees are particularly proud of their sponsorship of Fun Science for Families Day at the Oakwood Center. The event, which attracts up to 12,000 children, parents, and educators, is comprised of 50 booths (each booth has a teacher and a volunteer scientist) of hands-on learning of scientific principles. The main objectives are to demon-

strate that science can be fun and to promote parental involvement in their children's education. The event, which is a cooperative effort among Cytec, the Jefferson Parish Public Schools, and the Oakwood Center, has received national acclaim and has become a model for educational partnership.

Cytec employees are also among the most generous in the region when it comes to the annual campaign for the United Way, contributing more than $1 million since 1988.

Through these programs and others, the employees of the Fortier plant and Cytec have been widely recognized for their efforts in the community, working to make Louisiana a better place for everyone to live. ◆

Marrero Land & Improvement Association, Ltd., popularly known as "Marrero Land" and with roots reaching back to the turn of the century, has been a major player in the great story of the Westbank of Jefferson Parish, neighbor to and across the Mississippi River from the City of New Orleans. From its inception, Marrero Land has been an integral part of the growth and development of the Westbank, which has experienced one of the most dynamic industrial, commercial, and suburban residential expansions in the state of Louisiana.

When Louis H. Marrero, Sr., and his three sons founded the Company in 1904, the upriver area of the Westbank was largely a pastoral stretch of land consisting principally of historic plantations devoted to agricultural endeavors, and relatively isolated from the city. But the senior Marrero, a pioneer and visionary, saw the Westbank as an untapped resource with great potential for business and industry, complemented by commercial and residential development as the area made its transition from an agrarian to a modern day metropolitan economy.

From its early beginnings to the present, Marrero Land has worked tirelessly to make its founder's vision a reality, and its achievements are legion. Through the years, the company has played a major role in attracting business and industry to the Westbank, and is responsible for most of the major single family residential developments within the "villages" of Harvey and Marrero and within the City of Westwego. Throughout its history, Marrero Land has involved itself in the full spectrum of land ownership, management, and development from pasture leases to the joint-venture development of a major regional mall.

Since the early 1960's, and with the advent of "The Crescent City Connection," the second of two Mississippi River bridges, the Westbank has experienced explosive growth and development. Today, the Westbank's population is nearing 250,000 people constituting approximately 25 percent of the Greater New Orleans Metropolitan Area's population, and is a vibrant hub of residential, commercial, and industrial activity. Though Marrero Land has provided much of the land resources to accommodate such growth, it still remains as one of the largest owners of land still available for growth and development within the Metropolitan Area.

"We are proud of our record and feel fortunate and gratified to be a part of the Westbank's historic transformation and growth," says

N. Buckner Barkley, Jr., president of Marrero Land, alongside a portrait of his great-grandfather, Louis H. Marrero, Sr., founder of the Company. Photo by Joe Bergeron, M.Photo, C.C.P.

The Barkley Estates entrance and community park flanked by several attractive homes in this planned community development. Photo by Joe Bergeron, M.Photo, C.C.P.

N. Buckner "Buck" Barkley, Jr., great-grandson of Louis H. Marrero, and the Company's President and CEO. "Though we have holdings and interests elsewhere, our major focus has always been on the Westbank, the place of our birth, and we intend to continue to concentrate our efforts there."

In the late 1970's, Marrero Land gained widespread attention within the local development community and real estate markets with the opening of Plantation Estates, a 436-lot upscale residential development containing custom-built homes of varying sizes and styles. Located in the heart of the Westbank, off Barataria Boulevard, Plantation Estates is particularly noted for the quality of its environment and the beauty of its homes.

Among the Company's most recent achievements has been the development of the elegant and decoratively landscaped Barkley Estates, a 165-acre upscale residential community located in Harvey, Louisiana, north of Lapalco Boulevard, a major Westbank transportation artery. Opened in July 1994, Barkley Estates is a planned community development, with 416 spacious home sites, a boulevard entrance lined with historic live oaks, a community park, perimeter parks, a walking-jogging trail, and other amenities, all designed to provide the homeowner with a pleasant and enjoyable ambiance, and a consistent quality of life. Home construction in Barkley Estates, under strict design and construction controls, is very active and is reflected in a multitude of attractive homes of varying styles.

Emphasizing the concept of community over the more traditional subdivision style, Marrero Land, in its Barkley Estates development and through recorded deed and title restrictions, has established the Barkley Estates Community Association to govern the residential community and to maintain the quality level of each home and neighborhood, thus protecting, preserving, and enhancing the investment of each homeowner and the quality of life within the development.

But the concept of "community" is not new to Marrero Land nor limited to its properties and developments. Marrero Land maintains a philosophy that its growth and vitality are inextricably linked to the growth and vitality of the community in which its operates. Involvement in the community and community affairs is an essential element and a hallmark of Marrero Land's operations. Their involvement includes such community programs as "Adopt-A-School" and "Jefferson Dollars For Scholars," as well as membership in The Chamber/New Orleans and the River Region, and its Westbank Council; the Jefferson Business Council, the Harvey Canal Industrial Association, the Committee for a Better Jefferson, the Louisiana Landowners Association, the Metropolitan Area Committee, the Council For A Better Louisiana, and the Public Affairs Research Council.

Barkley himself currently serves on the Board of The Chamber, the Executive Committee of the Westbank Council of The Chamber, the Executive Committee and Board of the Jefferson Business Council, and the Board of "Jefferson Dollars for Scholars." He also serves on the Board and is a former president of the Louisiana Landowners Association, a past president of the Harvey Canal Industrial Association, and has served as Chairman of the Board of Commissioners For The Port of New Orleans.

As a community leader, Barkley, in 1993, was chosen as the recipient of the John W. Stephens, Jr., Award for service to the Westbank Council of The Chamber, and, in 1994, received the prestigious and coveted Role Model award given by the Young Leadership Council of New Orleans.

Barkley's prominence in the metropolitan scene has not deterred him from the vision and mission established by his great-grandfather nearly a century ago: to create a vital, vibrant, and long-lasting Westbank community. "This is our home and the place that has made us what we are today," says Barkley, "and this is where we intend to stay—growing and growing with the Westbank, and building on our reputation." ◆

For nearly 90 years, Domino Sugar Corporation's Chalmette Refinery has operated from a sprawling 70-acre site on the Arabi riverfront, just downriver from New Orleans.

Opened in 1909 by the American Sugar Refining Company, the refinery is referred to as the "Chalmette Refinery" because of its proximity to the Chalmette Battlefield. The American Sugar Refining Company later became Amstar Sugar Corporation, and was renamed Domino Sugar Corporation, in 1991.

With a history tracing back to 1807, Domino is the nation's leading cane sugar refiner. The company produces grocery, industrial, and institutional sugar products at plants in Arabi, LA, Baltimore, MD, and Brooklyn, NY.

With corporate headquarters in New York City, Domino has been under the ownership of the London-based food conglomerate, Tate & Lyle, since 1988. This parent company holds the distinction of being among the world's largest sugar processors.

Domino's Chalmette Refinery is one of St. Bernard Parish's leading employers with a workforce of 450. Refinery workers are involved in every phase of production, from raw sugar intake to product packaging and shipping. Offices dedicated to customer service, purchasing, finance, and district sales also are at the Arabi plant. Domino® Sugar products are the most popular of their kind in the metro area.

Originally designed to process 3 million pounds of raw sugar daily, the modern Chalmette Refinery has a daily capacity of more than 6 million pounds. The majority of its raw sugar supplies come from Louisiana, Hawaii, Texas, Florida, and countries in the Caribbean Basin and South America, and are transported to the plant via oceangoing ships, barges, and trucks. The refinery's 1,100-foot-long dock, with a water depth of more than 45 feet year-round, is equipped to handle raw sugar cargoes in excess of 90 million pounds. It can also handle the ships that arrive to load refined sugar for export to all parts of the world.

The plant's complex sugar refining process, a carefully monitored system that includes heating, centrifugation, carbonation, filtration, evaporation, crystallization, drying, and conditioning, produces the familiar white granulated sugar that fills the Domino® Sugar popular five-pound yellow, blue, and white bags, and a range of other sugar-based foods, including Confectioners Sugar, Light and Dark Brown sugars, Qwik-Flo® Molasses and other specialty sugars and syrups. A potable water plant processes approximately 2.5 million gallons of water each day, a portion of this water is used in boilers to generate steam for processing and electrical generation of up to 11,000 kilowatts per hour. In 1995 one of those products, Domino® Flavored Confectioners Sugar, was awarded an A+ overall rating by AcuPOLL® for new consumer products. AcuPOLL® Reports is a monthly marketing report published by Marketing Intelligence Service, Ltd.,

Pictured above is Bobby Ducros, Sugar Boiler, working with the new technology in the Processing Department at the Chalmette Refinery of Domino Sugar Corporation.

The Chalmette Refinery was recognized as the 1995 "Best of the Best" Quality Action Team by Domino's New York Corporate Office. The employees on this successful team (left to right) were: Johnny Vicknair, Quality Control Technician; Larry Grayson, Pan House Operator; Al Pierre, Supervisor; Ben Bernard, Department Manager; Clarice Barney, Sugar Boiler; Bert Dugas, Instrument Technician; and John Talbot, Supervisor.

the country's leading provider of new packaged goods information. Each month an expert panel selects the most significant new packaged goods introduced to the market place and measures consumer reactions to each product. Consumer responses are measured using advanced statistical methods and then translated into "A" to "F" grades that reflect how well the new product performs versus the active AcuPOLL database of more than 2,000 concepts.

In addition to the actual refining process, such quality control issues as packaging, laboratory analysis, environmental monitoring, water treatment, and equipment maintenance are addressed at the refinery site.

Finished products are shipped out of Arabi by truck, rail, barge, and ship to retail, commercial, and industrial customers throughout the United States as well as overseas.

Serving The Community

Being a good corporate citizen is of great importance at Domino's Chalmette Refinery. The company's Educational Partnership Committee, established in 1990, serves local elementary schools through several volunteer projects held throughout the year.

Focusing its efforts on two schools—Arabi and Borgnemouth elementary schools—refinery employees serve as volunteer readers during National Literacy Week in March. Domino also funds annual awards recognizing top honor roll students and those who have shown the most improvement over the academic year. Other recent efforts involving schools have included the donation of playground equipment, winter coat drives and the painting of the Arabi Elementary School cafeteria.

Domino's Chalmette Refinery also supports the Fellowship Foundation, a nonprofit effort aimed at getting high-school-age boys involved in organized athletics. The company donates volunteers, t-shirts, hats, and Dominade® to the foundation's annual May track meet.

Refinery employees participate in the annual "Christmas

"Best of the Best." A Quality Action Team is any group of employees who devise ways to improve operational efficiency or product quality. The Chalmette Refinery team won for its method to produce drier sugar, which led to a higher degree of customer satisfaction. Open to all employees, such teams are eligible for cash awards amounting to as much as $1,500.

Another employee program, Right Things Right, recognizes individual employees for doing "the right things right"—or taking prompt action on problems recognized during the course of a workday, such as stopping a production line to make a necessary adjustment. Program winners receive an award, and are featured in the employee newsletter. Other employee awards include those for years of service and annual perfect attendance.

Other activities enjoyed by refinery employees include annual wellness fairs and company-sponsored softball and golf outings In addition, an employee-run Site Safety Committee promotes safety in the workplace, and an on-site Computer Center offers employees opportunities to improve their computer skills in their off-time. ◆

Several of the original structures built in 1905 still stand amidst palm trees at the Domino's Chalmette Refinery located on the Mississippi River just downriver from the French Quarter in New Orleans.

in October" housing rehabilitation effort, focusing on homes in the the nearby Lower 9th Ward of New Orleans; contribute to the United Way and to programs benefiting the arts and civic groups. The company also makes donations of sugar to worthy causes such as the Ozanam Inn, various civic and charitable organizations, churches, and schools.

In Recognition of a Job Well Done

Training in the areas of technological improvement and communication are among the many benefits enjoyed by Domino employees.

In 1995, one of the Chalmette Refinery's Quality Action teams was recognized by Domino's corporate office as

Amstar Sugar Corporation, (formerly American Sugar Company), changed its name to reflect it's famous brand of Domino® Sugar in 1991. Pictured above is the familiar blue and yellow five-pound bags of Domino® Sugar.

St. Charles Borromeo, Early Childhood
Development Center.

Nearing its sixth decade of operation, Norco Construction Company, Inc., of Norco, Louisiana—some 20 miles to the northwest of New Orleans—has all of the business it can handle.

"We are having to turn business down for the first time ever," says Henry Friloux, the president of the company, noting that in a normal year Norco Construction does between $4.5 to $5 million in business. But by the beginning of 1996, "we already had more than $4 million in contracts. And in the immediate months to follow we picked up another $1 million in work."

How to explain such success? Friloux partly attributes it to the quality of his customers, some of whom have been working with Norco Construction since its founding in 1941. "One of our major contractors has been the New Orleans Public Service," he adds. "Since 1943 we have worked with their gas department providing labor to them under a labor agreement." What was supposed to be a 60-day contract is now nearing it's 60th anniversary.

Another long-time customer is the Shell Oil Company, for which Norco Construction has built foundations and operations buildings, while moving Shell's massive tanks to and fro.

Recently, Norco completed four zone shops for Shell, one with a construction price tag of more than $900,000. "The zone shops are basically maintenance shops measuring around 10,000 square feet with cranes and other equipment," explains Friloux. "We build the foundation and the building itself with the offices and ancillary facilities for their employees."

Other Norco projects include industrial buildings for the Monsanto Agricultural Company, expansion work for the Frito-Lay Company in suburban New Orleans, and renovation work on the historic Destrehan Plantation, one of the largest and oldest plantations in Louisiana. The skilled Norco workers left their imprint on virtually every corner of the plantation, renovating the central building's fireplaces, sweeping porch, and extensive roofing, as well as painting both the house's exterior and interior walls.

It is that diversity of skills and variety of product that has kept the Norco company, with its roughly 100 employees, competitive. Founded by Friloux's father, Henry "De De" Friloux, Norco Construction has also become more competitive in the 1990s with its design-built projects, bringing together the best-laid plans of engineers and architects in one working team to design and plan out any kind and variety of building.

Another important part of the Norco company's design-built abilities comes with its computer capabilities, allowing for customers to not only design their dream structure on screen, but to order it by specification electronically.

Friloux also credits a working staff composed of both skilled and semi-skilled employees for Norco's success. "These are people who are very good at what they do," he says. "I can send them to something like the Destrehan Plantation where they can rebuild a 200-year-old wall while still making sure it has the look of an old wall, and then send them to put up a brand new metal building for one of the industrial facilities we work with, and know I am going to get a high level of quality either way."

For those reasons and others, the future for Norco Construction looks as bright as its past. ◆

St. Catherine of Siena, Monsignor
Barrett Complex.

The New Orleans Saints Professional
Football Team Training Center is a 65,000
square foot state-of-the-arts facility.

Almost as bookends, two notable projects recently seen to completion by Carl E. Woodward, Inc. of New Orleans symbolize the busy firm's sensitivity to the past as it enthusiastically embraces the design and construction needs of the future.

In the heart of the French Quarter, inside a Beaux-Arts-designed police station and courthouse built after the turn of the century, the Woodward firm recently completed all of the historic renovation for an enterprise dedicated to the past: the Historic New Orleans Collection, an archive and library containing some 64 tons of rare books, manuscripts, letters, and photographs reaching into Louisiana's Colonial era.

Replete with polished wood and copper and brass fixtures, the archives is topped by a sweeping library reminiscent of some of Europe's grand public reading rooms.

Across town at the edge of the Central Business District, Woodward has also completed work on the new 47,000-square foot Channel 6 television station WDSU, the local NBC affiliate.

An $8 million project, the station is capped by a microwave tower more than 120 feet tall and contains state-of-the-art equipment and wiring to all of the station's vital arteries, including the studios, production suites, and giant outside satellite dishes. A clearstory newsroom utilized as a broadcast backdrop is the building's core component.

"Both of these projects provided a different challenge," says Armand LeGardeur, Woodward's chairman of the board. "But even so, they were only two of the many projects we do yearly."

Indeed, on an annual basis, the Woodward firm as design/build contractors might work on up to 20 major projects and nearly twice as many smaller efforts.

Woodward projects today not only line the metro New Orleans map, but have extended to such states as Virginia, Florida, and Texas. But the firm is also a regular contractor for such petrochemical companies as Union Carbide and Monsanto, along the Mississippi River's edge. "Sometimes one company may need a new warehouse, while another needs a new computer control building, or some other special structure for their particular uses," explains LeGardeur. "These companies have a select group of contractors they have come to rely upon."

That Woodward is one of those firms should come as no surprise. Founded in 1924 by the late Carl E. Woodward, the firm's first decades were spent designing and building homes in uptown and suburban New Orleans. After World War II, Woodward signed on as a Butler Manufacturing Company dealership, building hundreds of prefabricated buildings to accommodate the massive suburban expansion needs.

In the 1960s, the Woodward firm became a full-service construction design/build firm. "Usually the architect designs the building while the contractor builds it, but they don't always work together which can sometimes lead to cost overruns and other similar problems," explains President Paul H. Flower. "We decided to combine both efforts into one working team, so that, with the owner, you have a partnering effort that lasts from start to finish."

With nearly 50 employees in administration and sales, plus 150 working in the field as craftsmen and materials specialists, Woodward today enjoys a reputation transcending the city's borders with a vigorous annual output. "The mid-1990s have been good for us," LeGardeur adds. "And we look forward to continued growth in the future." ◆

A recent $8 million project of
Carl E. Woodward, Inc. is the new
47,000-square foot broadcast facility of
WDSU Channel 6 television station,
the local NBC affiliate. Photo by
Neil Alexander/Southern Lights Studio.

Business & Finance

The Chamber/ New Orleans and the River Region

Water means prosperity for the business community of Greater New Orleans, through shipping, tourism, travel, and seafood, from the Mississippi as well as Lake Pontchartrain. Photo by Jackson Hill/Southern Lights Studio.

Between 1987—when the impact of the oil downturn was fully felt—and 1996, the New Orleans region added more than 90,000 jobs. The job base for the city reached 650,000 in 1996, more jobs than ever before. Photo by Jackson Hill/Southern Lights Studio.

In June, 1996, the rest of the world discovered what The Chamber/New Orleans and the River Region has known all along. Our seven-parish area, with perhaps the most pervasive European, Caribbean, and African influences of any metropolis in the nation, is definitely All-American.

With The Chamber leading the effort, Greater New Orleans won its first All-America City and Community Award. The City of New Orleans last won the award in 1952. The honor is given to communities that bring a broad coalition of private citizens, community groups, business, and government together to solve the same problems that are common to urban areas all over the country. It is just another way that The Chamber is spearheading successful initiatives to make a difference in the New Orleans region.

One of the biggest of those differences is reflected in the improving job picture. To enhance the local economy, The Chamber has worked to encourage diversification, smart business strategies, and business relocations and startups. Its efforts have been a primary factor in what the *Times-Picayune* in 1996 called New Orleans' "home-grown recovery."

Between 1987—when the impact of the oil downturn was fully felt—and 1995, the New Orleans region added more than 80,000 jobs. The job base for the city reached 600,000 in 1995, more jobs than ever before. According to statistics cited by the *Times-Picayune* and gathered by the University of New Orleans Division of Business and Economic Research, taxable retail sales grew from $8.7 billion in 1987 to $12.7 billion in 1995, while per capita income more than doubled.

The growth will continue. According to Chamber projections, the area should gain 20,000 more jobs by 1998. The benefits touch all New Orleans area residents, because every time one $30,000 job is added to the region, at least $150,000 in additional economic growth results. Between 1991 and 1995, the New Orleans region also recorded an unprecedented $13 billion in capital investment and infrastructure improvements. It's one of the highest investment amounts, per capita, of any area in the country.

Industries creating these jobs include tourism, health care, shipbuilding and the maritime sector, petrochemicals, and construction. Small businesses, like those that make up more than 80 percent of Chamber membership, are primary contributors to this new wave of diversification.

The Chamber is clearly carrying out its mission, as it was redefined in 1996: "To create a favorable business environment and support the growth and development of business." We carry out our mission through advocacy, addressing issues critical to economic prosperity in the region, and providing information and services that support the success of member businesses.

The impetus behind much of the new economic power is workforce preparedness, and education. The Chamber focuses on preparing area citizens for work, through programs that include the School-to-Work initiative, Dollars for Scholars, Keyboards for Kids, and teacher/student recognition programs carried out by area councils.

The Chamber's top educational priority is School-to-Work, an initiative co-sponsored by the MetroVision Economic Development Partnership, an organization which is rooted in Chamber economic development efforts. School-to-Work links schools and the community to provide academic and career experiences for students, from kindergarten through college, to learn the knowledge, skills, and habits required to be successful adults. School-to-Work was one of the key efforts recognized by the All-America City and Community Award.

The Chamber has also been recognized as a national leader in building regional cooperation. Renowned national urban affairs columnist Neal Pierce hailed a new spirit among New Orleans area parishes: "A genuine dialogue about a more cohesive future for the region is dawning, driven by the overwhelming and shared necessity of economic survival." The first point of The Chamber's statement of philosophies notes that "The prosperity of the region depends on our ability to work together across jurisdictional and organizational boundaries to achieve common objectives."

The organization has developed an extremely successful framework for combining maximum regional cooperation with effective local impact and advocacy. Six Area Councils, including representation from Orleans, Jefferson, Plaquemines, St. Bernard, St. James, St. Charles, and St. John the Baptist parishes, are organized under the Chamber umbrella to establish positions and advocate for changes within their areas—as well as coming together to create the region-wide influence of The Chamber. This decentralization is a wellspring of flexibility and diversity, and a source of strength.

National kudos have also come to The Chamber for its leadership in forging new connections through technology. The Chamber Business Network was established in 1995 as the first of its kind in the nation, providing Chamber members with unlimited free access to the Internet. This pioneering effort allows thousands of businesses in the region to tap into valuable electronic mail services, user newsgroups, and to use the web as a marketing tool to promote their products and services globally—all as a part of Chamber membership. The program has become a model for dozens of similar organizations across the country.

On the edge of the global computer networking wave is the Chamber's participation in the International Business Exchange Program. Sponsored by the U.S. Chamber of

Commerce, the marketing tool links supply and demand internationally, using a network accessible from members' desktop computers to match buyers and sellers of products and services worldwide.

Members also benefit from a variety of marketing, networking, and other resources, including business referrals, a small business hotline, discounts on services as disparate as health insurance and long distance charges, and Chamber lobbying efforts on a local, state, and national level.

Since its founding in 1913 as the Association of Commerce and Industry, The Chamber/New Orleans and the River Region has been known for effective management, continual re-engineering of staff and processes, and excellence in implementation. That's why the U.S. Chamber has cited it as an exemplary organization, using fewer resources to operate at a level of service well above other chambers of its size.

With unified business leadership, involved and diverse membership, effective communications, support for public policies that promote economic growth, focus on initiatives that address local issues, emphasis on entrepreneurial enterprises, and contribution to creating a positive business environment, it's no wonder that The Chamber/New Orleans and the River Region has earned the All-American ranking. ◆

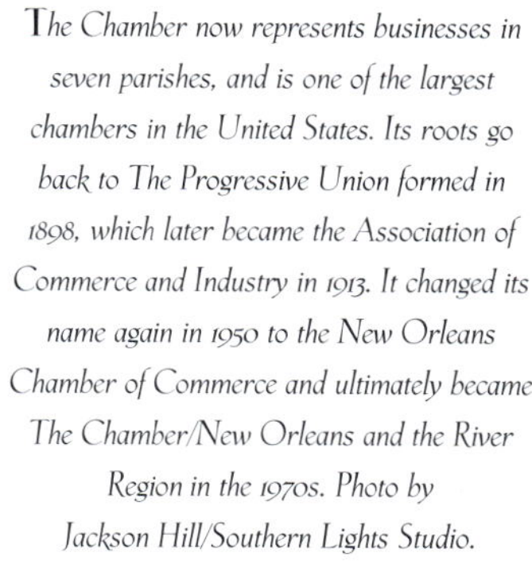

The Chamber now represents businesses in seven parishes, and is one of the largest chambers in the United States. Its roots go back to The Progressive Union formed in 1898, which later became the Association of Commerce and Industry in 1913. It changed its name again in 1950 to the New Orleans Chamber of Commerce and ultimately became The Chamber/New Orleans and the River Region in the 1970s. Photo by Jackson Hill/Southern Lights Studio.

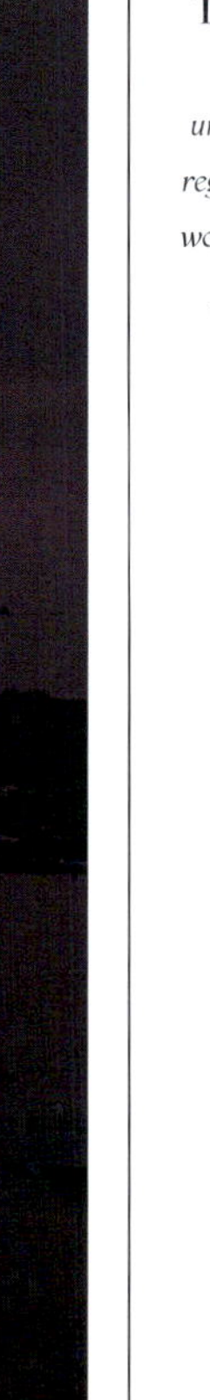

The Chamber/New Orleans and the River Region maintains a focus on the future, unifying the business community, developing regional solutions to common challenges, and working to make Greater New Orleans even greater. Photo by Jackson Hill/Southern Lights Studio.

Stewart Enterprises, Inc.

Operating with monumental success across our nation and the world, Stewart Enterprises, Inc., of New Orleans has managed to do nearly the impossible—to grow its family business to the point where Stewart is now the second largest U.S.-based, publicly traded death care provider in the world, while still maintaining the personal relationship reminiscent of the family business started by the Stewarts in 1910.

"The secret to our continued success since our founding in 1910," says Frank B. Stewart, Jr., chairman of the board and a third-generation executive, "is our constant commitment to serving families, first and foremost. And now, as a public company, with an increased pace and volume of acquisitions, the scope of families we serve is rapidly expanding. It now includes our client families, company employees and their families, and the family owners of businesses we have acquired, as well as our family of stockholders."

"We serve over 90,000 families each year, handling most of their death care arrangements," says Joseph P. Henican, III, vice chairman and chief executive officer of Stewart Enterprises, "but we serve each family's needs, one at a time." He explains: "When a family comes to us at their time of loss, they don't really care what we do for others; they care only about their own intensely personal needs and desires. Meeting those needs and desires through the delivery of quality, service, and value explains why Stewart Enterprises is regarded as a leader in its profession."

The Stewart name has endured since 1910, when the family acquired three small cemeteries and a marble shop. This "home-grown" company—proud to be headquartered in New Orleans— has evolved into an international company providing all three phases of death care need: (1) ceremony and tribute (the funeral service), (2) dignified disposal or burial, and (3) memorialization or remembrance—"fulfilling man's desire to be remembered as having been significant."

Stewart Enterprises has the largest *percentage* of combined operations, where a funeral home is located in a cemetery. This is important because it is the combined operation which "grows the business internally," as a result of the dynamic synthesis created by operating a funeral home on cemetery property. This concept enhances Stewart's attractiveness to financial analysts because it draws a more positive long-term picture of growth for investors. Stewart emerges as the leader long-term because it combines its strategic acquisition program with the development of combined operations and expertise in consumer preplanning. This latter aspect, helping families to prepare for "the inevitable" in advance of need, makes Frank B. Stewart, Jr., believe—like his father before him—that this profession is a "calling." And he believes that anticipating the needs and desires of families is the fountainhead of Stewart's success.

Since the company's initial public offering in 1991, Stewart's growth has been dramatic. During the subsequent years, the company has acquired premier funeral homes and cemeteries located in 21 states, Puerto Rico, Mexico, and Australia. "In the U.S.," says Stewart's President and Chief Operating Officer William E. Rowe, "the company has established a strong presence in major markets stretching from the Atlantic seaboard to the Pacific and Gulf Coasts. We are experiencing excellent growth in markets we've never been in before, and we think the potential for more growth throughout the Midwest and Far West is virtually unlimited."

As to presence in foreign markets, the company is considered the premier and largest provider of death care products and services in Puerto Rico. Stewart owns and operates Mexico City's most prestigious funeral service firm. In Australia, the company is a major funeral home operator in six of the country's top markets.

In addition to providing quality, service, and value, another hallmark of Stewart's reputation is the way it values the importance of local customs and traditions important to families and their communities. "We recognize that customs vary from country to country and from community to community. We are committed to preserving these traditions both in the U.S. and abroad," says Rowe.

To Stewart, preserving traditions includes keeping intact the fine local name and reputation of each funeral home and cemetery it acquires. When possible, it also retains each facility's local management and staff. "We aren't just buying bricks and mortar when we go into a new market,"

The international headquarters of Stewart Enterprises, Inc., located in Metairie, a suburb of New Orleans, Louisiana.

Frank B. Stewart, Jr.
Stewart Enterprises chairman
and chairman, Chamber of Commerce
New Orleans 1995–96;
William E. Rowe
president and chief operating officer;
Joseph P. Henican, III
vice chairman of the board and
chief executive officer.

Lake Lawn Metairie Funeral Home, located on the historic grounds of Metairie Cemetery in New Orleans.

insists Stewart. "We are acquiring the constituencies that give unique value to the local firm. In these times of ponderous federal, state, and local regulations; escalating operating costs, and a mountain of administrative paperwork; we simply add quality, service, and value through achieving economies of scale and scope, while at the same time retaining the goodwill established by the firm before we acquired it. This is a fact we respect and never lose sight of."

Nor is any sight lost of trends in consumer needs and desires. Industry analysts foresee the need to meet the growing demand by families for combined operations. Such a facility offers unparalleled service, convenience, and economy all at one convenient location. As a leader, Stewart will continue to respond to consumer demand for combined facilities, even as acquisitions continue apace.

"Over a third of our cemeteries have a funeral home located on cemetery property," explains Rowe, "and we plan to open three new funeral homes per year in the cemeteries that we already own. This demonstrates the continued commitment to the development of combined operations."

Another concept that Stewart utilizes is "clustering," i.e., the pooling of separate funeral homes and cemeteries in a common market. Clustering—while it does not provide all death care goods and services at a single location—does serve families through leverage, obtained by combining the operations of the clustered facilities for greater economy, then passing this economy on to the consumer.

More growth via consolidation through acquisition, clustering, and combining operations is expected to continue at Stewart. "Our plan for growth is well-considered and well-paced," explains Henican, who says that the Stewart acquisition pattern from its inception has always been deliberate and strategically long-term. "There is a tremendous amount of growth through acquisition still available to us. In fact, we see the next 10 to 15 years as our main era of consolidation. But that growth will not interfere with the mission to serve families, which has helped make Stewart an industry leader," Henican concluded.

Actually, Stewart's future seems to be merging with its past, as the firm upholds its tradition of bringing quality, service, and value to generations of families. His philosophy steeped in the history of his family's service to families, Frank Stewart explains: "It's a long-term tradition in which human beings care for other human beings from generation to generation. It involves *caritas* together with tough-minded fiscal responsibility, so we feel there is really a sacred side to our work." He concludes: "We take great pride in saying our home is in New Orleans, where the funeral and cemetery customs reflect the care of our people today for those who went before us. Truly, it is our heritage to believe in the 'eternal return.' " ◆

NASDAQ:NMS
Symbol: STEI

Lake Lawn Park Mausoleum, New Orleans, one of the largest community mausoleums in the United States.

Bank One

During the late nineteenth century, two banks were founded, nine years and more than one thousand miles apart.

Today, more than a century later, they are one. Bank One Corporation—among the top 12 banks in the U.S. with approximately $100 billion in assets. By far the largest bank holding company to maintain a physical presence in Louisiana. Bank One Louisiana, N.A. has more than 150 branches and $6 billion in assets statewide.

In 1877, a group of visionaries in Shreveport founded an institution that they named First National Bank.

Just a few years earlier, in 1868, a group of business leaders in Columbus, Ohio, founded Sessions & Co., which later changed its name to City National Bank & Trust.

Like the formation of the Mississippi River in the far reaches of the north that combines with the Missouri to become the mighty waterway that flows through New Orleans, these two events represent the headwaters of what we know today in our community and state as Bank One Louisiana.

Both institutions set upon a course of establishing strong reputations for attentive customer service and innovative financial products as they grew and prospered in their respective regions.

A few highlights of two illustrious banking histories bear out this common heritage of quality and innovation:

- City National of Columbus was the first bank outside California to offer what was then called Bank Americard service, an innovation in personal credit that would revolutionize contemporary consumer buying habits, which represent today some two-thirds of the American economy.

- Just a couple of years later, Louisiana National Bank of Baton Rouge (LNB) would become the first institution in our state to offer the Bank Americard.

- In 1975, LNB, which would later become part of the Premier Bank family, introduced a debit card that allowed customers to pay for purchases without writing a check.

- Just two years later, in 1977, LNB was the first institution in Louisiana to introduce Bill Payer, a system of paying bills over the telephone, eliminating the need to write checks at all.

At the time when Bank One began to expand to other states beyond its roots in Ohio in the 1980s, Louisiana laws changed to allow formation of larger, statewide banking organizations. In December, 1985, the first statewide bank holding company, Louisiana Bancshares, Inc., was formed by three predecessors of what today is Bank One, Louisiana, N.A.

In a short time, the alliance grew into Premier Bancorp, whose eight prominent community banks came together on

Unlike any branch of any bank ever seen in New Orleans, the Place St. Charles location features contemporary interior design that houses the most sophisticated array of technology and banking services available in the market.

Bank One's full-service branch in Place St. Charles, located in the heart of the CBD.

Bank One offers 22 branches in the metropolitan area such as this one at Metairie Road.

January 1, 1989, to form Premier Bank, dedicated to quality banking throughout Louisiana.

Premier's growth in New Orleans started just a year later.

The state's largest metro area was introduced to Premier's level of service and innovation in 1990, when Premier established its first presence in the New Orleans market with a local loan production office. By 1992, Premier introduced the most advanced banking presence ever seen in New Orleans with the opening of a full-service branch in Place St. Charles, located in the heart of the CBD.

Unlike any branch of any bank ever seen in New Orleans, Premier's Place St. Charles location features contemporary interior design that houses the most sophisticated array of technology and banking services available in the market.

The following year, Premier dramatically expanded its presence in the New Orleans market with the acquisition of Alerion Bank, which itself had been founded as American Bank & Trust in the 1920s. When Premier purchased 11 branches of a failed savings and loan association from the RTC the very next year, the stage was set for the marriage to Bank One at the beginning of 1996.

The merger with Bank One created a financial institution in Louisiana that is backed by the resources of one of the largest banks in the U.S., a bank with some $100 billion in assets, operating more than 1,500 branches across 12 states stretching from West Virginia to Arizona.

What those resources mean to individual and commercial customers alike is that Bank One Louisiana is able to offer a wider variety of products and services than ever before. For instance, corporate customers benefit from:

- Wider access to capital markets.
- Expanded international trade finance services.
- A wider array of investment management and trust services.
- The commercial lending power of the third-largest Small Business Administration (SBA) participant in the United States.

At the same time, individual customers can take advantage of an array of financial products and services that are unparalleled in Louisiana banking, including:

- At least five different choices for checking accounts alone, each designed to fit an individual's personal lifestyle and financial needs.

- Product options which permit customers to tailor their own unique relationship with Bank One.
- Improved access to the latest technology in on-line banking services.
- Dozens of other services and products to make financial life easier and more convenient, such as mutual funds, direct deposit, and automated bill-paying services.
- 24-hour telephone banking staffed by human beings, not voice mail menus.

The transformation of what began as a series of small community banks around the state into today's Bank One Louisiana is a story that is by no means ending. Rather, it is just beginning. As the financial needs of Louisiana's corporate and individual citizens change and grow to meet the challenges of the millennium just ahead, no institution in the state is more prepared to answer the call than Bank One Louisiana.

It's a far cry from the headwaters more than 100 years ago in Shreveport, Louisiana, and Columbus, Ohio. But, then, so was the Mississippi River. Like the natural waterway that has provided the life blood of the New Orleans economy for nearly 300 years, banking services reach New Orleans in full strength with Bank One Louisiana to lead our community into the next century. ◆

Bank One's interior lobby of the Metairie Road branch.

With a banking tradition more than a century-and-a-half old, First National Bank of Commerce (First NBC) is a member of the largest, most respected banking company in Louisiana. Together with its parent company, First Commerce Corporation, the bank's assets total $8.4 billion.

First Commerce Corporation also owns Central Bank in Monroe, First National Bank of Lafayette, Rapides Bank and Trust in Alexandria, First National Bank in Lake Charles and City National Bank in Baton Rouge.

First NBC traces its roots to March 5, 1931, when the New Orleans Canal and Banking Company was chartered to build the New Basin Canal, a now-defunct commercial waterway which stretched from the city's West End area to the Superdome.

In 1924, the bank merged with Citizens Bank, another prosperous institution dating from the 1830s. The bank is perhaps best known for issuing one of the most trusted $10 bills of the 19th century, the "dixie." The nickname, later a catchword for the South, stems from the American mispronunciation of the French word for ten—"dix"—which was printed prominently on the back of each bill.

Several mergers and name changes later, today's First NBC boasts 51 financial centers and over 2,500 employees in the metropolitan area. First NBC's corporate headquarters occupy over nine floors of the 52-story Place St. Charles, two blocks off Canal Street in the Central Business District.

A commitment to quality in customer service, coupled with a high performance strategy, is the cornerstone of First NBC's operation policy.

In the 1980s, First NBC was the first bank in the metro area to introduce the automatic teller machine. It now boasts the largest ATM network in the city, with over 200 sites.

First NBC also pioneered such improvements to customer service as a 30-minute response time to loan applications and a convenient Call First feature, which offers customers 24-hour bank-by-phone services such as transferral of funds between accounts and information on specific checks, current balance, and interest earned.

In 1995, First NBC became one of the first banks in the region to market credit cards on the Internet, and in 1996 was the first in the state to issue the PayTM card, a debit card that allows individuals without bank accounts to access their payroll funds through ATMs and point-of-sale locations.

Business men and women need look no further than their local branch of First NBC for reliable, up-to-the-minute financial services and advice.

First NBC's Business First option teams business customers with a business relationship manager who helps them custom tailor a plan to suit their specific needs. The business relationship manager sees customers through every step of their entrepreneurial journey, from early financial concerns over issues such as expansion, loan options, investments and cost-cutting, to long-term planning and retirement issues.

In 1994, First NBC demonstrated its faith in the local economy by setting up a licensed Small Business Investment Company, which allows the bank to invest up to $2 million in promising small business ventures through the purchase of a company's stock.

First NBC prides itself in offering clients a complete range of products and services to meet their every financial need. Marquis Investments, a wholly owned subsidiary of First NBC, provides customers with a full range of investment options. At the division's kiosks, customers have access to up-to-the-minute stock market information that allows them to monitor their investments.

First NBC's reputation as New Orleans' premier business bank was underscored in 1995, when its credit card division, First Bankcard Center, signed a contract to issue and process proprietary credit cards to enlisted men and women at U.S. Air Force bases nationwide. In 1996, the credit card account was expanded to U.S. Air Force bases around the world, including those in Japan, England, Turkey, Guam, Greenland, Italy, Korea, Germany, Portugal and Panama. These additions brought the total of Air Force bases involved in the program to over 100, with approximately 240,000 military accounts.

Being a good corporate citizen is an integral part of First NBC's mission.

When the bank established a $30 million mortgage pool designed in part to funnel more credit to minority families, it won praise from evaluators for that and other programs in compliance with the Community Reinvestment Act (CRA). The CRA is a federal act to increase the number of loans and business transactions between banks and members of minority communities.

In 1995, the bank's First Commerce Community Development Corporation (FCCDC) launched the Central City Initiative, a private-public partnership with the city of New Orleans to rehabilitate blighted houses in a 40-block area and sell them to low- and moderate-income buyers.

Since its debut, the FCCDC has become a statewide leader in neighborhood redevelopment by partnering with civic groups to renovate single-family homes, build new homes and transform abandoned buildings into affordable apartments for senior citizens in the New Orleans metro area, Lafayette, and Alexandria. The FCCDC plans on expanding its rehabilitation efforts into the Monroe, Baton Rouge, and Lake Charles areas.

First NBC's community consciousness is felt in almost every sphere of local life, from the military to the arts to programs for young people.

The bank's annual "Corporate Salute to the Red, White, and Blue" honors the contributions of the military to the local community through a month-long program of exhibits and a Flag Day observance.

First NBC also is involved in the activities of the Young Leadership Council and the Jazz and Heritage Foundation, and is a major sponsor of Habitat for Humanity, the annual N'Awlins Air Show at Belle Chasse Naval Air Station, and the Louisiana Dribblers. It also hosts a summer internship program, in conjunction with the Urban League, that gives young people a taste of careers in the banking field.

First NBC is a proud sponsor of local arts, including the New Orleans Museum of Art, the Louisiana Philharmonic Orchestra, the New Orleans Ballet Association, the WYES Showboat Auction, Jeff Fest, and the Jefferson Performing Arts Society. First NBC executives serve on the boards of these and many other nonprofit organizations.

Whether it be community involvement or products and services to meet the needs of individuals or businesses, First NBC proves to be the metro area's preeminent financial institution. ◆

First National Bank of Commerce's main office lobby in downtown New Orleans.

Hibernia National Bank

Hibernia National Bank, the oldest name in Louisiana banking, has been making it possible for people to achieve their financial goals and realize their dreams since 1870. As the bank "Where Service Matters," Hibernia has built the biggest and best financial services network in Louisiana—with almost 200 banking locations in 29 parishes as of mid-1996. About 88 percent of Louisiana's population lives in markets served by Hibernia. The company also will have a strong presence in two Texas counties when a pending merger with Texarkana National Bancshares is completed.

In every market, Hibernia is working hard to become a one-stop financial marketplace for individuals and businesses. Hibernia people are not waiting to see what competitors are doing; they are developing outstanding products, services, and systems to help customers realize their dreams. They are busy making progress toward one of the bank's primary goals—to be the leader in customer service.

Several key factors have come together. Hibernia has strong local market share, a real community focus, the drive to be the employer of choice, diversified commercial and consumer banking products, and an aggressive, want-to-do-business style. Combined with Louisiana's best delivery network, an understanding of customers' needs, the right products, and fast responses backed up by technology, it all adds up to unique banking strength.

Hibernia is rooted in a distinctive heritage. In 1870, a dozen men in New Orleans saw a window of opportunity. The economy was improving after the Civil War, but there were few healthy banks. Those men banded together to form Hibernia—named in honor of their native Ireland—and helped rebuild commerce in the city.

During the 13 decades since, Hibernia has been a leader, from building the city's first modern skyscraper and the tallest building in the South in 1921—a 23-story structure topped by the Hibernia Tower, a landmark that once was the official navigation light for Mississippi River pilots and continues to delight New Orleanians with its changing seasonal colors—to heading the bond-holding syndicate that underwrote the building of more than 10,000 miles of new roads in the state in the 1930s.

The bank's recent history is characterized by growth, derived from mergers and from the strengthening of the bank's existing statewide franchise.

Hibernia has been the most active of eight Louisiana financial institutions in merging with strong community banks. The 15 Louisiana mergers completed or announced by mid-1996 represent about one third of the announced transactions in the state since 1993. A 16th merger with Texarkana National Bancshares was announced at mid-year.

In mid-1992, Hibernia's market share in Louisiana was about 10 percent, with $4.5 billion in assets. In just three and a half years, the statewide market share grew to 17 percent, with almost $9 billion in assets following the completion of mergers. The growth has been balanced among Louisiana's geographical areas. In mid-1996, Hibernia had a 23 percent share in the North Louisiana market, a 20 percent share in the Southwest, and a 21 percent share in the Southeast.

Hibernia chooses merger partners carefully, seeking strong banks with excellent market positions and talented, community-based management teams with enviable records of customer loyalty. Hibernia, in turn, brings to merger banks an expanded menu of financial services and much greater access to technology-driven products.

Hibernia is an acknowledged leader in developing products and services that provide the flexibility, convenience and innovation that customers want. For example, Hibernia now has Saturday banking at about 40 percent of its offices and is the first major Louisiana bank to provide full-service Sunday banking at certain locations. It has achieved a technological edge, with an expanded ATM network, telebanking, and an Internet presence.

In 1870 Patrick Irwin was elected as the first president of Hibernia.

The main door to the vault in Hibernia's headquarters tips the scales at 24 tons and requires a 20-mule team to haul it to the building in 1921.

A new $35 million program at Hibernia increases Louisiana's available venture capital significantly, and the bank remains a leader in developing innovative products and services for small businesses—including rapid loan turnaround, one-page loan applications, and the state's first corporate credit card with a revolving line of credit. Response time for consumer and mortgage loan applications has been cut significantly.

A team approach to service is also key to Hibernia's growth and market position. In 1995, the bank launched a strategic initiative, drawing on the resources of every employee, to change the way it does business. "We are building a company that's radically different from the competition because we're harnessing the power of Hibernia people," says bank president Steve Hansel.

Vision 2000 is designed to do just that, bringing about changes that will result in improved customer service, productivity, communications, and career-development opportunities for employees. Vision 2000 includes redesigning processes so they add value for customers. Among its guiding principles: "Make service matter. Act like an owner. Make smart, common-sense decisions. Hustle. Continuously improve. Listen carefully. Create an environment in which people can excel, be rewarded, and have fun. Win in the marketplace as a team. Treat others with respect. Invest in the future to ensure long-term success." Thanks to Vision 2000, Hibernia people will have access to improved customer information as well as the authority they need to serve customers better and faster.

Accompanying Vision 2000 is the STARS program—Success Through Action, Redesign, and Service. STARS encourages employees to work together, be creative, and find better ways of doing their jobs. It is an effective catalyst for change, generating hundreds of solutions from employees.

The bottom line: Vision 2000, STARS, and other initiatives will distinguish Hibernia as the acclaimed service-provider in each of its markets even before the year 2000.

Hibernia is also known for its corporate citizenship, with $2.5 million going into communities throughout Louisiana in 1996. Education is the bank's top priority, but it also supports health and human services, art and culture, and civic and community causes. A new community development corporation will infuse resources into areas throughout the state, and a special statewide $46 million low-interest mortgage loan program benefits low- to moderate-income families.

From its roots in tradition, Hibernia has embraced change—to find the best way to provide truly outstanding service for customers, value for shareholders, and opportunities for employees. By managing change, Hibernia people are shaping a new corporate culture and finding the competitive edge in an increasingly challenging environment. ◆

*The Whitney clock, a symbol of strength
and stability since 1883.*

For generations, the Whitney has been serving the
financial needs of New Orleans families and businesses.
Founded in 1883, the Whitney is the city's oldest continuously operating bank. The bank got its name from three
of its founders: George Q., Charles M., and Maria Louise
Whitney. Other founders included New Orleans business
leaders and a future Chief Justice of the United States
Supreme Court. Long respected for its strength and stability,
it is the only major New Orleans bank to remain open
during the depression.

Many of the city's businesses bank with the Whitney
because of the skill of its relationship managers and the
individualized service the bank offers. The Whitney has
also specialized in international banking, helping local
companies with the financial complexities of the
import/export market.

Since 1990, the Whitney has made major investments
in the consumer, trust, and investment businesses. The
bank operates 34 branches throughout the New Orleans
market, and has over 70 Automated Teller Machines (ATM)
systemwide, many in gas stations and
other convenient locations. The bank
has even purchased a mobile ATM
to dispense cash at the city's many
festivals and events.

Unlike many banks, the Whitney is
investing heavily in branches. Many are
being renovated, and the bank opened
two new branches in the growing St.
Tammany parish since early 1996.
Several other branch sites are under
development around New Orleans,
and a new operations center opened
in mid-1996.

Located in the new operations center
is the bank's customer service staff. The
Whitney offers toll-free account information 24 hours a day. During banking
hours, customers can also phone the
bank's well-trained customer service

staff for assistance. Additionally, the Whitney Loan by Phone
service takes credit applications.

Realizing that an investment in technology is critical to
the future, the bank has converted to a new core banking
system and installed dedicated software for specialized
operations. An integrated personal computer network and a
state-of-the-art platform and teller system are being installed.

The Whitney has also invested heavily in trust and
investment services. As part of its offerings to its commercial customers, the Whitney has developed employee
benefits services. Companies have found that benefit
packages help attract and retain good employees, and the
Whitney has helped many set up 401-K plans and other
programs. The Whitney also offers personalized portfolio
management for individuals and businesses.

Because many families and companies do business
along the Gulf Coast, the Whitney recently expanded across
southern Louisiana and into Alabama and Florida. Since
1994, the bank has expanded from one branch in Baton
Rouge to a projected 13 branches by 1997. A 1996 merger
added branches in St. Mary and Iberia parishes, and two
new branches have been built in Lafayette.

In 1995, the Whitney was the first Louisiana banking
company to enter Alabama, and this was followed in 1996
with the announcement of mergers in Pensacola, Florida.
The bank has determined that there are many cultural
similarities and shared traditions along the Gulf Coast.
Indeed, a Whitney customer can get the same personal
attention and Whitney service in any branch, no matter
which state the branch is located in.

While the bank has made significant investments in
technology, branches, and expansion, it has continued to
post strong financial performances, quarter after quarter.
Whitney Holding Corporation, the parent company of
Whitney National Bank, is publicly traded on the NASDAQ
stock market. ◆

*For generations the Whitney has been building
relationships that build New Orleans.*

The Jefferson Business Council is an independent, not-for-profit organization of Jefferson Parish business leaders dedicated to promoting good government practices and examining quality of life issues impacting the parish.

Comprised of the chief executive officers of Jefferson Parish's 45 largest employers, the council was founded in 1991, when a group of Jefferson-based members of the New Orleans Business Council decided to form a similar organization focusing exclusively on their home parish.

Since its founding, the business council has financed and published for community education purposes independent studies of Jefferson's criminal justice system, sheriff's office, and parish government.

"The studies have heightened public awareness on important community issues," said Russell Protti, the business council's executive director.

The multi-dimensional issue of criminal justice was taken up as an area of interest early in the organization's history, when a series of voter referendums asked Jefferson Parish voters to approve additional sales taxes to finance the building of new prisons.

Increasing the sales tax was not a viable alternative to voters, the business council argued, until a thorough study of the parish's criminal justice system could be conducted.

"We wanted the parish to look at criminal justice comprehensively; for example, to look at innovative types of

Joseph J. Krebs, Jr., chairman of Jefferson
Business Council.

incarceration—not just maximum security prisons," Protti said.

The business council's opposition to additional sales taxes contributed to the measures' defeat and broadened the prison debate to include how criminal cases move through the system, from arrest to incarceration. The business council's study of these issues prompted the parish council to form a citizens' committee charged with examining criminal justice as an integrated system.

To demonstrate its ongoing commitment to good judicial practices, the business council is a major contributor to the Judicial Watch Program, a joint initiative of metro area business groups evaluating the efficiency of the courts.

The business council was also the catalyst behind the 1994 reform of the Jefferson Parish charter, a document dating from the 1950s.

Upon completion of an independent analysis of the parish charter, the business council submitted recommendations to the parish council that eventually formed the nucleus of a charter advisory committee and a voter referendum to amend the charter. Amendments to the charter included such new provisions as veto power for the parish president, term limitations for public officials and rules on succession of power, as well as updated language on the budget and procedures.

In an era in which hospitals are increasingly closing or restructuring themselves in response to market demands, the business council has become a leading advocate for enhanced public debate on the futures of its two not-for-profit hospitals.

In 1995, the business council submitted a successful position paper urging the parish council to study the pros and cons of all restructuring options, and open up the issue to public debate.

"Our position is that the elected council should make the decisions on public hospital reform based on all the facts. These decisions should be made in the light of day, in public forums— not behind closed doors," said business council chairman Joseph Krebs, Jr.

The business council's educational interests extend to individual citizens as well. The organization co-sponsors the Jefferson Dollars for Scholars program, which raises money and grants university scholarships to young people to enhance their educational opportunities.

While the business council has been successful in helping to shape public policy and attitudes, it neither endorses candidates for public office nor supports lobby groups.

"We view ourselves as a small group of citizens who have the money and wherewithal to build coalitions and examine quality of life issues within the parish community," Krebs said.

Admission to the Jefferson Business Council is by invitation only. Copies of its studies are available through the Bureau of Governmental Research. ◆

Professions

KPMG

KPMG's New Orleans partners are (seated left to right) Raymond J. Jeandron Jr., Deke G. Carbo, Albert J. Richard III, Robert L. Perez, (standing left to right) James H. Browning, Gerard A. Brechtel, Robert L. Champagne, Harold J. Bouillion. (Hardy B. Fowler not pictured.)

From Small Beginnings

In 1909, the New Orleans office of Marwick & Mitchell opened in the Hibernia Bank Building. From those beginnings, the New Orleans practice of KPMG Peat Marwick LLP has grown apace. Today, the KPMG New Orleans office in One Shell Square is the anchor office of this international firm's Louisiana practice, serving clients from Baton Rouge and Shreveport locations as well.

In New Orleans, nine partners provide leadership, delivering the firm's accounting, auditing, tax, and consulting services. The firm's client list ranges from some of our area's most prestigious private companies to large international public companies as well as state and local government agencies, individuals, health care organizations, and educational institutions.

Accounting firms are traditionally known for auditing and tax services. But KPMG also provides a full range of consulting and business support in such areas as due diligence reviews for potential mergers, medical claims review of a firm's insurance carrier, and advice on tax structure for expansion to Mexico, to name a few examples. And the firm's strategic services consulting is available to assist clients with business performance improvement in world-class finance, sales force automation, enabling technologies, and operations strategy and systems.

A Team Approach to Service

Client service teams are a strength in the New Orleans office and throughout the firm. KPMG continually strives to meet client needs through client teams organized along industry lines: manufacturing, retailing, and distribution (which includes the chemical and energy industries); financial services, public services, information, communications, and entertainment; and health care and the life sciences. A team comprised of partner, manager, and professional staff is assigned to each client. Team personnel have knowledge and expertise related directly to the special needs of the client and provide the client with industry- related experience and continuity of service, from one year to the next.

Client service teams also include professionals from a variety of technical disciplines. Auditors, tax advisors, and consultants work together to address the client's issues and industry-specific needs. Rigorous training requirements and frequent communications keep KPMG teams abreast of the issues facing industries and the services that can be provided to each client.

"As the result of this approach, which is unlike any other major professional services firm," comments New Orleans managing partner Harold Bouillion, "we are always increasing our understanding of the industries in which our clients are operating. We bring more specific expertise and better resources to address our clients' full range of needs, from consulting services such as performance improvement, systems integration, and sales force automation, to traditional accounting services."

Continues Bouillion, "Our structure also reflects the growing impact and demands of the global economy. While every company is concerned with minimizing the cost of doing business and maximizing performance, a fast-growing number of our clients are also facing direct competition from Europe, China, Canada, Mexico, South America, and elsewhere. The companies that are world-class in quality and efficiency will be success stories of the 21st century, and KPMG will do our best to help ensure that our clients are among them."

KPMG uses cutting-edge technology to better serve their clients.

The Resources of the Global Leader

Enhancing KPMG's New Orleans professionals' ability to serve their clients is an unmatched resource: the worldwide network of KPMG. On a global basis, KPMG is the leading auditor of the top 1,000 commercial and industrial companies in the world. More than 76,000 KPMG people serve clients through 1,100 offices in 131 countries. The full resources of this global network can be brought to bear on any client engagement. This depth of resources is a considerable strength, and one of which the firm is justifiably proud.

The firm itself will mark its 100th anniversary soon, celebrating its 1897 founding by two Scotsmen, James Marwick and Roger Mitchell. The company today is the result of steady growth and a number of mergers that culminated in 1987 in a worldwide merger with Klynveld Main Goerdler, to become KPMG Peat Marwick LLP, The Global Leader.

Commitment to New Orleans

KPMG's New Orleans people, from partners through support staff, are active in civic, social, and business organizations throughout the area. Bouillion has said that community involvement has contributed to client retention and to the firm's ability to attract top graduates from universities around the country.

"And it's the right thing to do," affirms Bouillion. "We believe in the spirit of progress in the people of New Orleans; we are proud to be part of this dynamic business community and part of one of the unique cities of the world." KPMG's professionals, processes, and commitment to quality will continue to provide momentum for participation in the future of New Orleans. ◆

Reputation for Quality

KPMG backs up its commitment to clients with a client survey to provide feedback to the firm about its service teams. The yearly client survey aids the firm in allocating resources, identifying and correcting problem areas, and maintaining the top-quality service that is the base for KPMG's reputation.

According to recent information from Securities Data Co. and *Public Accounting Report*, KPMG ranked number one among the world's top 10 merger and acquisition advisors. KPMG was the first firm to assist in the privatization of Eastern European economies, as well as the pilot privatization of Vietnam. KPMG was the first of the Big Six accounting firms to be granted ISO 9000 Registrar status and the first professional services firm of any kind to obtain this status in Hong Kong. KPMG has also received high grades from the banking and high technology industries, according to independent client surveys. The Emerson Company's 1995 survey of chief executive officers of banks places KPMG at the top of the Big Six firms in knowledge of business, involvement in and contribution to the industry, audit and accounting services, information technology services, contribution to the success of the business, regulatory consulting services, and other consulting and advisory services.

According to Bouillion, "KPMG's long-standing client satisfaction commitment and orientation to our industry lines is obviously paying dividends. And while we are extremely pleased to be ranked so prominently in client satisfaction surveys, we realize that what is ultimately most important to our clients is that we understand their business environment in the same terms they do. We'll keep striving in that direction, no matter how good the surveys look."

W.H. Linder & Associates, Inc.

With a diverse client base that includes major petrochemical companies, shipbuilders, and even the country's space program, W. H. Linder & Associates, Inc. (LINDER), has also continued its long-lasting ties to the state's massive oil and gas industry, emerging as one of the principal players in a new era of deepwater exploration.

"The key projects we have participated in, giving us international recognition, have been the oil and gas developments in the deepwater of the Gulf of Mexico," explains Bill Gieseler, marketing manager of LINDER, which is based in the New Orleans suburb of Metairie.

To date, LINDER has participated in five historic deepwater projects, which have broken records for the water depths in which they are installed. For Shell Offshore, Inc., and partners, LINDER served as the consulting engineers for the Auger TLP Project, installed in 2,860 feet of ocean water; the Mars TLP Project, in 2,930 feet; the Ram-Powell to be installed in 2,900 feet; and the Ursa TLP Project in 3,200 feet. A joint Texaco-Marathon project known as Petronius, will be installed at a depth just under 1,800 feet in the Gulf of Mexico.

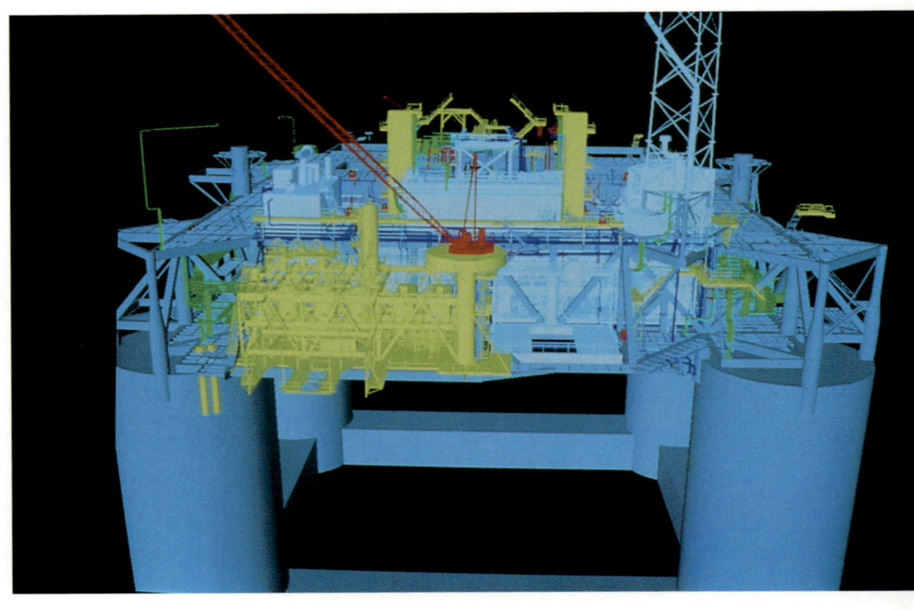

3–D CADD Model of Oil & Gas Production Facility.

The deepwater project reaffirmed the prominence LINDER has always enjoyed in the region's oil and gas industry. Founded in 1981 by Civil Engineer, William H. Linder, the firm began with an initial core staff of seven, and its work was exclusively oil and gas related.

In the past decade, LINDER, which now employs upwards of 175 people and enjoys annual revenues in the $12 to $14 million range, has jumped into a wide variety of other projects including public sector work, refining and petrochemical plant work, projects outside the New Orleans metropolitan region, and the placement of contract technical employees.

Among the non-oil and gas clients that make up a growing 25 percent of LINDER's workload is the Port of New Orleans, where LINDER participated in a recent $400 million expansion and modernization effort. LINDER was responsible for the design of loading ramps, terminal lighting, fire protection systems, water lines, and communications systems for the new Port office building.

LINDER is a multi-disciplined engineering firm specializing in Civil, Structural, Mechanical, Process, Electrical, and Instrument Engineering. LINDER's suite of services consist of Project Management, Feasibility Studies, Detail Design and Drafting, Environmental, Development, Plant Turnaround, and Start-up support.

During the past decade LINDER has participated in approximately 500 projects, expending as little as a few hours to over 300,000 man hours. "We stay with a project from conception to startup," explains Gieseler. "We play some role in the project from the front end with conceptual and preliminary engineering studies and go forward from there as the project develops."

But even after a project is completed and all of the design details have become reality, LINDER remains involved: "You continue to service your clients by helping with engineering support requirements they may have for a year or two after start-up."

With projects in a variety of states, including oilfield work in Houston and Bakersfield, California, as well as work for such companies as Texaco in their overseas

Shell Offshore, Inc.'s, Auger Tension Leg Platform Topside Facility under construction in Amelia, Louisiana.

The Auger project, officially known as the Auger Tension Leg Platform Topside Facility, is capable of processing up to 70,000 barrels of oil and 150 million cubic feet of gas per day.

Among the tasks completed by the LINDER firm for the Auger project were: the complete design of the oil and gas production facilities and utilities, as well as the design of the control system for the bilge/ballast system for the hull, and regulatory submittals to the US Coast Guard for some 17 topside modules and skids.

operations, LINDER today is a fully competitive, technologically advanced firm where skilled designers create drawings using state-of-the-art CAD systems.

Those technological innovations combined with LINDER's Project Team approach have been providing day to day plant engineering support for the LaRoche Chemical Gramercy Plant for over three years, while similar services have been performed for the Agrico Chemical Plant in Uncle Sam, Louisiana.

LINDER's relationship with the Shell Oil Company Lube Oil Plant in Metairie dates back to 1985 and the design of Shell's slurry ratio control facility, drum dumping station and the slurry plant gangue removal facility, are among the nine major design projects LINDER has done for the plant.

LINDER has also been responsible for updating of piping and instrumentation diagrams for Exxon Production Company Gas Plants in order for them to meet federal OSHA regulations. For the Chevron Chemical Company, the firm helped develop an environmentally sound waste-water treatment process, and was responsible for designing a new barge and loading facilities, marine vapor recovery systems, and a variety of other support systems for CYTEC (formerly American Cyanamid).

In order to cool the test stands for the NASA rocket engines, massive amounts of water are pumped by some ten huge diesel powered pumps through a cooling system composed of pipes as large as 112 inches in diameter. Those pipes have corroded in unusual ways, requiring the LINDER engineers to not only identify the source of the corrosion, but also which pipes need replacing and how to prevent future corrosion from occurring.

"Almost all of our work is intense by its very nature,"

CO_2 Compression and Dehydration
Facility in St. Charles Parish
Chemical Plant.

explains Gieseler, "which means that we have to work closely with our clients every step of the way."

The LINDER engineers not only size up a project's problems and potential with repeated on-site visits and inspection, they work in a hands-on manner with clients, emphasizing the importance of communication.

As LINDER enters the next century, the firm plans to expand its non-oil and gas business, while "making sure," says Gieseler, "that we do not see a decrease in the amount of work we do with our oil and gas clients. Because we have the skills and expertise as consulting engineers to work in a variety of fields, we believe we can grow in all of them at the same time." ◆

Waldemar S. Nelson and Company, Inc.

Building on more than 50 years of success and growth, Waldemar S. Nelson and Company, Inc.—one of New Orleans' most successful and long standing professional engineering and architectural firms—is planning for the next 50 years that will see it enhance and expand its technological capability and geographic diversity.

The variety of specialized skills under the Nelson and Company name is one reason why the company has thrived now for five decades. "In the late 20th century the technical drive is more and more for the concentration of abilities on the part of the individual," says Charles W. Nelson, president of the company. "From the corporate standpoint we are large enough to have eight different departments, and within each one of those departments are individuals who concentrate in one given area. So we end up with a number of specialties, and through that we get diversity as well."

That approach has served Nelson and Company well. Among its major clients are Shell, Exxon, Texaco, Amoco, and British Petroleum, for whom Nelson is designing topside oil & gas production facilities for those operator's deepwater Gulf of Mexico projects. For Freeport-McMoRan, Nelson is doing the design work for the expansion of the company's huge copper mines in Indonesia. Other major clients include Conoco, Chevron, Mobil, Agrico, Cytec Industries, and Allied Signal.

In fact, upwards of 80 percent of the work produced at Nelson and Company is classified as heavy industrial: "A typical client for us, in terms of the roughly 200 to 300 projects that we execute each year, would be an industrial client," says Nelson, who adds that "Individual assignments can range from a one man inspection lasting a few days up to large, integrated design teams of over 100 people working for several years".

On the topic of technical innovation, Nelson says "We are doing a lot of in-house data management and control

*W*aldemar S. Nelson, standing, chairs the Executive Committee of (seated, l–r) Richard Cabiro, Treasurer; Charles Nelson, President; Tom Ehrlicher, Secretary; and Jim Cospolich, Executive Vice President. The Committee of professional engineers with a wide variety of experience builds on the firm's past and plans for its future.

as it relates to the design experience. We are advancing our computer-aided engineering, and are compiling information on the drawings we generate into a data base management system that then results in the information required for the construction process."

With an extensive network of hardware and software, Nelson and Company has devoted much of its capital resources in recent years to the acquisition of even more hardware equipment and software components to interact with an already-existing company system. Meanwhile, the more than 330 employees of Nelson and Company, working in such diverse departments as chemical process, mechanical, civil, electrical, instrumentation and control system engineering, construction management, environmental science and architecture, all have extensive computer expertise.

With projects today both overseas and across the U.S., Nelson and Company is particularly well positioned for the technological and economic challenges of the future: up to 90 percent of its business in any given year is repeat business, a vote of confidence from its clients that Nelson takes seriously.

"Our clients' success has been the reason for our success," adds Nelson, "and with them we expect to grow for the future." ◆

*W*aldemar S. Nelson and Company provided design and procurement assistance for Shell Offshore's "Mars" Tension Leg Platform which set a Gulf of Mexico water depth record.

For over a century the diverse and creative talents of the attorneys at the law firm of Montgomery, Barnett, Brown, Read, Hammond, & Mintz, L.L.P., have produced a hard working partnership dedicated to providing the best in legal representation and counseling. A full service law firm with a local, regional, national, and international practice, its attorneys handle all aspects of corporate, real estate, and business law; admiralty, products liability, insurance and professional liability defense; environmental, energy, oil and gas; bankruptcy, tax and estate planning. As Montgomery Barnett approaches the 21st century, it will continue to employ the talents and experience of its attorneys to efficiently and effectively serve the needs of its clients.

Montgomery Barnett's managing partner, Daniel Lund, emphasizes the firm's successful philosophy: "We operate under simple principles. We set a goal on each matter to provide our client with prompt and effective representation, properly staffed for the particular matter involved. We have never varied from this benchmark. We have never forgotten that we are professional service providers and we must satisfy our clients. Our broad client base demonstrates our solid position in the legal community. The legal community itself recognizes our experience as many lawyers and law firms have retained us to advise them regarding their professional liability issues. Our clients like our philosophy and approach to handling their legal matters."

Because cases frequently include complex and overlapping issues, Montgomery Barnett often pools the talent and experience of attorneys from different practice areas in teams to offer its clients the best possible legal representation for a particular situation. Each team is headed by a lead attorney who is charged with knowing the status of each matter and notifying the client of any significant developments. This approach permits Montgomery Barnett to task-orient its practice with the result that the client gets the best and most cost-effective representation.

Montgomery Barnett's modern offices on the 32nd and

33rd floors of the Energy Centre are conveniently located near the federal and state courthouses in downtown New Orleans and house attorneys with experience covering the entire spectrum of civil law practice. Its maritime practice encompasses a wide range of matters including pollution, maritime products liability, marine insurance, and hull and cargo claims. Montgomery Barnett's extensive work defending a series of class action suits—including the nationwide representation of medical device and asbestos manufacturers—has enhanced the firm's reputation as leading product liability litigants. Over 20 major insurance companies rely on Montgomery Barnett to manage their defense of personal injury, property damage, malpractice, errors and omissions, construction, and occupational disease claims.

Located in one of the nation's most prolific oil and gas regions, Montgomery Barnett has represented major and independent oil companies and landowners since the 1940's at all stages of exploration, development, and production of oil, gas, and other minerals. National, regional, and local lenders as well as institutional and individual borrowers seek Montgomery Barnett's advice in commercial and secured lending transactions. The firm's veteran attorneys handle complex business litigation and routinely litigate cases involving all significant areas of private and governmental practice.

Montgomery Barnett's attorneys take pride in their professional abilities, dedication, and concern for their client's interests. Tie this to a group of concerned citizens involved in a diverse set of community services and projects, and a picture emerges of a dynamic, hard-working, community-oriented law firm. That Montgomery Barnett brings pride-of-work, state-of-the-art technology, experience, innovation, and caring to its practice of law does it and the City of New Orleans proud. As it faces the next century, Montgomery Barnett will continue to reflect those values and deliver the results its clients have come to expect. ◆

In conference at the firm's Energy Centre offices are (left to right) partners Patrick J. Browne, Albert Mintz, John B. Gooch, Jr., Christopher E. Carey, and John Y. Pearce. Photo by Mike Posey.

At the Unites States Fifth Circuit Court of Appeals: managing partner Daniel Lund (at podium) and partners (left to right) Kim E. Moore, Lawrence G. Pugh, and Quentin F. Urquhart, Jr. Photo by Mike Posey.

Juxtaposed against the growing dynamic of minority enterprise, Tucker & Associates, Inc. has witnessed nearly two decades of growth on their way to becoming a local firm with a national reputation.

With information technology, support services, facilities management, project management and administrative services, engineering and technical services, and training and education, Tucker & Associates, Inc. has grown from a small business, run almost single-handedly by Robert H. Tucker Jr. and Janee "Gee" Tucker in 1980, to a major New Orleans firm with more than 120 employees and annual revenues of approximately $9 million.

A consultant firm specializing in management and technical services for both the private and public sectors, Tucker & Associates, Inc. has won headlines for the better part of the decade due to the large number of important contracts it has competed and won.

Among its many business triumphs has been the awarding of a $25 million Department of Energy contract for management and technical services work on the Strategic Petroleum Reserve; a $7 million contract with the Department of Navy to provide records management services for the Naval Reserve; and a $12 million contract with the Department of Navy for facilities management and telecommunications support services.

Robert H. Tucker Jr. serves on the governing boards of the Port of New Orleans, the World Trade Center, and the Regional Transit Authority, in addition to advising mayors in several cities including New Orleans. Janee Michelle Tucker serves as president and chief executive officer. A former free-lance actress under contract with multiple studios in the 1960s and 1970s, Janee Tucker coordinated the employee training programs for a major fast food company between 1977 and 1985. She has also emerged as a major role model in the local community for her prominence as an African-American business leader.

As Tucker & Associates' revenue base has jumped from $6.7 million to nearly $9 million between 1993 and 1996, its marketing presence has expanded geographically into new territories in Massachusetts, Washington, D.C., and California.

Tucker & Associates, Inc. is headquartered in downtown New Orleans and has other project sites in the city and the suburb of Harahan.

Bob and Janee founded another company in 1994 that will help increase the Tuckers' local business community profile: Integrated Logistical Support, Inc. (ILSI) specializes in engineering services, project, and construction management.

Already the company's revenue has jumped from $200,000 in 1994 to more than $1.5 million in 1996 and Tucker believes ILSI will see revenues of more than $3.5 million by 1998.

Like Tucker & Associates, Inc., ILSI, Inc. reflects the dominant philosophy long voiced by Robert H. and Janee Michelle Tucker: no dream is impossible. ◆

Tucker and Associates has grown from a small business, run almost single-handedly by Robert H. Tucker Jr. and Janee "Gee" Tucker, to a major New Orleans consultant firm specializing in management and technical services for both the private and public sectors.

With a client list that includes many of the nation's largest insurers, foreign underwriters, and an impressive list of self-insured corporations, the New Orleans law firm of Hailey, McNamara, Hall, Larmann & Papale has emerged as one of the region's most active and prominent firms engaged in a wide variety of litigation. The firm's legal expertise includes personal, commercial, and industrial casualty claims, both state and federal workers' compensation claims, professional malpractice, employment practices, RICO claims, public utility regulation, officer and director's litigation and insurance regulatory law.

Among the area's outstanding admiralty law firms, Hailey, McNamara has, since its inception, represented offshore operators, drilling contractors, vessel owners, and service companies in the defense of maritime litigation.

Founded in 1976, the Hailey, McNamara firm in suburban Metairie is now the largest law firm in all of Jefferson Parish.

Another of the firm's important areas of work, giving it national recognition, is in the field of environmental litigation involving occupational exposure to asbestos, chemicals, and other substances, as well as toxic tort and hazardous waste claims.

Founded in 1976, the Hailey, McNamara firm in suburban Metairie has grown to the point that it is now the largest law firm in all of Jefferson Parish, and one of the largest litigation firms in the vast metropolitan reach of New Orleans. Hailey, McNamara is primary counsel throughout Louisiana for many clients and has attorneys admitted to practice in several states.

With a roster of clients stretching across the Deep South and reaching into such countries as Japan and England, Hailey, McNamara has been one of the city's most aggressive players in the area of state-of-the-art technology, used to better enhance its client service. Communication between attorney and client is aided by the efficient use of computerized word processing, billing systems, and invoicing procedures.

Enhanced technology also includes the regular use of Westlaw Computer Research, which gives the firm access to not only all of the prominent law libraries and reporters across the country, but also the valuable Med-Line service, as well as a host of other data information sources, critical to building enhanced defense strategies in the frequently complex medical and products cases handled by the firm.

Hailey, McNamara has also elevated the importance of communication one step further with the publication of a quarterly newsletter designed to assist its many clients in far away places by keeping them informed of the latest damage awards, precedent and statutory enactments, and other litigation trends.

The firm has also won national recognition for its white-collar criminal defense work, including representation of witnesses before grand juries and conducting internal corporate investigations—a strength enhanced by the presence of former assistant United States Attorneys on the Hailey, McNamara team.

Its far-reaching abilities, however, have not deterred Hailey, McNamara from the founding principle of the firm: to provide the best representation at the lowest possible cost. For that reason, the firm has long emphasized the importance of efficiency, affording a particularly valuable service to insurers with large volumes of cases, as well as corporate and professional clients facing complex and precedent-setting lawsuits.

By utilizing its extensive experience, resources and the latest technology, the firm provides the most aggressive and cost efficient legal representation available. Hailey, McNamara is uniquely postured to meet the evolving needs of its clients in order to respond to the challenges of the 21st Century. ◆

The New Orleans law firm of Hailey, McNamara, Hall, Larmann & Papale has emerged as one of the region's most active and prominent firms engaged in a wide variety of litigation.

Education & Quality of Life

For more than 75 years, Delgado Community College has been providing New Orleans and its citizens with education that works.

Delgado is the oldest and largest community college in Louisiana, with four campuses in the New Orleans area, an enrollment of about 14,000, and an alumni body of more than 100,000. It was founded in 1921, funded by a bequest from Isaac Delgado. A Jamaican immigrant who became a wealthy New Orleans businessman, Delgado bequeathed part of his fortune to the city to establish an institution to educate youth in trades and skilled crafts.

The skills Delgado students learn have changed dramatically in three-quarters of a century, but the mission of the community college remains congruent with the vision of its founder. Some 70 percent of Delgado students come for a job-related reason—for the degree, certificate, or courses that will lead to a new job or advancement in their current career.

"Delgado is particularly strong at putting well-prepared graduates into the workforce," says President Ione H. Elioff. "We are responsive to the educational needs of the economy, and we help grow jobs for local residents." Through customized training and more than 70 associate degree and certificate programs in technology, allied health and nursing, business, arts and humanities, and the sciences, Delgado prepares a well-trained workforce to meet the needs of the South Louisiana economy.

In 1996, Delgado is working closely with the MetroVision regional economic development efforts and its school-to-work programs. By the year 2000, according to MetroVision statistics, about 65 percent of the jobs in the local area will require one to two years of post-high school education,

Delgado Hall named for Isaac Delgado, a New Orleans businessman who donated money and land to establish the College.

20 percent will require bachelor or graduate degrees, and only 15 percent will require a high school diploma or less.

A recent summit meeting of 120 top business and civic leaders and Delgado administrators led to a carefully crafted series of six Workforce Development Clusters. The clusters outline a seamless link joining occupations identified as high-growth by the Workforce 2000 task force—and the skills those occupations demand—with school-to-work programs in public elementary and secondary schools, high school career academies for vocational training, and Delgado associate degree programs.

The clusters reflect Delgado strengths as well as the economic needs of New Orleans. The maritime and transportation cluster focuses on Delgado offerings in technology and international business, for example. Adding to Delgado's depth in this area is a new associate degree program in safety and health technology to help meet a growing demand from the petroleum and shipbuilding industry in the Mississippi River corridor. Similarly, the business and information management cluster is tied closely to Delgado's business studies program. The college's programs in maritime and industrial firefighting and radar training, which attract people from all 50 states and 20 foreign countries, are important resources for employers in the shipping industry.

The construction and engineering cluster involves 18 Delgado technology associate degree programs, and many specialized concentrations, including a new Programmable Logic Controller sequence that offers state-of-the-art training in operating and repairing the "smart" sensors that can control anything from a traffic light to the rate at which oil is pumped from the floor of the Gulf of Mexico. The

Delgado has the latest computer equipment and software for hands–on training.

health care cluster has a dual focus on patient care and health care management, with a close relationship to Delgado's 16 programs in allied health and nursing—the Gulf South's largest two-year nursing program. Because hospitals have a need for care providers with multiple skills, Delgado has just introduced a 12-hour program to cross-train health care professionals in phlebotomy, the art of drawing blood. In an additional indicator of quality, every graduate of Delgado's Radiologic Technology program passed the national certification exam—for the 20th year in a row. The national pass rate is about 85 percent.

The human and public services cluster focuses on teaching, social work, public safety and recreation and leisure, based on Delgado associate degree programs in early childhood education, general studies, criminal justice, fire technology and physical education.

The New Orleans cluster draws from Delgado programs in hospitality and tourism, music, performance and media arts, commercial art, interior design and fine arts, and print and broadcast journalism to prepare people for various aspects of the hospitality, music, visual and performing arts, and Mardi Gras industries. New degree and certificate programs in hospitality prepare students for jobs in New Orleans's fastest-growing industry, while a new jazz concentration within Delgado's music degree program helps energize an old New Orleans tradition. The culinary arts program, with a three-year, 6,000-hour apprenticeship under the master chefs of New Orleans, was named as a national model for workplace-based education by the National Center for Research in Vocational Education. Its graduates are found in fine restaurants from coast to coast.

While many Delgado students plan to go straight to the job market, about 20 percent attend the community college for two years before transferring to a four-year college. Delgado administrators continue to work with the state's four-year schools to make the transfer process as easy as possible. It makes economic sense, too. Delgado's tuition is one of the most affordable in the region, and more than half its students receive financial aid. The college has an open admissions policy for most programs, with an average class size of 21 and personalized counseling programs. Delgado even offers courses in how to negotiate the job world—or how to succeed in college.

Delgado reaches deep into the New Orleans community to make sure its courses are accessible. The main campus— City Park— enrolls more than 10,000 students a year, with another 2,500 attending the West Bank campus, some 800 enrolled at the Slidell Learning Center in suburban St. Tammany Parish, and students in allied health and nursing studying at the Charity School of Nursing campus in downtown New Orleans. In addition, the college offers selected courses at nine other locations in the metropolitan area.

As Delgado Community College begins looking toward its centennial, it will continue to extend its resources into the community. It will work with employers to determine the qualities they need in their workforce. It will help create jobs for the people of the region. It will prepare citizens at all economic levels of the New Orleans region for careers, for continuing their education, and for success in life. It's the Delgado tradition. ◆

(top) Delgado is the largest provider of allied health and nursing professionals in the New Orleans area.

Delgado's Culinary Arts program follows the tradition of European culinary apprenticeship programs.

Once a rural expanse of woods and swampland to the west of New Orleans, Jefferson Parish has evolved into the fastest growing parish in the state over the course of its 175-year history.

Once regarded as a mere suburb or "bedroom community" of New Orleans, Jefferson Parish is now a self-sufficient metropolitan area in its own right, and an acknowledged state leader in retail, industry, and tourism. With a 1995 population of 479,000, it is the second most populous parish in Louisiana.

Named in honor of President Thomas Jefferson, the parish was created by the Louisiana Legislature in 1825 out of land formerly designated as the City of New Orleans. Bisected by the Mississippi River, Jefferson Parish is home to 17 communities: Avondale, Barataria, Bridge City, Crown Point, Grand Isle, Gretna, Harvey, Jean Lafitte, Marrero, McDonoughville, Waggaman and Westwego, on the west bank; Harahan, Jefferson, Kenner, Metairie and River Ridge, on the east bank. The parish president is Tim Coulon.

Jefferson Parish boasts many statewide claims to fame. For example, its residents enjoy the state's highest per-capita income and level of education. The parish's annual average unemployment rate of 5.3 percent is one of the lowest in Louisiana.

Home to the largest concentration of retail shopping space in the state and the immediate Gulf Coast region, the parish was the site of a record $5.5 billion in retail sales in 1995, which represented some 60 percent of all retail sales in the metro area. In that same year in Jefferson Parish, nearly 8,100 jobs were created, housing starts rose 7.5 percent, and the economy grew by 4 percent, the highest parish growth rate in the state.

Tourism in the parish, which reached record heights in 1995, is expected to grow into the 21st century. In 1995,

Named in honor of President Thomas Jefferson, the parish was created by the Louisiana Legislature in 1825 out of land formerly designated as the City of New Orleans.

tourist-related spending totalled some $570 million. The parish currently supports over 8,500 tourism related jobs and boasts more than 6,000 first-class hotel and motel rooms.

A major player in Jefferson Parish's tourism explosion is the 50,000-square-foot Pontchartrain Center, located in Kenner. Fast becoming one of the Southeast's most popular convention facilities, the center hosts an average of 55 shows

Built in 1907, this Baroque style structure now serves as the Gretna City Hall to the City of Gretna which is one of Louisiana's largest historical districts.

per month, and welcomes more than 350,000 visitors annually. In 1995, the center created a parishwide economic impact of $20.7 million, a figure that is expected to increase when a $3.8 million, 20,000-square-foot expansion is completed in the spring of 1997.

Gaming, one of Jefferson Parish's newer industries, is flourishing in Jefferson Parish. Harvey's Boomtown Belle and Kenner's Treasure Chest Casino—the latter which features a new land-based entertainment complex—draws locals and tourists alike. An annual array of festivals, including the popular music and food extravaganza, Jeff Fest; cultural events, museums, top-flight restaurants, home tours, and nature trails are among the other tourist attractions that can be enjoyed on both banks of the parish.

Also bringing new recreational and business opportunities to residents and tourists is the $13 million Bayou Segnette sports and recreational complex in Westwego, to be built alongside the similarly named 580-acre state park that already offers picnicking, fishing, camping, a wave pool, and swamp tours. Scheduled for completion in 1998, the $13 million, 77,000-square-foot facility will be home to local, regional, and national sporting events, as well as four volleyball courts, eight team locker rooms and three multipurpose activity rooms.

Other major sporting enterprises based in Jefferson Parish include the New Orleans Zephyrs baseball stadium in Metairie, scheduled for completion in 1997; the New Orleans Saints Training Camp, also in Metairie; and the state's most visited park, Jean Lafitte National Historic Park and Preserve.

Despite such impressive growth, Jefferson has managed to provide residents with a neighborhood-based quality of living that is unparalleled in South Louisiana. An excellent record of public safety, first-rate public schools, and safe streets enhance Jefferson Parish's standing as an ideal place in which to raise a family and locate a business. Additionally, unlike citizens living in other suburban communities across the country, Jefferson Parish residents pay no local income or earnings tax.

Founded in 1988 to stem the tide of unemployment and businesses leaving Louisiana, the Jefferson Economic Development Commission (JEDCO) is dedicated to giving parish-based businesses the tools they need to be successful.

With dual goals of attracting new businesses to the parish and aiding those already in existence, JEDCO offers a business incubator program that provides fledgling entrepreneurs with start-up services such as affordable office space and secretarial support. Other JEDCO services include programs to help firms secure financing from banks, the federal government, and private sources; a Latin American program encouraging trade between Jefferson-based businesses and Latin America; and the latest information on such business concerns as office availability and tax incentives and exemptions for Jefferson Parish companies.

Home to New Orleans International Airport, the Huey P. Long Bridge, the Lake Pontchartrain Causeway, Interstate-10 and other major roadways, Jefferson Parish is an important regional distribution and transportation center. Among the ongoing efforts to repair or expand the parish's transportation systems are a $650 million capital improvement program for the airport in Kenner, and a $90 million road improvement program.

In response to the booming Jefferson Parish economy, the Port of New Orleans has approved the construction of a $40 million, 150,000-square-foot dockside cargo facility in the parish that will provide cold-storage space for chilled and frozen import and export cargoes. While the exact Jefferson Parish address of the 50-acre site has not yet been determined, planners chose to locate it in Jefferson Parish for good reason: the parish is headquarters to more than 40 percent of the firms listed in the Port of New Orleans directory, and to 49 percent of those firms' employees.

As Jefferson Parish faces the next century, it will be equipped with goals outlined by its 1995 quality-of-life summit, Jeff 2000. Top priorities include increasing jail space, improving roads, continued enhancements to the parish's tourist industry, and the continued vitality of the parish's two public-owned hospitals: East Jefferson General Hospital in Metairie, and West Jefferson Medical Center in Marrero. ◆

A major player in Jefferson Parish's tourism explosion is the 50,000-square-foot Pontchartrain Center, located in Kenner. Fast becoming one of the Southeast's most popular convention facilities, the center hosts an average of 55 shows per month, and welcomes more than 350,000 visitors annually.

Lafreniere Park is the largest park in Jefferson Parish and is host to various festivals, concerts, races, and athletic events and shows.

Xavier University of Louisiana

In a city known for its old-world charm and traditional architecture, the Xavier University of Louisiana skyline stands out as a symbol of the change and energy that has made the school both a regional and national institution to watch.

As a centerpiece of the construction and growth that never seems to stop at the university, Xavier now features one of the best university libraries and archives in the Deep South with a $14 million, six-story Library Resource Center, a building whose aqua-colored rooftop can be seen from miles away. It is connected to a new addition to the College of Pharmacy, which features bio-environmental, bio-chemical, and medicinal chemical laboratories, as well as a Clinical Trials Unit.

Other recent improvements on the 23-acre campus include a $7 million academic science complex that will soon have a $12.3 million addition, as well as increased campus housing and office space.

With 3,500 students today, Xavier's enrollment has nearly tripled in the past quarter-century. One of the oldest and most respected universities in the South, Xavier is the only university in the United States that is both historically black and Catholic.

Offering degrees in more than three dozen majors on the undergraduate, graduate, and professional levels, Xavier's major academic units include its College of Arts and Sciences, the College of Pharmacy, and the Graduate School.

Xavier's most distinguished record has been in the sciences. Xavier ranks first in the nation in placing African Americans into medical schools and has trained more African American pharmacists than any pharmacy school in the country. The university also ranks first nationally for the number of black graduates with physical science and life science degrees. In 1995, the National Science Foundation was so impressed with the university's record that Xavier was selected to participate in the Model Institutions for Excellence Program and was awarded a $12.3 million grant to develop the institution's infrastructure and student support activities aimed at increasing the number of minority students getting doctorates in the sciences.

Xavier has remained true to its tradition of producing top-notch educators and professionals. Over the past several years, 100 percent of Xavier's education majors have passed the National Teacher's Exam before graduation. In 1994, the campus newspaper became the first paper at a historically black college inducted into the Associated Collegiate Press Hall of Fame. Xavier also has produced many artists, including faculty member John T. Scott, a MacArthur Genius Grant recipient whose work has been displayed at the White House.

In addition, Xavier has distinguished itself for the scope and variety of innovative programs. The Center for Environmental Programs is on the cutting edge of research on environmental concerns. The Center for the Advancement of Teaching, established in part with a $3 million Kellogg Foundation grant, is designed to prepare faculty and students for the technology of the new millennium. The Drexel Center is a community outreach and adult education program.

Xavier's performance has won the university praise from the national press, including the *New York Times Selective Guide to Colleges*, which has described Xavier as a "school where achievement has been the rule, and beating the odds against success a routine occurrence," and *Newsweek*, which referred to Xavier as "a science-education powerhouse."

Under the guidance of long-time president Norman C. Francis, Xavier University's future promises to be as sterling as its past, a past as rich in history and culture as the city and region the university serves. ◆

Xavier ranks first in the nation in placing African Americans into medical schools and has trained more African American pharmacists than any pharmacy school in the country. Photo by Irving J. Johnson III.

One of the oldest and most respected universities in the South, Xavier University of Louisiana is the only university in the United States that is both historically black and Catholic. Photo by Irving J. Johnson III.

From a single flight cage built in Audubon Park in 1916 to nine world renowned nature facilities today, the Audubon Institute has emerged as a model of success through public/private partnerships.

Over the past two decades, the Audubon Institute has earned or raised more than $150 million, reinvesting these funds to build and improve its various facilities, creating a virtual New Orleans mecca for families and nature lovers.

The Audubon Institute rebuilt the Audubon Zoo, located in pastoral Audubon Park, into one of the nation's best. The Institute also opened the Aquarium of the Americas, revealing a Mississippi Riverfront vista for the first time in a hundred years and prompting the construction of Woldenberg Park, now enjoyed by thousands daily. Adjacent to the Aquarium is the Entergy IMAX® Theatre, drawing capacity crowds for eleven "in-your-face" 3D big-screen nature adventures every day. The Audubon Institute has, in addition, assumed operations of the Louisiana Nature Center, a wooded and unspoiled retreat for hiking and birdwatching. Across the Mississippi River, the Institute created a new scientific compound seeking answers to the world's endangered species issues: the Freeport-McMoRan Audubon Species Survival Center and the Audubon Center for Research of Endangered Species. Located on the site: Wilderness Park, a secluded picnic spot for group activities and workshops.

While these have been endeavors of the heart for the business and civic leaders of New Orleans, the Audubon Institute is framing an economic vision as well. That vision, according to CEO Ron Forman, is "to create a unique collection of living science facilities under one umbrella management organization...all financially healthy, all with the mission of 'Celebrating Life Through Nature'."

Audubon is a not-for-profit corporation closely tied to the City of New Orleans and patterned after the Smithsonian Institute. With over 600 employees and a like number of volunteers, the Audubon Institute receives minimal public operating subsidies, depending instead on the revenue generated from over 2.5 million paid admissions at its four public attractions and its 120,000 members to support the operations of the parks and research compound.

Capital investment is carefully planned. For example, the Aquarium and IMAX Theatre represent a development of some 170,000 square feet of prime riverfront property and anchor a park that showcases 17 acres of green space. Initiated in 1992 with completion planned by 1997 for the final extension of the Park, this project is debt free, financed by a combination of tax supported bonds and private investment.

These financial strategies make it certain that generations of New Orleanians into the future will always have access to the wonder of the natural world right around the corner. ◆

The Audubon Institute rebuilt the Audubon Zoo, located in pastoral Audubon Park, into one of the nation's best. Photo courtesy of the Audubon Institute.

Inside the Caribbean Tunnel at the Aquarium of the Americas, visitors enjoy talking with divers that are equipped with special helmets to answer questions about this aquatic environment. Photo by David Bull.

UNO's mission and charter are dedicated to creating opportunities for today's students and tomorrow's leaders by strengthening the meaningful links between the university and the community it serves.

The University of New Orleans is preparing to enter the 21st century with a new foundation built on partnership and committed to excellence, leadership, and a stronger, more dynamic community.

Overlooking the city from the airy shores of Lake Ponchartrain, the University of New Orleans symbolically and substantively represents New Orleans' future. Indeed, UNO's mission and charter are dedicated to creating opportunities for today's students and tomorrow's leaders by strengthening the meaningful links between the university and the community it serves.

That goal is made more cogent by the sweeping Partnerships 2000 campaign, the university's first-ever capital campaign specifically designed to enhance UNO's already diverse academic programs, and to build and expand its facilities for the technological needs of the coming century.

With an enrollment of nearly 16,000 students, UNO, which only opened in 1958, has already reached into the community with a stunning variety of innovative programs, making it a highly effective presence among regional institutions of higher education.

Among notable projects are:

The **National Center for the Revitalization of Central Cities**, the only university-based research group to focus on mechanisms to revitalize the country's urban sector;

The **School of Hotel, Restaurant, and Tourism Administration**, ranked among the top 16 such programs nationally and 13th in faculty research productivity worldwide;

The **Institute for the Comparative Study of Public Policy**, established with the University of Innsbruck, Austria, to sponsor public policy symposia and generate the exchange of ideas between students and teachers in both countries; and

The **Community Learning Center** at Lake Forest Plaza, UNO's Downtown, Jefferson, and Slidell campuses, and a broad range of public school partnerships which further weave UNO into the fabric of the community.

UNO has become a strategic voice in the region's economic growth through such initiatives as:

The **International Program for Port Planning and Management**, one of the premiere maritime executive training programs in the world;

The **Division of Business and Economic Research**, which facilitates growth through research and analysis;

The **UNO Technology Enterprise Center (TEC)**, which, with its business incubator and **Small Business Development Center**, is expected to generate an annual economic impact of $25 million in new spending through the support of small and new businesses;

The **UNO Business/Higher Education Council**, an alliance between the business community and higher education committed to economic development; and

The **Real Estate Market Data Center**, which provides accurate data information on real estate market trends throughout southeast Louisiana.

Future UNO projects include:

The **Center for Energy Resources Management (CERM)**, which as the anchor tenant of UNO's 56-acre Research and Technology Park will focus research on energy sources, conservation, and the environment;

The **Roger H. Ogden Museum of Southern Art**, part of the UNO-Lee Circle Center for the Arts which promises to revitalize historic Lee Circle and the Warehouse Arts District;

The **National D–Day Museum**, an interactive facility, also planned for historic Lee Circle, which will focus on issues of war and peace; and

The **Homer L. Hitt Alumni Center**, which will provide a permanent campus home for UNO's more than 40,000 alumni.

With a capital campaign of $100 million, bolstered by growing corporate and alumni support, the University of New Orleans is preparing to enter the 21st century with a new foundation built on partnership and committed to excellence, leadership, and a stronger, more dynamic community. ◆

With a mission to provide and broaden access to history, literature, philosophy, language, and culture, the Louisiana Endowment for the Humanities is an independent, nonprofit affiliate of the National Endowment for the Humanities.

Fueled by a conviction that economic prosperity hinges on a well-educated citizenry, the LEH, established in 1971, has directed its energies into two primary areas: the initiation of innovative programs promoting literacy and teacher-education for a better educated Lousiana, and the awarding of grants funding public projects in the humanities.

LEH–Initiated Programs

Since 1985, the LEH has sponsored *Summer Teacher Institutes*, an annual series of university-based seminars which in its first ten years gave more than 1,600 Louisiana middle and high school teachers new perspectives in such studies as literature, philosophy, women's studies, and history. Recent summer institutes have investigated such topics as the Harlem Renaissance, Louisiana in film, and the works of Mark Twain. During their first decade of operation, these enhancements to Louisiana teacher education enrolled a quarter of the state's humanities teachers and benefited nearly a quarter of a million students statewide.

Prime Time-Family Reading Time, a literacy series based at public libraries, brings at-risk families together with storytellers and humanities scholars to share the joy of reading while improving literacy skills. The unique program, which draws on children's literature rich in culture, history, and values, is designed to help families talk about books in ways that help children in school. In 1995, over 125 parents and their children participated in the program. Half of those families are now off public assistance.

The LEH's library-based reading program for adults, *Readings in Literature and Culture* [RELIC], brought the joys of literature to over 42,000 people in 64 parishes in its first 12 years of existence. Recent sessions have brought scholars and the out-of-school public together to read and discuss stories associated with Southern folklore, Louisiana history, and Native-American culture.

Louisiana Cultural Vistas, the statewide quarterly magazine of the LEH, brings the best of the state's art, history, culture, and literature to the printed page for more than 90,000 readers. The magazine's content ranges from profiles of and literature by Pulitzer prize-winning Louisiana writers and the state's most renowned artists to articles about Huey Long's political legacy and the origins of Cajun Mardi Gras.

LEH Grant Program

An extensive grantmaking program offers historians, filmmakers, photographers, museum directors, and other champions of the humanities opportunities to increase scholarship in and public appreciation of their respective fields of interest.

In 1995, LEH grants totaling over $255,000 supported 52 programs reaching 7,672,155 people in 57 cities and towns statewide, as well as nationwide television audiences for selected documentaries.

While all cultural studies are considered for funding, LEH is especially committed to projects illustrating the diversity of Louisiana culture. Recent grants have funded studies of Irish immigration in New Orleans and the history of Louisiana sugarcane cultivation.

The LEH also provides seed money for major projects, such as films for local and national public television, radio programs, photographic displays, and museum exhibits. An ongoing LEH grant funds the Humanities Resource Center, the state's largest repository of film and video materials on humanities-related topics, located in the State Library in Baton Rouge.

With an annual budget of $1.4 million, LEH obtains one-third of its funding from corporate, foundation, and private entities; one-third from the NEH; and one-third from the state of Louisiana, the Board of Elementary and Secondary Education, and the Board of Regents.

The LEH is operated by a 27-member board of directors, comprised of university professors along with business and civic leaders, representing all regions of the state, six of whom are appointed by the Governor of Louisiana. ◆

Louisiana Cultural Vistas, the quarterly arts, culture, history, and literature magazine of the Louisiana Endowment for the Humanities, covers a wide range of Louisiana topics, from interviews with Pulitzer Prize–winners and renowned artists to stunning photo essays on Cajun Mardi Gras and the historic state capitols.

Nunez Community College

Opening its doors in an era when Louisiana is expected to see dynamic community college growth across the state, Elaine P. Nunez Community College has emerged as one of the most energetic and innovative higher education institutions of its kind in the region by emphasizing the need for training and educating tomorrow's skilled workforce.

Established by an act of the state legislature in 1992, Nunez Community College—named in honor of long-time civic activist and supporter of education Elaine P. Nunez, who is also the late wife of Samuel B. Nunez Jr., the former president of Louisiana's state senate—has been a place of nearly magical transformations.

Located on an 18-acre site which once housed a regional technical institute, Nunez Community College has seen the construction, achieved in part by the help of some of the college's technical students, of a new 18,000-square-foot classroom building which also houses the Arts & Sciences faculty offices, Health Sciences faculty offices, laboratories and a general meeting area for large gatherings. In addition, an extra 3,400 square feet of science classrooms and laboratories have since been built alongside the structure which houses the college's technical shops.

Located in suburban Chalmette along the Mississippi River south of New Orleans, Nunez Community College has seen its enrollment increase to nearly 2,200 students, while its faculty stands at more than 130 full-time and part-time professors and instructors.

With a stated curricula mission of focusing on the development of the total person through a blend of occupational technologies coupled with arts, sciences and humanities education, Nunez Community College offers two-year associate degrees in more than 20 major programs including accounting, computer science, culinary arts, emergency medical technology and environmental technology, among other disciplines.

The college's 20 certificate programs, meanwhile, include air conditioning, heating and refrigeration; carpentry and building contruction; computer engineering technology; diesel mechanics; electrical construction; home health aide; practical nursing and welding.

With its focus on occupational training—one of the most rapidly growing student markets in the U.S.—Nunez Community College has also worked with local and regional businesses and industry providing courses designed to upgrade employee skills and education. Lifelong learning courses for both adults and children represent another area of growth for the college.

Accredited by the Commission on Colleges of the Southern Association of Colleges and Schools, Nunez Community College has also seen its 18,000-volume library nearly double in size since its opening. Nunez also has signed articulation agreements with four-year institutions such as the University of New Orleans and Nicholls State University, and it has won approval and funding from the state legislature to begin construction of a new library and classroom building.

That expansion, coupled with a student enrollent that has increased by approximately 7 percent a year since its 1992 opening, promises a Nunez Community College filled with diversity, growth and potential for a bright future. ◆

Students learn how to handle hazardous waste through the Environmental Technology Program at Nunez Community College. Photo by Nijme Renaldi.

Each summer Nunez Community College students participate in the Kiddie Kollege daycare internship program as part of the college's Early Childhood Education curriculum. Photo by Nijme Renaldi.

Health Care

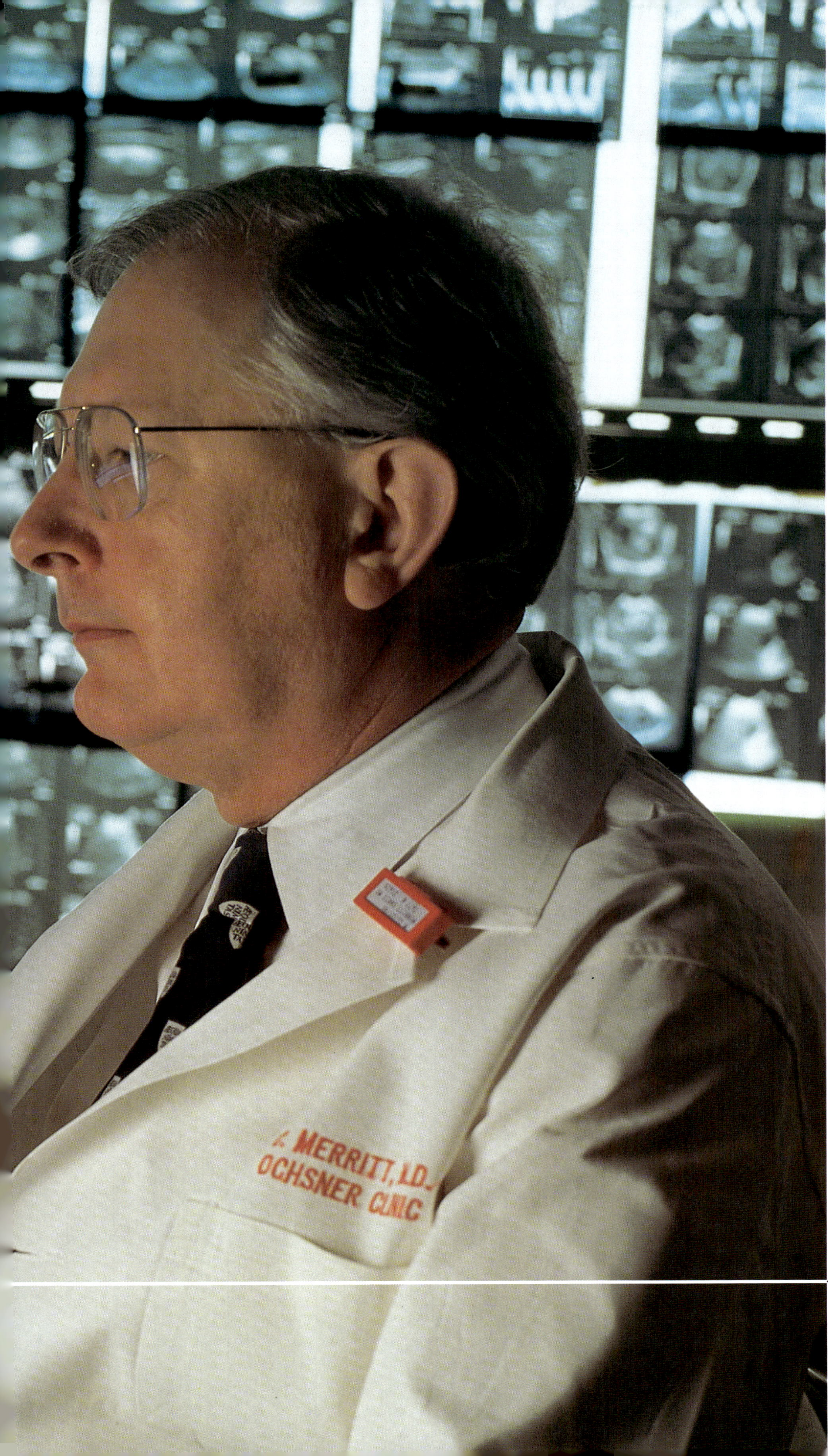
MERRITT, M.D.
OCHSNER CLINIC

CHAPTER 19

Responding to the growing need for managed care on an affordable basis, Southeast Medical Alliance (SMA) of New Orleans has emerged as one of the industry's major players, after nearly a decade of explosive growth.

SMA, founded in 1988, is owned by East Jefferson General Hospital, Lakeside Hospital, Slidell Memorial Hospital, Tulane University Medical Center, and West Jefferson Medical Center. Since its inception, SMA has seen its membership steadily increase from its initial first-year numbers of just over 2,500 to 5,500 by 1990; 75,000 by 1991; and now more than 425,000 as a preferred provider organization (PPO).

Meanwhile the popularity of the SMA's health maintenance organization (HMO) has proven equally volcanic. Established in January of 1995, the HMO now serves nearly 13,000 people, of which 8,000 live in the metro New Orleans area.

"We have been successful because we are providing an essential service," explains Barbara Louviere, president of SMA, "but also because all of the data clearly indicates that more and more organizations, as well as more and more employers, are looking to managed care organizations like ours to provide health benefits to their employees at a fixed rate."

That trend has seen SMA emerge as one of the largest and most extensive managed care providers in the state, not only adding more than 200,000 new clients to it's membership rolls in the past two years alone, but also contracting with a large number of additional hospitals including St. Tammany Parish Hospital, Terrebonne General Hospital, and Our Lady of the Lakes Regional Medical Center, among other institutions.

There are today more than 120 hospitals under contract to SMA, not to mention some 5,200 physicians. The alliance has just over 70 full-time employees and is based in the New Orleans suburb of Metairie in an ever-expanding space of offices. In addition to it's PPO and HMO services, SMA offers an Exclusive Provider Organization and a Point of Service program.

Officially known as SMARTPlan, SMA's health maintenance organization is a physician network primarily servicing southern Louisiana and comprising more than 300 personal care physicians and nearly 1,100 specialists.

SMARTPlan offers a comprehensive package of benefits that includes doctor's office visits, inpatient and outpatient surgery, and preventive care. SMARTPlan also provides maternity and 24-hour emergency care, as well as a roster of

Officially known as SMARTPlan, SMA's health maintenance organization is a physician network primarily servicing southern Louisiana and comprising more than 300 personal care physicians and nearly 1,100 specialists.

physicians and specialists in such fields as oncology, neurology, and gastroenterology—all selected by the patient.

"I think people see programs like the ones we offer here and right away wonder whether or not there will be any savings with them, not to mention if it is quality-driven," says Louviere. "When they see that those are the two things we care about the most, they want to sign on with us."

The response to the alliance's SMARTPlan, for example, has been overwhelming. Because its mission has been to provide both affordable healthcare while maintaining its quality, SMARTPlan has seen its membership expand on practically a monthly basis.

In addition, because of the large number of local and regional hospitals SMA works with and for, the quantity of qualified physicians—the all-important doctor-to-patient ratio—shows no sign of abating.

"It has been extremely important for us to maintain both our physician as well as our hospital relationships," continues Louviere. "In fact, we right now have such a large number of physicians and hospitals in our group that we don't have to worry at all about either the hospitals or physicians being maxed out. On the contrary, they are still accepting patients."

SMA has emerged as one of the largest and most extensive managed care providers in the state.

Offering 100-percent coverage with only a small, fixed co-payment, SMARTPlan also features for its members outpatient surgical procedures or hospitalization covered at the 100-percent level, after a fixed co-payment chosen by the employer, and even includes such hospital benefits as room and board, anesthesia, and inpatient hospital admission services all paid for at the 100-percent level.

Professional services 100-percent-funded include hospital maternity care, emergency care, both diagnostic and therapeutic services. Physicians signing on to SMARTPlan have also pledged themselves to not only providing quality, low-cost care, but to handling all of the patient's paperwork—no small thing in the era of duplicate and oftentimes confusing forms.

In an ongoing effort to reduce and maintain costs, SMA also features a medical review panel, explains Louviere, to "help assure that no inappropriate surgeries take place," as well as a local physicians' oversight, and a tracking system measured against national normative data.

With such features, it is not surprising that SMA's membership list has more than quadrupled in the 1990's. But the alliance, although coming about during a time of similar managed care efforts across the country, has distinguished itself as one of the few to succeed under the ownership of multiple hospitals.

Those hospitals have also committed themselves to supporting SMA's network expansion of services and physicians, at the same time that the alliance has maintained ever-scrupulous control over its own performance standards and product design.

And because SMA has emphasized patient convenience since its inception, its specialists under the SMARTPlan can be found virtually anywhere in the region: from cardiologists in Baton Rouge to pediatricians in New Orleans, oral surgeons in Mandeville—north of Lake Ponchartrain—and general surgeons down in Abbeville.

"We are always trying to find not only new services for our members, but new ways to make our services more available," says Louviere. "The emphasis is always on their short-term and long-term healthcare needs. That's what has made us successful."

The hospitals, personal care physicians, mental health providers, ancillary providers and pharmacies, among others, can be found throughout New Orleans and in an arc that encompasses the city for hundreds of miles.

"The bottom line is always keeping people well," says Louviere. "If somehow we can't do that, then we want to do whatever we can to get them well as soon as possible. That remains our number one mission." ◆

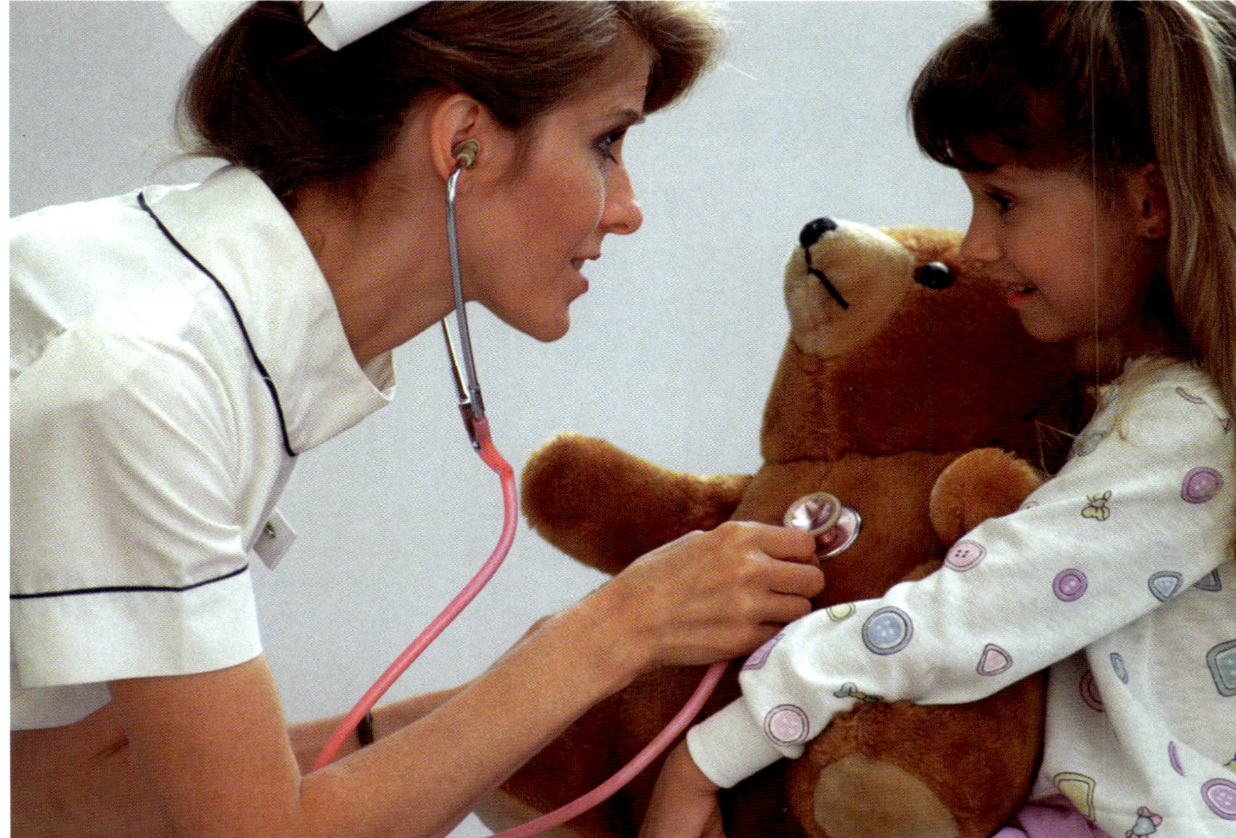

SMARTPlan also provides maternity and 24-hour emergency care, as well as a roster of physicians and specialists in such fields as oncology, neurology, and gastroenterology— all selected by the patient.

The Ochsner Medical Institutions

Serving the primary, specialty, and tertiary health care needs of patients from throughout the United States and Latin America, the Ochsner Medical Institutions are an alliance of two major health care organizations—the Ochsner Clinic and the Alton Ochsner Medical Foundation. For over 50 years, Ochsner physicians have earned a reputation for treating the Gulf South's most complex medical cases with state-of-the-art technologies.

The second largest private sector employer in Jefferson Parish and the third largest private sector employer in the metro area, the Ochsner Medical Institutions employ 5,300 professionals and staff and has an annual payroll of over $200 million.

The Ochsner Clinic

Opened to patients in 1942, the Ochsner Clinic began as a diagnostic and treatment center of 19 physicians and staff in uptown New Orleans. The clinic, organized as a private partnership, was founded by five local surgeons. It was named after one of them, Dr. Alton Ochsner, an internationally known surgeon and teacher who was the first physician to link smoking with cancer of the lung.

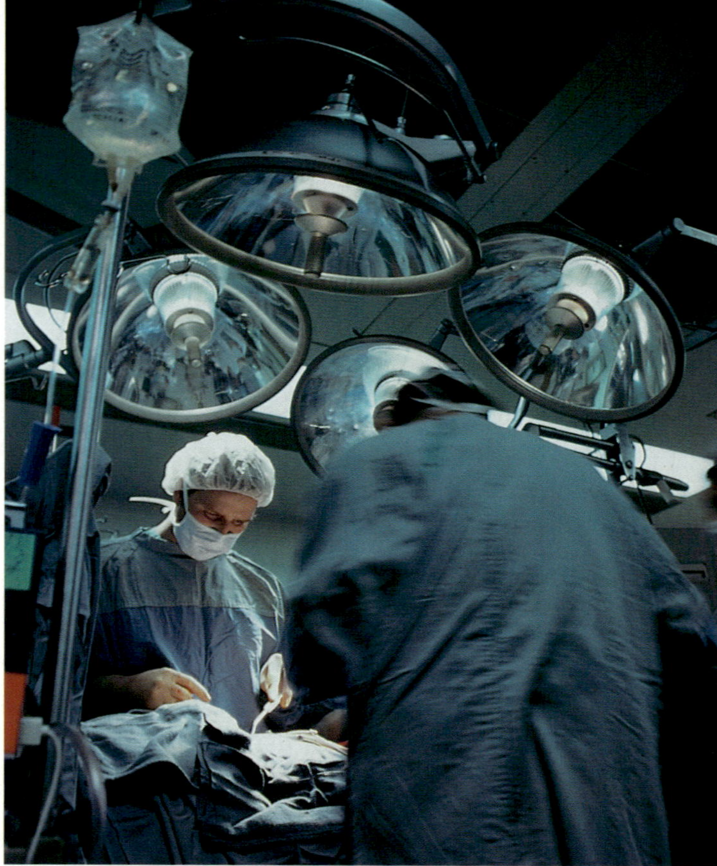

For over 50 years, Ochsner physicians have earned a reputation for treating the Gulf South's most complex medical cases with state-of-the-art technologies.

Today the clinic operates as a multi-specialty group medical practice of 375 physicians and surgeons in 64 medical specialties. Serving over 700,000 patients annually, the clinic handles specialized, highly technical procedures that are usually referred to major medical institutions and university medical centers. Employing a support staff of 1,300, it ranks fourth among New Orleans-area private sector businesses based on revenue generation.

Over the years, the Ochsner tradition of health care excellence has spread throughout southeastern Louisiana. Ochsner Clinic of Baton Rouge, a multi-specialty group of 95 physicians and surgeons representing 30 specialties, opened in 1986. Twenty-two additional neighborhood clinics provide convenient and comfortable family medical care to patients throughout southeastern Louisiana.

The clinic operates as a multi-specialty group medical practice of 375 physicians and surgeons in 64 medical specialties.

The Alton Ochsner Medical Foundation

The other partner in the Ochsner Medical Institutions is the Alton Ochsner Medical Foundation, chartered in 1944 as a nonprofit entity dedicated to patient care, medical education, and clinical research activities.

Carrying out the Foundation's commitment to patient care is the 532-bed Ochsner Foundation Hospital, a teaching hospital admitting 18,000 patients annually. Located at its current 21-acre site between Jefferson Highway and the Mississippi River since 1954—directly adjacent to the Ochsner Clinic—the hospital is the site of 12,000 surgical procedures each year. Its emergency department treats an additional 30,000 patients annually on an outpatient basis.

With recent accolades including recognition in the publications "The Best Doctors in America" and "The Best Hospitals in America," the hospital is accredited with commendation by the Joint Commission on Accreditation of Health Care Organizations, placing it above 87 percent of all hospitals in the United States.

Ochsner is a member of the Louisiana Hospital Association; Voluntary Hospitals of America, Inc.; American Hospital Association; Metropolitan Hospital Council of New Orleans, Inc.; and the National Council of Community Hospitals.

Since its initial commitment to support medical education, the Foundation has grown to become one of the largest non-university-based physician training programs in the country. The foundation sponsors 25 fully accredited graduate medical education training programs for over 250 residents and fellows annually.

In addition, the Ochsner School of Allied Health Sciences provides fully accredited training in three allied health professions: radiology technology, diagnostic medical sonography, and respiratory care.

To ensure that its medical staff remains on the cutting edge of medical technology, the Ochsner Continuing Medical Education Department conducts 40 courses a year for practicing physicians and other health professionals. The Foundation's Learning Resources Center, featuring a comprehensive medical library and fully equipped medical editing, medical illustration, audio visual, and photographic departments, serves the foundation's mission of medical education.

The Ochsner Research Division conducts clinical and scientific research that provides patients with innovative therapies and the latest in treatment options. Recent and ongoing studies include those in the areas of AIDS, viral hepatitis, hypertension, cellular transplantation therapies, organ preservation, molecular genetics, diseases of the bone, and angioplasty technology.

Ochsner Health Plan

The Ochsner Health Plan, established in 1984, is Louisiana's first fully integrated statewide health care network — linking physicians, hospitals and managed care in one comprehensive system of health care delivery. The Ochsner Health Plan now has over 140,000 members receiving services from a network of 29 acute care hospitals and over 1,000 physicians statewide.

All of the Ochsner Health Plan's managed care products feature: competative pricing, no claims forms for in-network care, a choice of many convenient locations, a growing list of providers and affiliated hospitals, a focus on wellness and preventive care, virtually no paperwork, and world-wide access to emergency care.

Special Programs at Ochsner

Heart Care

The Ochsner Heart and Vascular Institute is a world-class facility offering comprehensive preventive, diagnostic, acute,

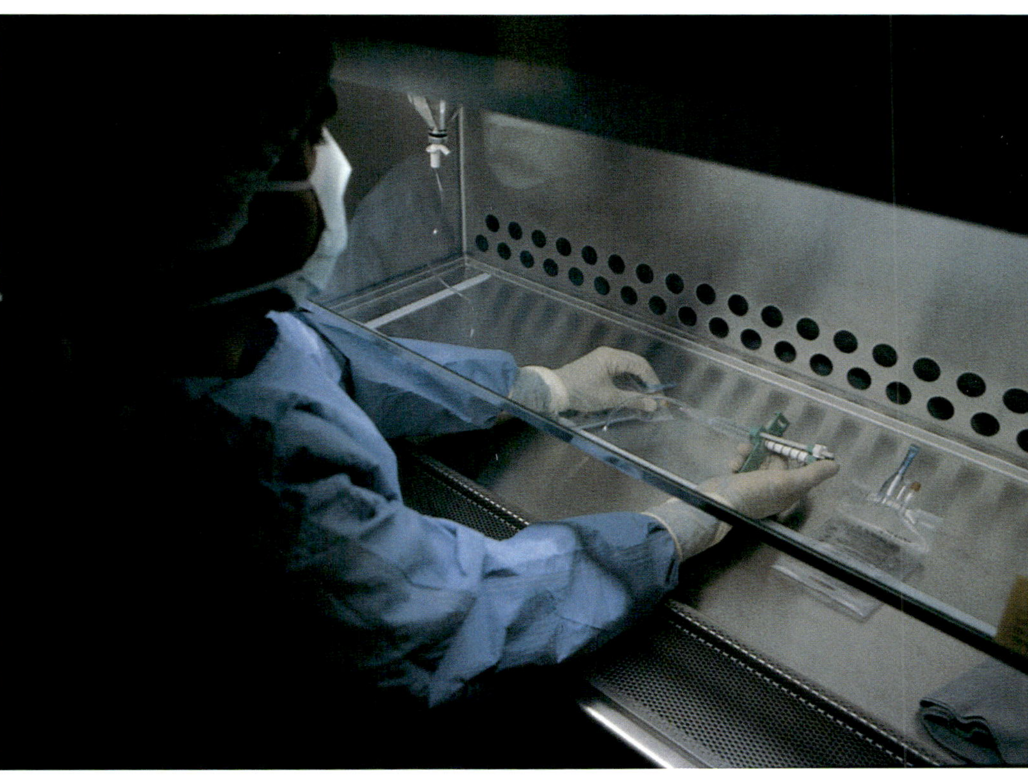

The Oshsner Research Division conducts clinical and scientific research that provides patients with innovative therapies and the latest in treatment options.

The Ochsner Heart and Vascular Institute is a world–class facility offering comprehensive preventive, diagnostic, acute, and rehabilitative care for virtually every cardiac and vascular problem.

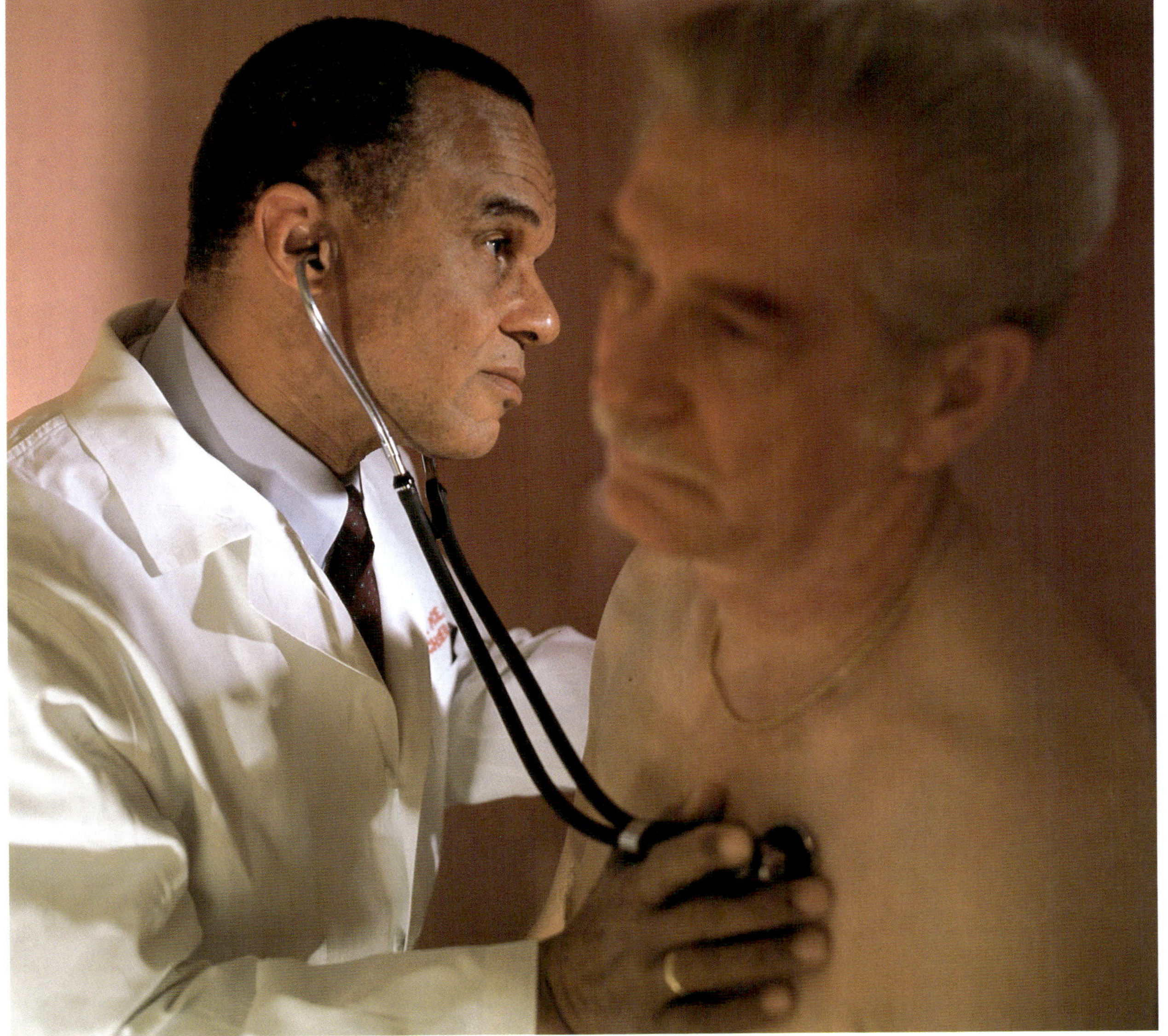

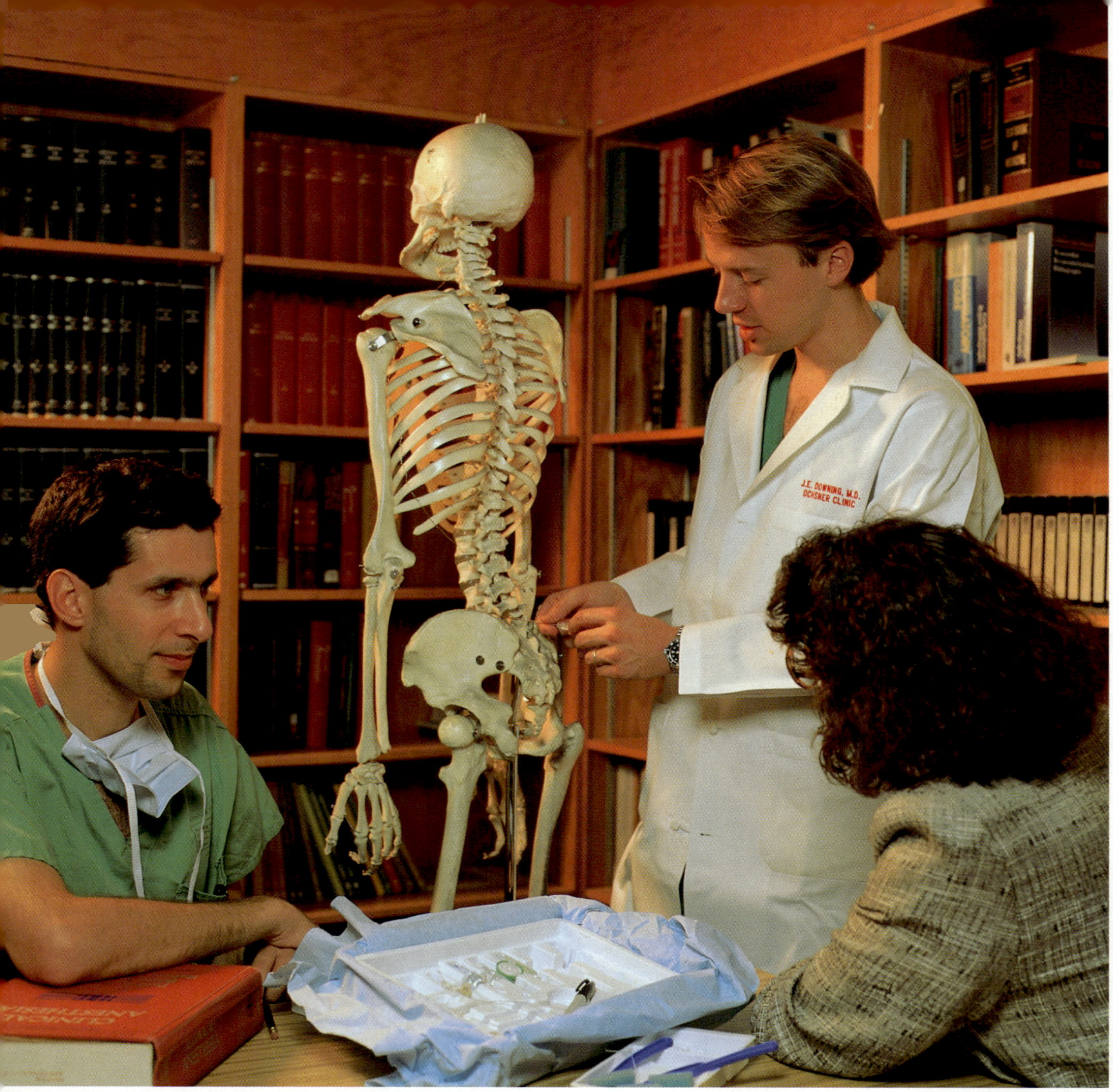

and rehabilitative care for virtually every cardiac and vascular problem. In 1996, *Good Housekeeping Magazine* named Ochsner in its listing of "The Best Heart Doctors in America."

In addition to pioneering the latest techniques to remove coronary and peripheral artery obstructions, Ochsner was the first hospital in the United States to use angioscopy, an imaging technique which allows physicians to view the arteries of a beating heart. The hospital also performed the nation's first heart valve replacement.

The institute's Cardiovascular Health Center offers a full spectrum of preventive health services including a human performance lab, cardiac rehabilitation, and programs on weight control and smoking cessation.

Cancer Care

The Ochsner Cancer Center provides extensive outpatient cancer services and the highest level of inpatient care. The Ochsner Center for Radiation Oncology offers the most advanced radiation treatment procedures, including standard external beam radiation therapy, hyperthermia, stereotactic radiosurgery, and radiation implants.

Cancer control studies play a major role in the center's Clinical Research Program, offering patients innovative therapies before they are generally available elsewhere. Ochsner participation in national cancer prevention trials for breast and prostate cancer may provide new insights into the design of strategies to reduce cancer risks.

Organ Transplantation

In 1970, Ochsner Foundation Hospital was the site of Louisiana's first heart transplant. Today the hospital boasts the fifth largest heart transplantation program in the United States.

A regional pioneer in the area of organ transplantation, Ochsner physicians also performed the first successful single-lung, the first double-lung, the first liver, the first liver-kidney, the first pancreas-kidney and the first heart-lung transplantation surgeries in Louisiana.

Established in 1984, the Ochsner Multi-Organ Transplant Center was the site of over 1,000 organ transplant surgeries in its first 11 years of operation. The center is a national leader in one-year survival rates following transplantation surgeries.

Women's Services

The Ochsner Center for Women provides a wide range of services for women of all ages, including routine obstetric

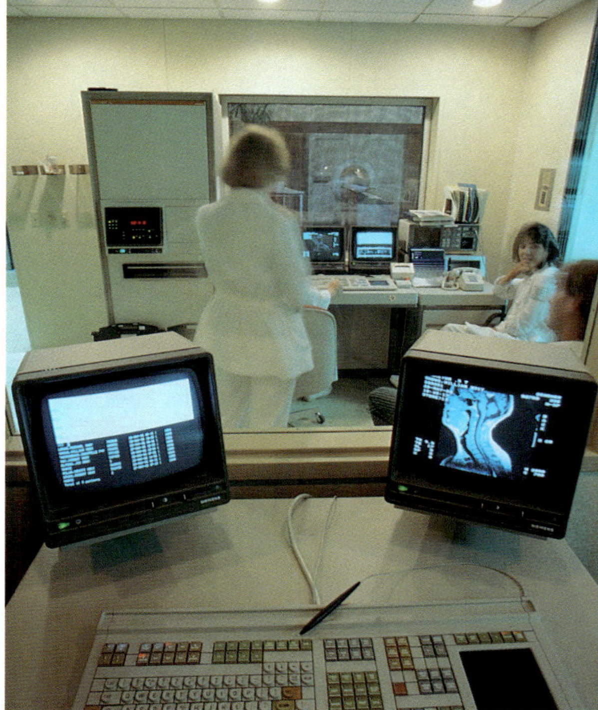

and gynecologic care, management of high-risk pregnancy, cancer, health screenings, osteoporosis, and infertility.

The Ochsner Birth Center features comfortable, home-like rooms for labor, delivery, and recovery. Patients have access to Ochsner experts in high-risk pregnancies, complex deliveries and critical care of newborns.

The Ochsner Breast Center offers educational and screening services such as instruction in breast self-examination, mammography, ultrasound, and stereotactic core biopsy.

Children's Services

Providing everything from critical care of newborns and children of all ages, to diagnosis and treatment of common childhood illnesses, the Ochsner pediatric staff comprises one of the largest single groups of physicians within the Ochsner medical complex.

Sub-specialty pediatric care is available in allergy and immunology, anesthesiology, cardiology, child development, endocrinology and nutrition, gastroenterology, hematology and oncology, neurology, psychiatry and psychology, and surgery.

A specially designed unit for inpatient care of adolescents includes rooms equipped with TV, VCR, video games, and a small refrigerator, and a teen activity room with an entertainment center, games, and a computer.

Orthopedic Services

The Ochsner Department of Orthopedics provides diagnosis and treatment of virtually all diseases, disorders, and injuries of the musculoskeletal system. Ochsner offers specialized orthopedic care for pediatric patients and cancers of the musculoskeletal system, as well as programs in sports medicine, reconstructive and implant surgery, hand surgery, microsurgery, and podiatry.

Colon and Rectal Services

Diseases of the colon, rectum, and anus are treated on both an inpatient and outpatient basis by the Ochsner Department of Colon and Rectal Surgery. The department features a fully equipped Colonoscopy Suite and an Anorectal Physiology Laboratory. Helping physicians diagnose and treat such disorders as incontinence, pelvic floor abnormalities, rectal cancer, anal sphincter injuries, and anal fistulas are ultrasonography and anorectal manometry.

Digestive Disorders

The Ochsner Department of Gastroenterology and Hepatology is nationally respected for its diagnosis, treatment, and research protocols in a range of digestive diseases including chronic hepatitis and ulcer disease, and in the management of patients who require liver transplantation.

Dialysis

The 19,000-square foot Ochsner Dialysis Center features dialysis machines at 36 stations and three isolation rooms for patients with contagious illnesses. Videos and stationary bicycles can be enjoyed while patients are on dialysis machines.

Other Services

Meeting the needs of Ochsner patients, their families, and guests is the Brent House Hotel, which provides comfortable and convenient lodging in a hotel-quality environment. Located directly adjacent to the clinic and hospital, the hotel features 450 rooms and offices, a six-story climate-controlled atrium with fountains, greenery, and comfortable furnishings, a heated outdoor swimming pool, two dining areas, beauty and barber shops.

The Ochsner owned, full-service Elmwood Fitness Center, offers programs for the entire family. The center features indoor and outdoor pools, childcare facilities, two full-size aerobic studios, raquetball, volleyball, and basketball courts; weight training, and aquatics. The Cardiovascular Health Center, which provides cardiac rehabilitation, and Kidsports, a facility dedicated to children's fitness and play activities, round out the center's offerings. Corporate memberships are available at a reduced rate if five or more individuals sign up.

Ochsner Home Health Services, Inc., provides skilled nursing and home health services to individuals in the greater New Orleans and Baton Rouge areas who are acutely ill or have chronic health problems but do not require hospital care. Home health care services range from a single visit to 24-hour, seven-days-a-week monitoring.

Community Service

In 1995, Ochner and its employees contributed $250,000 in funds, food, clothing and other in-kind items to individuals and organizations in our area. Over the same time period, they volunteered over 16,000 hours to the community. The Ochsner Medical Institutions sponsor about 140 community health education seminars and suport groups annually.

Ochsner is the proud sponsor of community events including the annual Crescent City Classic. ◆

Founded in 1931, LSU Medical Center is an important part of the larger Louisiana State University System and includes two Schools of Medicine, in New Orleans and Shreveport; a School of Graduate Studies on each campus; the only School of Dentistry in the state; a School of Nursing that is one of only two in the nation to offer all four levels of nursing education; Louisiana's only School of Allied Health Professions, with programs in New Orleans and Shreveport and the LSU Hospital on its Shreveport campus, which has been ranked as the nation's #1 public hospital. With facilities throughout Louisiana, LSU Medical Center continues to house an exciting array of cutting edge medical and scientific research and technology confirming its reputation as a national institute of note.

In 1995, LSU Medical Center won a much-coveted planning grant from the National Cancer Institute, giving it funds and support to transform its already-prestigious Stanley S. Scott Cancer Center into a Comprehensive Cancer Center as designated by the National Cancer Institute—one of only 27 in the country.

But LSU Medical Center has merited recognition for myriad other reasons as well, including its Neuroscience Center of Excellence, where current work includes advances on brain cell regeneration and the prevention of epileptic seizures, as well as developing new drugs for the advancement of stroke recovery.

At the LSUMC's Cardiovascular Center, the latest technology and scholarship are being applied to the vast new world of genetic manipulation, spurring heart cells into regrowth after a heart attack.

LSU Medical Center educates about 70 percent of Louisiana's health care professionals.

At the LSU Eye Center, meanwhile, research has made it possible for millions of nearsighted people to correct their vision without glasses or contact lenses.

That so much activity springs from one institutional source can easily be seen by the number of people who make up the LSU Medical Center family. With its campuses in Shreveport and New Orleans and educational programs and patient care that span the state, the Medical Center has upwards of 3,000 students enrolled in programs touching all of Louisiana's 64 parishes. As a state resource, LSU Medical Center provides the opportunity for Louisiana students at all economic levels to enroll in its health professions schools. To support its activities, LSU Medical Center generates some 20,000 primary and secondary jobs.

LSU Medical Center students are Louisiana residents. With a unique complement of health professions schools, it is not surprising that LSU Medical Center educates about 70 percent of Louisiana's physicians, 80 percent of its dentists and 90 percent of its allied health professionals.

Well ahead of the nation's attention turning to primary care, LSU Medical Center developed innovative programs to increase the number of Louisiana's primary care physicians. Paired with initiatives in Family Medicine, the Area Health Education Center (AHEC) program has made great strides in encouraging medical students to specialize in family practice or other primary care disciplines in rural or under-served urban settings all over the state.

LSU Medical Center physicians care for the people of Louisiana with more than 1.5 million outpatient visits a year in hundreds of hospitals, clinics, and health care settings across the state. This enormous ambulatory care contribution is in addition to the care provided to thousands of patients admitted to the more than 1,400 hospital beds in the state attended by full-time LSUMC faculty physicians.

Outreach efforts include creating a telemedicine program that is linking the resources of LSU Medical Center to physicians and other health care professionals and their patients in far-flung parts of the state and with state institutions such as long-term care facilities, public health clinics and others where the potential for improving access to care and lowering costs is very significant.

LSU Medical Center health care professionals are the major providers of care in Louisiana's Charity Hospital System.

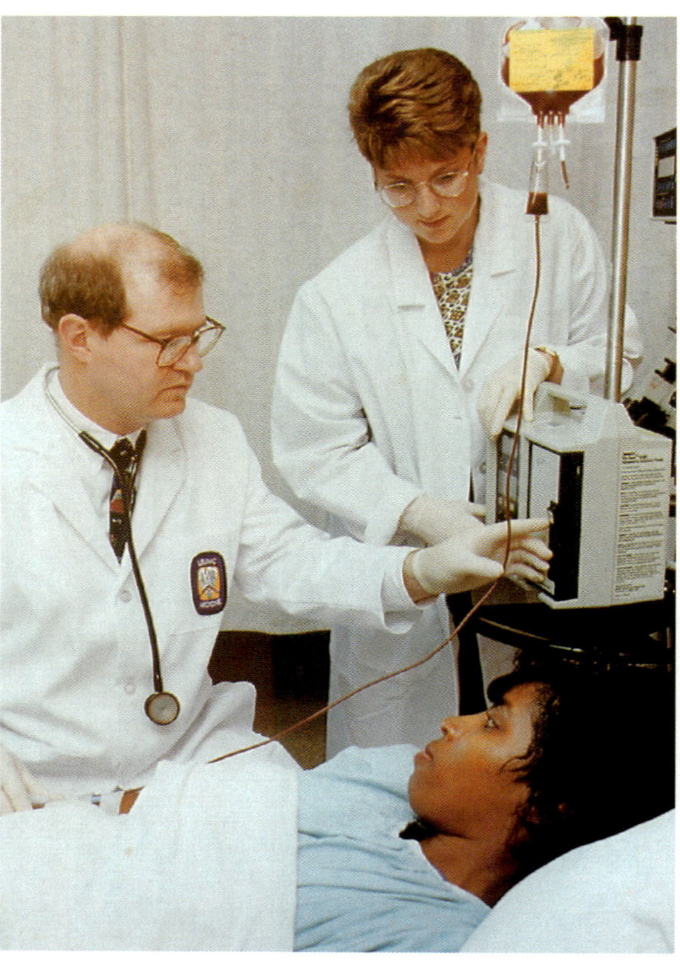

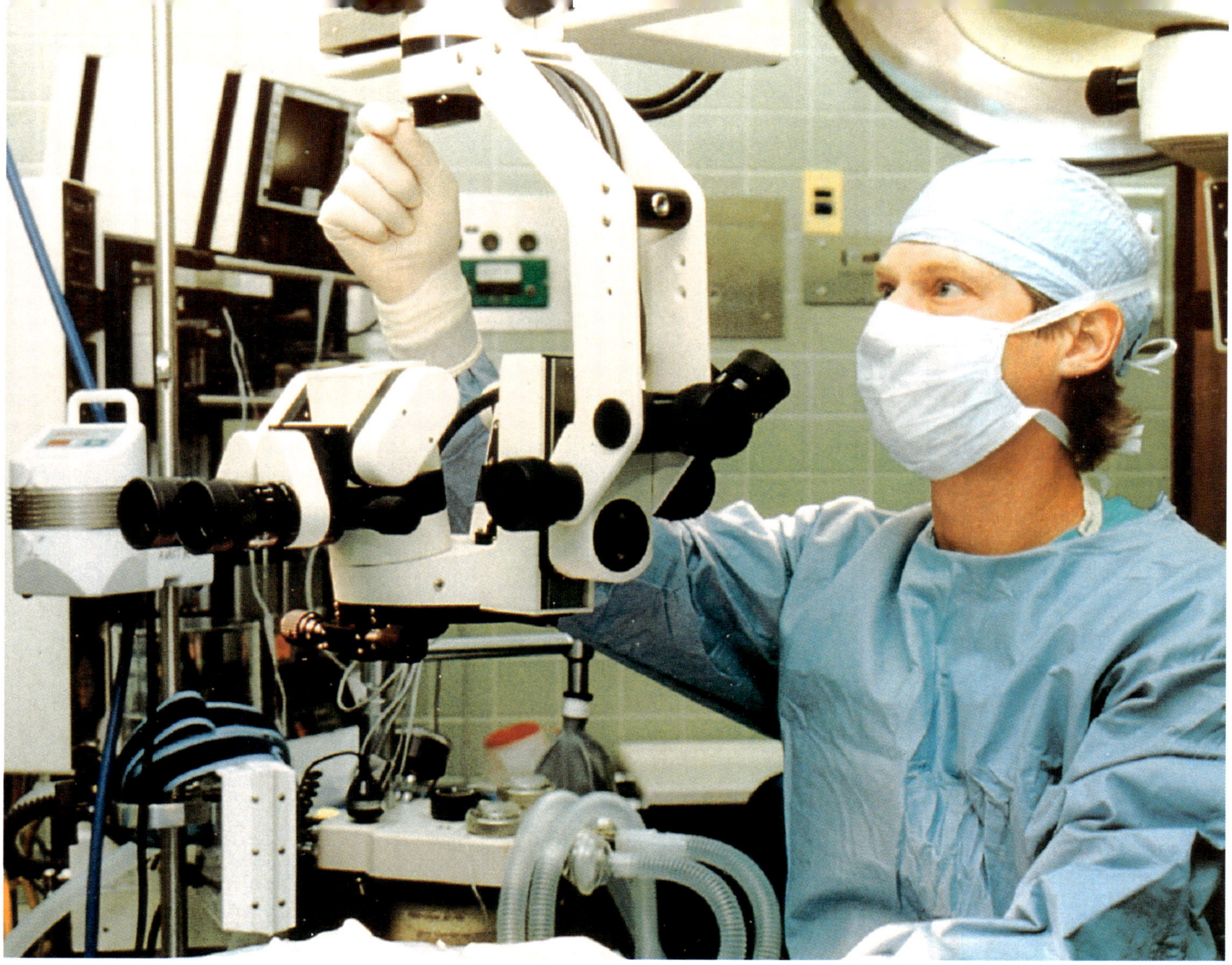

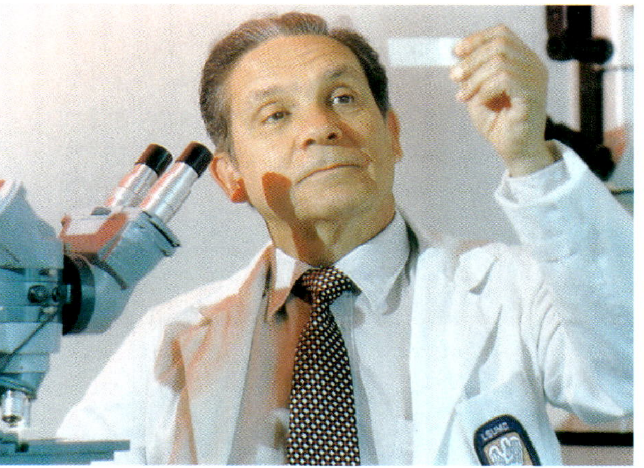

LSU Medical Center contributes significantly to the health of Louisiana's economy as well. With an annual economic impact of more than $1 billion, LSU Medical Center is the largest holder of National Institutes of Health grant money in the state. The value of LSU Medical Center research grants and contracts is more than $66 million. Such support helps drive the historic and oftentimes precedent-setting medical research and development technology that is constantly taking place on the various LSU Medical Center campuses.

Research at LSU Medical Center has given birth to a wide variety of breakthrough technology and innovations. Among research accomplishments, scientists at LSU Medical Center may have found the means to render the deadly Ebola virus harmless; were the first in the world to link smoking to one of the major causes of heart disease; have developed a new way to pinpoint hidden cancers undetectable by conventional tests; and have invented a device that will replace cumbersome head gear for those with braces.

LSU Medical Center has the oldest Bone Marrow Transplant program in Louisiana and is the only one certified as a transplant center in the state by the National Marrow Donor Program. In addition to transplanting the first long-term successful transplant for leukemia, LSUMC physicians also performed the first bone marrow transplant for sickle cell disease in the state and have an innovative research program using bone marrow transplants for recurrent breast cancer.

Caring for Louisiana's most ill is a strength of the LSU Hospital in Shreveport. Operating Louisiana's only designated Burn Center, combining full critical care, convalescence and research, it also operates one of the nation's few unit-based outpatient clinics for burn patients on a round-the-clock basis. The Neonatal Intensive Care Unit is a 40-bed unit that carries a Level III designation—the highest classification denoting the highest level of capability. And premier among the hospital's unique services is the Level I Trauma Center. Staffed around the clock by multi-disciplinary teams of highly trained specialists, the Trauma Center team is assembled to handle the most critical injuries the moment the patient arrives. LSU Medical Center physicians and others were also successful in obtaining a Level I Trauma designation for their program at Charity Hospital in New Orleans.

Given such triumphs in education, patient care, research, and community outreach, it is not surprising that LSU Medical Center has fulfilled the vision of its founders as the "finest Medical Center of its kind." ◆

LSU Medical Center faculty have pioneered treatments that have saved countless lives.

Through research and other activities, LSU Medical Center generates 20,000 jobs with an annual economic impact topping $1 billion.

Methodist Health System

The face of health care is changing and Pendleton Memorial Methodist Hospital is actively involved in determining how it will look in the 21st century.

As Methodist Hospital approaches three decades of caring, it maintains an outstanding reputation as a leader in the greater New Orleans health care and business communities. For more than a quarter of a century, the hospital has also maintained its founding philosophy and long-standing tradition of courtesy, concern, kindness, and compassion. As national and local health care fields experience significant transformation, as East New Orleans develops and matures, and as emerging technology increases options, Methodist has remained constant in its primary mission of meeting the health care needs of the community.

Methodist Hospital was founded by members of the Gentilly Methodist Church, dedicated and concerned volunteers who recognized the needs and visualized the projected growth of East New Orleans. Since its opening in the fall of 1968 as a nonprofit, community hospital, Methodist has continued to grow, expand, and change to serve East New Orleans.

In keeping with its Christian philosophy, the Methodist Health System promotes health and wellness through healing, caring, serving, and educating the people of East New Orleans and the surrounding communities. Emphasis is placed on quality and the delivery of superior services to enhance the health and well-being of those served. Care is delivered in an atmosphere that reflects the hospital's mission to treat the whole person —physically, mentally, and spiritually.

Under the leadership of Fred Young, Jr., President of the Methodist Health System, Methodist Hospital is positioning itself for the start of the 21st century with the addition of a new 131,000-square-foot East Tower, and an expansion and renovation program, setting the foundation for additional medical advances in patient care and comfort. The 1995 completion of the East Tower represents a significant exterior face change and symbolizes the internal changes necessary for a contemporary, successful health care institution.

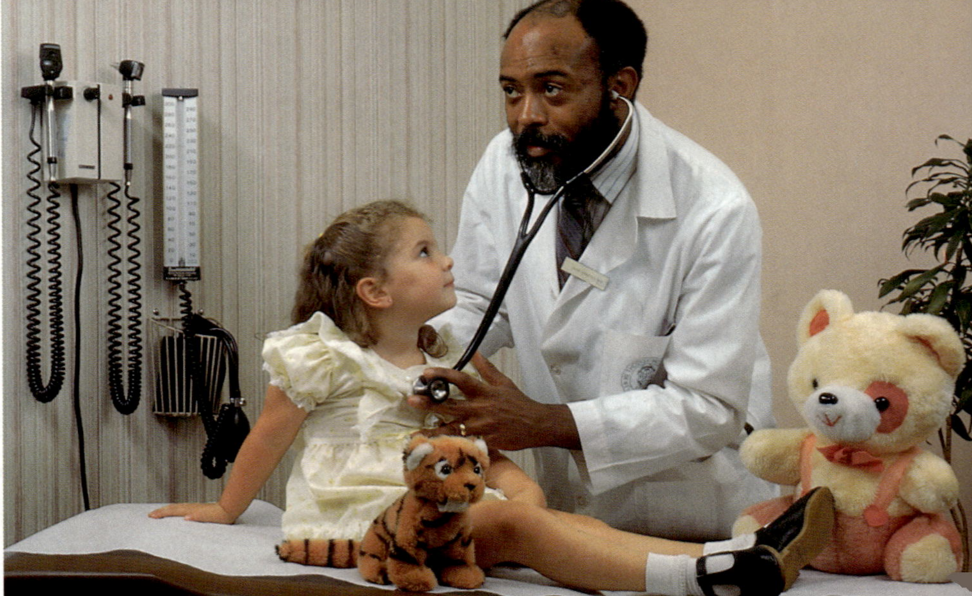

The Methodist Medical Staff represents a wide range of specialists to meet the needs of the growing East New Orleans Community.

The first major expansion since the 1978 addition of patient floors to the original hospital, the East Tower features resource restructuring for a more efficient, convenient arrangement of services with an emphasis on outpatient care. The addition of the East Tower opens opportunities for Methodist to develop a plan to offer all private patient rooms to enhance the comfort of inpatient stays. The facility houses a variety of patient service departments including physical therapy, respiratory therapy, occupational therapy, endoscopy, a 29-bed intensive care unit, and a Women's Center.

During its years of physical growth, Methodist has also concentrated on the quality of patient care with the addition of advanced technology. Advanced radiology equipment and procedures, open heart surgery, a Cancer Center, Advanced Surgery Center, and Ambulatory Surgery Center, for example, are integral parts of the Methodist Health System campus. Ever mindful of its mission to enhance the quality of life in the community, Methodist also offers a variety of wellness programs and health screenings as well as support groups to assist individuals in the prevention of disease as well as the recovery process.

In addition to a variety of advanced programs, Methodist has recently introduced the Methodist Health Alliance (MHA), an ambitious managed care program. The Methodist Health Alliance is a bold answer to decreasing hospital-based revenues and increasing movement toward alternative treatments. An integrated health care delivery system, the Methodist Health Alliance is a comprehensive coordination of physician and hospital services which contracts and works with managed care organizations and other payors to increase cost efficiency while ensuring that participants receive high-quality care. The MHA is a logical progression in the health care evolution and represents a decade of effort to develop the elements of a comprehensive integrated delivery system on the Methodist campus.

The community will continue to find the highest quality of care and top-flight service at Methodist Hospital as it grows even stronger as a multifaceted, flexible, prime choice for managed care companies. Methodist and its medical staff will increasingly be an attractive option for employers, payors, and specifically targeted managed care companies. The move is a proactive adaptation to health care industry

The 1995 completion of the East Tower represents a significant exterior face change and symbolizes the internal changes necessary for a contemporary, successful health care institution.

changes and re-engineering for a more efficient system that ensures high quality care at appropriate service levels.

The trend toward managed care is a contributing factor in the increasing number of partnerships, mergers, and alliances taking shape in the greater New Orleans area—as well as throughout the United States. In response to the changes in health care and to maintain a strong position as a community-based hospital, Methodist, in 1995, signed a Memorandum of Agreement with several other leading hospitals to develop a community-based health care network of institutions in the greater New Orleans area. This venture offers opportunities for non-profit facilities to retain their own personal identity and directions during a transformation age in health care.

Methodist Hospital's success remains grounded in its innovative approach to care that extends not only to the East New Orleans community but more and more to the Gulf Coast region. The hospital has not only added new technology and procedures but has expanded into a comprehensive health care campus including:

- Pendleton Memorial Methodist Hospital, a 317-bed acute care facility offering a full range of inpatient treatment and outpatient diagnostic services.
- Methodist Ambulatory Surgery Center, a freestanding, same-day surgery center, offering outpatient treatment in all major specialties.
- Methodist Behavioral Resources, the parent company for Methodist Psychiatric Pavilion, a 36-bed mental health and chemical dependency treatment center; and Psychotherapy Associates, a network of four outpatient clinics, providing therapeutic intervention on an inpatient and outpatient basis.
- Methodist Cancer Center, the only hospital-affiliated, freestanding facility of its kind in the East New Orleans community, offering a comprehensive range of treatment services.
- Methodist Child Care Center, offering quality care to the children of hospital employees and the East New Orleans area.
- Methodist Health System Foundation, dedicated to providing, supporting, and developing health-related programs and services to the community.
- Methodist OB/GYN Clinic, offering a specialized range of diagnostic treatment and surgical services related to pregnancy, menopause, infection, pain, and the general needs of all women.
- Methodist Occupational and Industrial Medicine Clinic, for employees of metropolitan area businesses, providing a wide variety of services from emergency treatment for injured or ill employees to rehabilitative care.
- Methodist Outpatient Diagnostic Center, providing laboratory, radiology, and electrocardiogram (EKG) services.
- Methodist Physical Medicine Center, a comprehensive state-of-the-art preventive and rehabilitative program.
- Physicians Medical Plaza, with custom designed suites to meet the individualized needs of each physician.
- Medical Center of East New Orleans, providing office space for over 80 physicians of the East New Orleans area.

Keeping ahead of the needs of the community and the evolving medical trends and technology is a tradition for Methodist Hospital. Expanding and renovating to serve a growing area, while providing comfort and care for patients and their families is vital to the Methodist philosophy. As the face of Methodist Hospital changes, its foundation of courtesy, concern, kindness, and compassion remains stronger than ever as a new world of health care approaches.

In 1995, Methodist Hospital served more than 85,000 patients, with 25,410 emergency registrations and 26,879 outpatient visits. These figures indicate distinct growth in an era of overall declining hospital census on a national basis. Total assets for Methodist have also continued to grow; from $48 million in 1992 to $78 million in 1994, and $81 million in 1995. With a medical staff of more than 400 and 1,100 employees, the economic impact of the hospital complex is estimated at more than $90 million annually. Methodist Hospital is the second largest employer in East New Orleans.

Accredited by the Joint Commission on Accreditation of Hospitals, Methodist Hospital is a member of the American Hospital Association, the Louisiana Hospital Association, the Orleans Parish Medical Society, the United Methodist Conference, The Chamber/New Orleans and the River Region, and the East New Orleans Economic Development Council. ◆

Personalized attention and patient comfort are priorities at Methodist.

East Jefferson
General
Hospital

East Jefferson General Hospital, a not-for-profit, community-owned hospital, is often referred to as a "jewel" of Jefferson Parish. Located just minutes from downtown New Orleans, the hospital provides tertiary care and other services to the residents of East Jefferson Parish and surrounding communities, and serves as a provider for major managed care organizations.

The hospital's opening on Valentine's Day in 1971 marked the culmination of a community effort that began in 1959. The rapidly growing Jefferson Parish had a core group of business and civic leaders who worked tirelessly for public support of the bond issue that would lay the groundwork for their community hospital. Many of these individuals and countless other community members have remained closely involved with East Jefferson General over the years.

East Jefferson General Hospital follows a mission of providing personalized care and health-related services consistent with quality medical and ethical standards to improve the health status of individuals in the East Bank of Jefferson Parish and surrounding communities. In carrying out this mission, the hospital fulfills the commitment to deliver quality care and services at a price which represents value to patients, employers, and insurers.

Today, the 556-bed hospital boasts a broad-based medical staff of over 800 primary and specialty physicians. These doctors admit over 18,000 patients and order some 112,000 outpatient visits each year.

With more than 2,000 full-and part-time team members (employees), the hospital is one of Jefferson Parish's top five employers. The hospital creates an average annual economic impact of $600 million, directly or indirectly supports over 6,000 jobs, and conducts over 80 percent of its purchasing business with Louisiana-based vendors.

At East Jefferson General Hospital, physicians, clinical and support staff, and almost 1,000 volunteers work together within a culture geared to guest relations. President and Chief Executive Officer Peter J. Betts, F.A.C.H.E., shares these thoughts. "Our patients and other customers expect two kinds of quality. First is clinical, or technical, quality. This is demonstrated by our accreditation with commendation, the highest recognition awarded by the Joint Commission on Accreditation of Hospitals and Healthcare Organizations. The second kind of quality expected of us is expressed in terms of 'how I am treated as a person' or guest relations. We strive to understand the expectations of our patients, their families, and our other customers and then to meet or exceed these expectations. Quality health care is very personal, and we want to be known for our personal touch."

East Jefferson General Hospital borrowed advice from the experts at Disney and translated it to a healthcare setting. Standards for customer service are high, and ongoing surveys demonstrate that these standards are being met. Ninety-six percent of our patients state that East Jefferson General Hospital has met or exceeded their expectations.

Meeting The Medical Need

With myriad diagnostic tools, interventional procedures, and a strong rehabilitative program, East Jefferson General's Gulf South Heart Center offers state-of-the-art care for diseases and abnormalities of the heart. Its nationally recognized staff was the first in the metro area to provide biplane-digital angiography, a now-routine imaging procedure that offers two views of the heart simultaneously. Today, additional cath labs and other diagnostic areas along with an expanded rehab program, ongoing patient education, and family support programs meet increasing patient needs.

The Center For Living With Cancer provides a full range of treatments and diagnostic procedures for inpatient and outpatient care. The oncology inpatient unit helps to provide a holistic approach to health care, as the unit features a well-stocked kitchen, beds for overnight stays, and comprehensive support services for every family member. A full range of treatment and diagnostic procedures are available on an outpatient basis including chemotherapy, antibiotic therapy, blood component transfusion, and the latest in radiation therapy.

East Jefferson General has remained on the cutting edge with radiation therapy. Another first to the metro area provided by the hospital was stereotactic radiosurgery. Used in the treatment of inoperable brain tumors or malformations, the procedure employs multiple beams of radiation that converge directly on the tumor, leaving the surrounding healthy tissue relatively untouched.

From the high tech needs of the radiation therapy patient to the sometimes soft touch required with rehab patients, East Jefferson General responds. Rehabilitative Services offers the benefit of a full gamut of programs all geared to returning the patient to an optimal state of well being post-

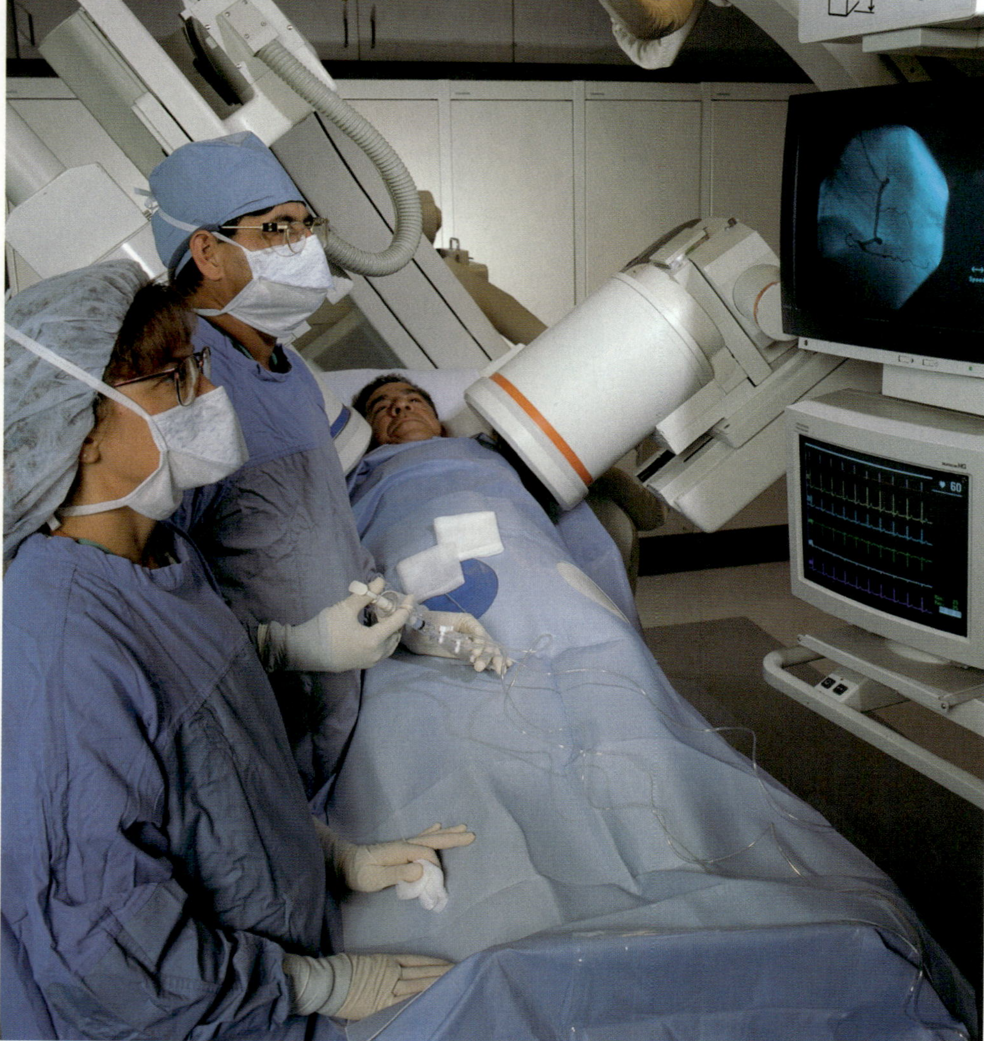

*With myriad diagnostic tools, interventional procedures, and a strong rehabilitative program, East Jefferson General's Gulf South Heart Center offers state-of-the-art care for diseases and abnormalities of the heart.
Photo by Paul Taylor.*

surgery or trauma. Rehabilitative Services includes physical, occupational, and speech therapies, and skilled nursing as well as the Occupational Medicine Clinic for the diagnosis and treatment of work-related injuries and illnesses. The clinic works in conjunction with the Emergency Department at East Jefferson General to give businesses 24-hour emergency room access, prompt feedback, case management, and timely return to work.

When it comes to the special needs of women, East Jefferson General Hospital is there to meet those needs from infancy through elder years. Woman & Child Services includes obstetrics, neonatal intensive care, inpatient pediatrics, and gynecology as well as a strong education component. Value-added services are Transition To Home (a cost-free, 12-hour continued stay after delivery for support and education), The Breastfeeding Center, Woman's Advantage membership program, and home health. East Jefferson General Hospital also offers a Parenting Center in affiliation with the local Children's Hospital.

While cardiology, oncology, rehabilitation, and woman and child services are centers of excellence, there are other standout services offered by East Jefferson General Hospital. One is the Wound Care Center®. The only one of its kind in the metro area, the Wound Care Center® treats chronic, non-healing wounds on an outpatient basis. Another standout is the hospital's Intensive Care Unit. This 20-bed unit was nationally recognized for meeting both functional and humanitarian needs while providing a supportive environment for the entire critical care team from patient and family member to nurse and physician.

Meeting The Community Need

Throughout its quarter-century of existence, East Jefferson General Hospital has consistently delivered state-of-the-art care guided by a humanistic approach that places the best interests of the community over the hospital balance sheet. Strong leadership is provided by a volunteer board of directors (appointed by the Jefferson Parish Council and Parish President) who live on the East Bank, Jefferson Parish.

Several programs and services bring to mind the true spirit of community service reflected at East Jefferson General.

Elder Advantage for example, the first hospital-based senior program in the state of Louisiana, now boasts over 44,000 members. Some love it so much they even volunteer their time in the Elder Advantage office. A wide array of benefits such as insurance paperwork processing, free and low-cost health screenings, special preferred pricing on pre-scriptions, merchant discounts, education programs, and social events, help make Elder Advantage the program of choice for seniors in the area.

With Woman's Advantage, members can enjoy interest-free payment plans for copayments and deductibles, free and low-cost health screenings, upgrades from semiprivate to private rooms (based on availability) and free Lamaze classes for members who deliver their babies at East Jefferson General. When a member turns 50, her membership rolls over to Elder Advantage, free of charge.

The Comprehensive Education And Early Detection

(CEED) program provides low-cost screening and education programs along with mobile mammography to the entire metropolitan area and beyond. And CEED meets the local business community's needs by conducting worksite wellness programs encouraging healthier lifestyles through education and behavior modification.

Community commitment doesn't stop here. East Jefferson General Hospital's ambulance service is the official "911" provider for the entire East Bank of Jefferson Parish. The hospital also manages the Parish's Mobility Impaired Transportation Service (MITS), which transports thousands of disabled residents throughout Jefferson and Orleans Parishes each year.

Meeting The Needs Of The Future

A slate of construction projects, scheduled for completion in 1998, anticipates the national trend away from long, inpatient hospital stays towards preventive and outpatient-based health care.

The new Joseph C. Domino Healthcare Pavilion (named in honor of a popular and respected charter hospital board member) is a 228,000 square foot state-of-the-art outpatient facility designed to provide quality care with the highest level of convenience for patients, their families, visitors, and physicians. "East Jefferson General Hospital recognizes the key to success in the future is convenience, quality, pricing, and patient-focused care. The Domino Pavilion, a one-stop medical mall, provides all of these ingredients." says President and CEO Peter Betts.

"We've come a long way since our beginning, and much about the delivery of health care has changed. East Jefferson General Hospital has anticipated most of these changes and has responded in a timely, efficient, and effective manner. With the support of our Board, community, and elected officials, we have formed a truly integrated system that provides services ranging from critical care to home care. Our first and foremost priority is to meet the healthcare needs of our friends and neighbors on the East Bank of Jefferson Parish." ◆

Browne–McHardy Clinic

In its nearly 50 years of operation, the Browne-McHardy Clinic of Metairie has established a position in suburban New Orleans making it an innovative ambulatory care setting. Beginning in 1949 as the practice of Dr. Donovan Browne and Dr. G. Gordon McHardy, the clinic quickly distinguished itself as one of the first in the region to offer an integrated group of specialists practicing in various disciplines of surgery and medicine.

Today, those disciplines include: allergy/immunology, audiology, cardiology, cardiovascular surgery, dermatology, facial plastic and reconstructive surgery, gastroenterology, general surgery, gynecology, hematology, infectious disease, internal medicine, neurology, obstetrics, oncology, ophthalmology, orthopedic surgery, otorhinolaryngology, head and neck surgery, pediatrics, pediatric cardiology, pulmonology, rheumatology, urology and urologic surgery.

Headquartered in a five story facility adjacent to the East Jefferson General Hospital, Browne-McHardy Clinic partners with more than 200 physicians in the metropolitan area. The clinic is a vital source of skills and talent and has doubled in the size of its physician staff and affiliated physician panel in the past five years. Over 80 of these physicians practice medicine at the Metairie and satellite locations. Browne-McHardy Clinic's patient load has increased as well. The number of patients has grown by more than 80 percent, with an increase in managed care enrollees of over 50 percent. Browne-McHardy has successfully balanced growth with continued quality care. Long term relationships are built on trust and performance. At Browne-McHardy Clinic, patients have been treated like family since 1949.

In 1985 Browne-McHardy Clinic was the first ambulatory care provider to participate in managed care contracting in the New Orleans metropolitan area. Today, its precedent-setting traditions continue with a greater and more extensive involvement in managed care. This involvement is an important facet of the clinic as the health care industry continues to transform to a more competitive managed care market.

Browne-McHardy Clinic, with satellite locations in New Orleans and New Orleans East, has also distinguished itself with its specialty care medical services some of which include: the Outpatient Surgery Center, for patients whose required surgical treatment exceeds the capabilities of the physician's office while not requiring overnight hospitalization; the Cosmetic Facial Surgery Center, where same-day surgical procedures include surgery of the nose, eyelids, face, and neck; the Browne-McHardy Laboratory, which provides valuable and immediate information from tests ordered by Browne-McHardy physicians; and the Imaging Center, which includes the latest in radiographic diagnostic equipment for both preventive and prescriptive medicine, chemotherapy infusion services, in-house pulmonary function testing and diagnostic tests in many other fields such as cardiology, OB/Gyn, urology, gastroenterology, pulmonology, and rheumatology.

In addition, there is the Browne-McHardy Hearing Center for the evaluation, fitting, and service of hearing instruments and the Optical Shop which offers a wide selection of frames and sunglasses at competitive prices.

The Clinic's specialty medical services coupled with one of the most loyal patient bases in the Deep South and a strategic link with a number of independent IPAs, group practices, and physician hospital organizations ensures a future for Browne-McHardy Clinic as it continues to deliver efficient quality care as it has provided for nearly 50 years. ◆

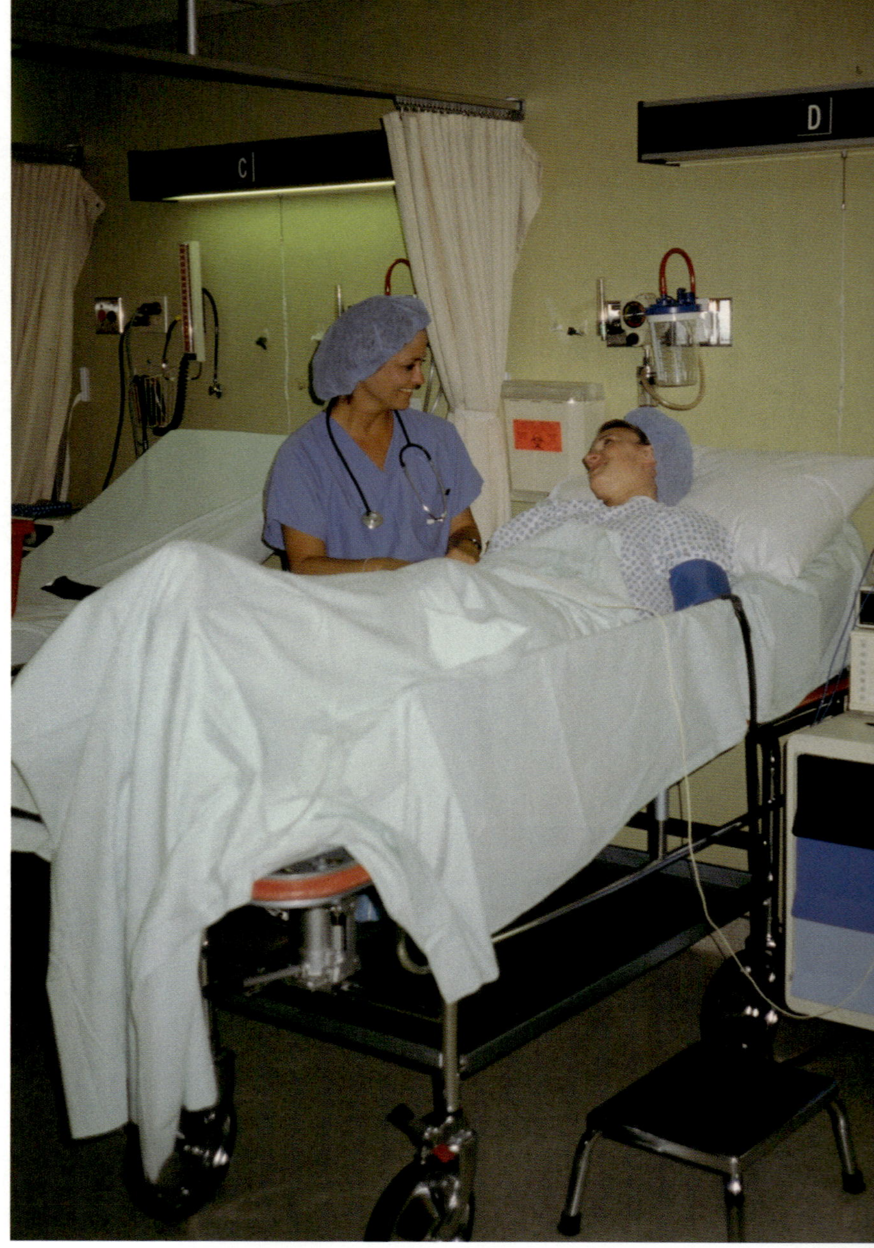

All Browne–McHardy Clinic personnel strive to satisfy the concerns of patients of all ages.

Headquartered in a five story facility adjacent to East Jefferson General Hospital, Browne–McHardy Clinic partners with more than 200 physicians in the metropolitan area.

Six leading hospitals of the Greater New Orleans area are building an alliance to ensure that their traditions of providing high-quality health care and sensitive community service prosper into the next century.

The institutions—Children's Hospital, Ochsner Foundation Hospital, Methodist Hospital, Slidell Memorial Hospital, St. Tammany Parish Hospital and Touro Infirmary—are working together to compete in the region's highly competitive health care marketplace.

The alliance was borne out of recognition that major health care institutions throughout the country are coming together to streamline operations and reduce costs to better serve the community. By forming the alliance, each of these six hospitals is working to preserve its unique heritage and culture while remaining viable and competitive.

Each of these hospitals is recognized in its community for the exceptional care it provides to patients. Some, in fact, are recognized for their clinical excellence throughout the world. Together, this coalition of hospitals is a team able to provide the full range of health care services this region needs.

THE ALLIANCE MEMBERS

Children's Hospital

The only full-service hospital in Louisiana exclusively for children, Children's Hospital in New Orleans treats inpatients and outpatients from the entire Gulf-South region in more than 40 subspecialty areas. With more than 380 physicians, the hospital is a teaching facility for the Louisiana State University School of Medicine.

Six leading hospitals of the Greater New Orleans area are building an alliance to ensure that their traditions of providing high-quality health care and sensitive community service prosper into the next century.

Methodist Hospital

Located in eastern New Orleans, Methodist Hospital was founded in 1968. The general acute care hospital recently underwent a significant renovation that included updating all rooms and departments and the addition of a 31,000-square-foot tower which houses administrative and clinical offices.

Ochsner Foundation Hospital

Admitting 18,000 patients annually, Ochsner is known for its pediatric, cancer, cardiology, organ transplantation, and orthopedic programs. The facility boasts one of the largest non-university-based graduate medical education programs in the country.

St. Tammany Parish Hospital

Serving western St. Tammany Parish and part of Washington Parish, the Covington-based hospital offers acute and diagnostic care services in a wide range of areas, including invasive and non-invasive cardiovascular services, obstetrics, magnetic resonance imaging, endoscopy and emergency care.

Slidell Memorial Hospital and Medical Center

Serving eastern St. Tammany Parish and parts of the Mississippi Gulf Coast, Slidell Memorial is a facility featuring a cancer care center, cardiac catheterization lab, outpatient diagnostic services, women's center, sports medicine and fitness center, and neonatal intensive care unit.

Touro Infirmary

Founded in 1852, Touro is the oldest private, not-for-profit hospital in New Orleans. Its multispecialty staff of nearly 500 physicians provides both primary and tertiary care. Centers of excellence at the hospital include oncology, cardio-pulmonary services, and obstetrics and gynecology. ◆

Touro Infirmary

Few institutions and even fewer names summon up the rich history of New Orleans and its people as does the renowned Touro Infirmary and its founder Judah Touro, a legendary philanthropist who made his fortune in real estate in the first years of the city's growth in the early 1800s.

It was Touro—a mysterious, reclusive figure whose life included service in the War of 1812 and ended just six years before the Civil War—who left behind property and a bequest to open the infirmary's first home, a plantation-style mansion near the waters of the Mississippi River in a still-rural piece of the city.

From the start, the infirmary's mission was ambitious—not only did it pledge itself to caring for all sick people regardless of race, color, or religion, but it was also determined to treat the victims of yellow fever, a disease that devastated New Orleans in the 1870s and eventually spurred the building of a new infirmary to accommodate the hundreds of people felled by the then-deadly disease.

More than a century later, Touro Infirmary thrives on more than 1 million square feet of space in 10 buildings off the Uptown corner of Prytania and Delachaise. Its skilled staff treats more than 100,000 patients a year.

"For over 145 years, Touro has been a cornerstone of New Orleans tradition, caring for generations of New Orleanians," explains Gary M. Stein, Touro's CEO and President, "As a community based, not-for-profit teaching hospital, we've become one of the Gulf South's leading health care institutions, sustaining Judah Touro's legacy to the New Orleans community, its people, families, business and future."

Today, Touro Infirmary, frequently lauded for its unparalleled cancer treatment, cardiology, obstetrics and gynecology, rehabilitative medicine, and in- and out-patient psychiatric programs, has a staff composed of more than 1,500 employees and over 500 physicians. Under strong leadership, Touro has an estimated $150 million economic impact each year on the local economy from its vast operations.

"Touro's success has had a lot to do with the fact that we have become both horizontally and vertically integrated in the 1990s," says Stein. And that means that such services as a managed care company, a home health agency, a free-standing surgery center and a fitness center have become Touro mainstays. "We see our future role as being a leader in providing wellness and prevention services that augment our outstanding clinical capabilities," Stein adds.

Touro also offers, among other things, advanced research of such maladies as age-related retinal disorders at the infirmary's Eye Research Institute, a new Family Birthing Center, and New Orleans' only Chest Pain Emergency Room.

Leading edge technology coupled with research and teaching, has given the infirmary national prestige and the confidence of a bright future as it faces the year 2000 and beyond.

"The rest of the decade looks very promising," says Stein. "We had our best year ever—in terms of both the hospital's clinical and financial performance—last year. And we're looking forward to building on that for the next 150 years." ◆

Touro Infirmary, a community based, not-for-profit teaching hospital, has become one of the Gulf South's leading health care institutions.

Touro Infirmary also offers a new Family Birthing Center.

Since its 1956 founding, West Jefferson Medical Center has been a regional leader in the provision of acute, preventive and rehabilitative care tailored to the needs of business and industry.

The 462-bed hospital, located on a 20-acre campus in Marrero on the west bank of Jefferson Parish, is just 10 minutes from Downtown New Orleans.

West Jefferson's proximity to vast industrial corridors, including the Harvey Canal and the Gulf of Mexico, led it in 1979 to establish the first hospital-based emergency helicopter service in Louisiana. Today it is the only such service in the metro area that flies offshore with registered nurses certified in advanced life support and under instrument flight rule conditions.

Acute care services for the business and industry customer include streamlined emergency care and drug screen collections. West Jefferson is the 9-1-1 service provider for the entire West Bank of Jefferson Parish.

The West Jefferson Center for Occupational Health, on the main campus, and satellite Family Doctor clinics offer convenient, occupational care for landbased and offshore industry. Pre-employment physicals and occupational injury treatment are just a few of the services that are available.

In 1993, the hospital opened its Industrial Return-to-Work Center, a human performance laboratory offering services such as work-hardening, functional capacity evaluation, pre-work screens, ergonomic analysis, back-to-school, and cumulative trauma prevention. The center is equipped to simulate nearly every occupational and industrial duty, from barrel-lifting to rope-swinging to toolwork. Its occupational therapists test injured workers on fine- and gross-motor skills, and provide those test results to employers.

The center also screens non-injured individuals during the pre-employment phase to help employers assess whether they are up to the daily tasks of a given job. In addition, job-site analysis is available to advise employers on how to create safer, more productive workplaces.

As the primary provider of workers compensation care for the West Bank of Jefferson Parish, West Jefferson is committed to getting employees back to work as soon as possible.

To assure effective injury management, the hospital takes a proactive role in keeping employers informed through monthly tracking reports apprising them of their employees' medical status, expenses, and ongoing medical care. The hospital's Business Advantage program, an umbrella of value-added services available exclusively to the business customer, coordinates a company's every occupational health need.

Preventive care and corporate fitness are not forgotten at West Jefferson. A comprehensive series of wellness, prevention, and safety programs are available, many at significant discounts to business customers and most of which can be brought to the worksite upon request. West Jefferson has a business and industry nurse to assist companies with their specific needs.

The two-story Health Center for Fitness and Rehabilitation, on West Jefferson's main campus, features 26,000 square feet of space for rehabilitative services and a complete array of general wellness programs including aquatic therapy and physical therapy. The center, which offers corporate rates, is staffed by exercise physiologists who can conduct lifestyle assessments and provide customized exercise plans.

West Jefferson Medical Center has a comprehensive Employee Assistance Program.

In addition to serving the special needs of business, West Jefferson is a full-service acute-care facility offering a continuum of care, including home health. The community-owned, not-for-profit institution has 1,700 employees and an annual payroll of more than $45 million. In its first 40 years of operation it pumped over $1 billion into the local economy. ◆

The West Jefferson Medical Center is a 462-bed hospital located on a 20-acre campus in Marrero on the west bank of Jefferson Parish.

West Jefferson's Industrial Return-to-Work Center is equipped to simulate nealy every occupational and industrial duty.

Acknowledgements

On the following page are many of the books I've read, in all or part, that have helped inform and shape this portrait of New Orleans. Even more influential in driving most chapters has been information from articles in newspapers and magazines, particularly the *Times-Picayune* and its ever-useful "Money" section. Many individuals have also given me a wealth of information about their organizations or enterprises—especially the always helpful and efficient Beverly Gianna at the New Orleans Metropolitan Convention and Visitors' Bureau. Her press packets are a model for the world! For business statistics, I'm happy to have access to the resources of researcher Bob Folse, with MetroVision and The Chamber/New Orleans and the River Region. His reports give an in-depth, accurate picture of virtually every aspect of the area. Thanks to everyone who provided information so graciously—and quickly. This book wouldn't have existed without you.

Bibliography

Bultman, Bethany Ewald. *New Orleans, A Compass American Guide*. New York: Fodor's Travel Publications, Inc., 1994.

Chase, John Churchill. *Frenchmen, Desire, Good Children and Other Streets of New Orleans*. 3rd ed. New York: Collier Books, 1979.

Davis, Edwin Adams. *Louisiana: The Pelican State*. Baton Rouge: Louisiana State University Press, 1975.

The Federal Writers' Project of the Works Progress Administration. *The WPA Guide to New Orleans*, (with a new introduction by the Historic New Orleans Collection). New York: Pantheon, 1938 (intro 1983).

Flake, Carol. *New Orleans*. New York: Grove Press, 1994.

Hardy, Jeanette and Elizabeth Mullener, eds. *The Times-Picayune Insider's Guide to New Orleans*. New Orleans: The Times Picayune, 1988.

Kuralt, Charles. *Charles Kuralt's America*. New York: G.P. Putnam's Sons, 1995.

New Orleans Magazine. 30th Anniversary Issue. New Orleans Publishing Group, January, 1996.

Seligman, Craig, ed. *Fodor's 1994, New Orleans, The Complete Guide*. New York: Fodor's Travel Publications, Inc., 1993.

Starr, S. Frederick. *New Orleans Unmasqued*. Edition dedeaux. New York: New Orleans, 1985.

Trade and Culture Magazine. May-June, 1995.

U.S./Latin Trade Magazine. Special section. "New Orleans: New Goals, New Focus." July, 1995.

Zenfell, Martha Ellen, ed. *New Orleans Insight City Guide*. Hong Kong: APA Publications (HK), Ltd., 1992.

Enterprise Index

Index

This book was set in Phaistos Roman, Phaistos Italic, Phaistos Bold, Garamond Light, and Garamond Light Italic at Community Communications, Montgomery, Alabama, and printed on 80 pound Warren Flo Text.